❦ Evidence and Meaning ❧

MAKING SENSE OF HISTORY
Studies in Historical Cultures
General Editor: Stefan Berger
Founding Editor: Jörn Rüsen

Bridging the gap between historical theory and the study of historical memory, this series crosses the boundaries between both academic disciplines and cultural, social, political and historical contexts. In an age of rapid globalization, which tends to manifest itself on an economic and political level, locating the cultural practices involved in generating its underlying historical sense is an increasingly urgent task.

For a full volume listing, please see back matter

EVIDENCE AND MEANING

A Theory of Historical Studies

Jörn Rüsen
Translated from the German by Diane Kerns and Katie Digan

berghahn
NEW YORK · OXFORD
www.berghahnbooks.com

Published in 2017 by
Berghahn Books
www.berghahnbooks.com

The translation of this work was funded by Geisteswissenschaften
International – Translation Funding for Humanities and Social Sciences from
Germany, a joint initiative of the Fritz Thyssen Foundation, the German
Federal Foreign Office, the collecting society VG WORT and the Börsenverein
des Deutschen Buchhandels (German Publishers & Booksellers Association).

Library of Congress Cataloging-in-Publication Data
A C.I.P. cataloging record is available from the Library of Congress

British Library Cataloguing in Publication Data
A catalogue record for this book is available from the British Library

ISBN 978-1-78533-538-9 hardback
ISBN 978-1-78533-539-6 ebook

When the great Rabbi Israel Baal Shem-Tov saw misfortune threatening the Jews it was his custom to go into a certain part of the forest to meditate. There he would light a fire, say a special prayer, and the miracle would be accomplished and the misfortune averted.

Later, when his disciple, the celebrated Magid of Mezritch, had occasion, for the same reason, to intercede with heaven, he would go to the same place in the forest and say: 'Master of the Universe, listen! I do not know how to light the fire, but I am still able to say the prayer', and again the miracle would be accomplished.

Still later, Rabbi Moshe-Leib of Sasov, in order to save his people once more, would go into the forest and say: 'I do not know how to light the fire, I do not know the prayer, but I know the place and this must be sufficient.' It was sufficient and the miracle was accomplished.

Then it fell to Rabbi Israel of Rizhyn to overcome misfortune. Sitting in his armchair, his head in his hands, he spoke to God: 'I am unable to light the fire and I do not know the prayer; I cannot even find the place in the forest. All I can do is to tell the story, and this must be sufficient.' And it was sufficient.

God made men because He loves stories.

—Elie Wiesel, *The Gates of the Forest*, pp. 6

Contents

Tables and Figures

Preface

This book would not have been written had I not received an invitation via Waltraud Schreiber to be the visiting Otto von Freising professor at the Catholic University of Eichstätt in the summer semester of 2007. The invitation included a request for me to present an overview of my theory of history (or metahistory). In Eichstätt, the theory of history in general and of historical studies in particular is at the core of historical didactic thinking. In Eichstätt, theory of history plays an important role in research, teaching, teacher training and cultural and political consultancy, as well as in practical work with history schoolteachers in all types of schools. During intensive discussions that I was able to have with graduate students of history didactics I was intensely struck by the way in which theory on history didactics can be made use of in practical research.

I gladly accepted the challenge to systematically develop a theory of history in only eight lectures. My work on the subject, the three volumes of *Grundzüge einer Historik*, is already over twenty years old.[1] Of course, discussions on the theory of history have evolved during this time, and I have participated in them. It is only logical that I should attempt to respond to these new developments in my updated metahistory.

It is not easy to update one's own work. The relevant new discussion should be incorporated as comprehensively as possible. But that would have meant writing something entirely new. At the same time, the old would have had to be seamlessly incorporated into the new. However, this is difficult to achieve because the contexts of the theoretical considerations in the 1980s and those of the present are vastly different. We cannot iron out these differences with a continuous argumentation running from 1980 to now. In this sense, I must compromise. I draw on my earlier considerations to various degrees and only go beyond my original argumentative horizon whenever I can draw on my own later work, and when I think the subject matter demands it.

Notes for this section begin on page xiii.

A lecture about metahistory at the University of Jena in January 2011 on the occasion of the professional representation of the chair of Volkhard Knigge (with support from Axel Doßmann) was a welcome opportunity for me to present a first draft of my updated work for discussion. I thank the attentive and critical audience for their suggestions.

Finally, I was able to test the intercultural claims that my metahistory makes in a seminar for advanced students that I organized in the autumn of 2012 in the Graduate Institute for National Development at National Taiwan University. I thank my partner Chang Chih-Ming for his interest and his many critical questions and objections.

Anthropological perspectives have played an important part in my meta-history since the very first version. The anthropologically fundamental and universal ability of humans to intellectually penetrate and appropriate their world and themselves in relation to others, that is, their cultural human-ness, serves as a guideline for argumentation. I have further developed this guideline and expanded it into a more complex argumentation. My years of cooperation and friendship with Klaus E. Müller have been extraordinarily stimulating and helpful. His profound knowledge of archaic life forms and his insight into fundamental structures of human ways of life have always anchored the theoretical abstractions in condensed syntheses of knowledge.[2]

Furthermore, I received many especially helpful suggestions in the framework of a larger research project. This research project was 'Der Humanismus in der Epoche der Globalisierung – Ein interkultureller Dialog über Menschheit, Kultur und Werte' ('Humanism in the Age of Globalization – An Intercultural Dialogue about Humanity, Culture and Value'), funded by Stiftung Mercator, which I led in cooperation with colleagues from neighbouring universities at the Kulturwissenschaftliches Institut in Essen between 2006 and 2009.[3]

Finally, the debates about my concept of metahistory in the journal *Erwägen Wissen Ethik* provided me with many ideas for the ending of this book.[4] I cannot mention all the critics individually – this book is simply too small.

I am pleased to thank all those who have helped me to realize this book. First of all, I must thank Waltraud Schreiber, her impressive synthesis of per-sistent inquiries and her sensitive contributions. I thank my colleagues and friends Estevao de Rezende Martins, Klas-Göran Karlsson, Georg Essen and Jürgen Straub for their interest in my theoretical work – and especially with its connection to history didactics. Their participation presented me with the pleasant challenge of not reproducing what I had already achieved. I would like to thank the Kulturwissenschaftliches Institut in Essen for their logisti-cal help, and the Institute for Advanced Study in Humanities and Social Sciences of the National Taiwan University and its Director Chun-Chieh

Huang for several research stays that granted me a welcome opportunity to work on metahistory. Thank you to Christoph Antweiler, Achim Mittag and Henner Laass for their critical comments.

I owe special thanks to those who have helped me overcome the difficulties of translating my German text into English, especially Diane Kerns, who produced a draft translation, and Katie Digan, who edited that text. It has become clear that my use of the German language does not really have an English equivalent and that many important concepts do not have an English counterpart. I thank the translators for their resourcefulness and patience in overcoming these difficulties. Additionally, I thank the editors of Berghahn books, especially Caroline Kuhtz, for their thorough reading. I also thank David Carr, Stefan Berger, Georg Iggers, Richard Vann and Krishna Winston for their good advice.

Special thanks go to Angelika Wulff for her critical review of the text. She brought many inadequacies to my attention that were improved upon by her useful suggestions. Of course, I alone am responsible for the end product presented here.

My wife Inge has helped me tremendously with her unwavering willingness to listen to my unfinished ideas and to help me find clarity. But most of all, I thank her for her patient and intensive work on the intellectual and linguistic improvement of my text.

Notes

1. J. Rüsen. 1983. *Historische Vernunft: Grundzüge einer Historik I: Die Grundlagen der Geschichtswissenschaft*, Göttingen: Vandenhoeck & Ruprecht; J. Rüsen. 1986. *Rekonstruktion der Vergangenheit: Grundzüge einer Historik II: Die Prinzipien der historischen Forschung*, Göttingen: Vandenhoeck & Ruprecht; J. Rüsen. 1989. *Lebendige Geschichte: Grundzüge einer Historik III: Formen und Funktionen des historischen Wissens*, Göttingen: Vandenhoeck & Ruprecht. I quote these titles as *Grundzüge I*, *Grundzüge II*, and *Grundzüge III*.

2. The most striking example is his book: K.E. Müller. 2009. *Die Siedlungsgemeinschaft*, Göttingen: Vandenhoeck & Ruprecht; see also idem. 1987. *Das magische Universum der Identität*, Frankfurt am Main: Campus; idem. 1999. *Die fünfte Dimension*, Göttingen: Wallstein. Concerning the importance of this ethnology for historical studies, see J. Rüsen. 2000. 'Vom Nutzen und Nachteil der Ethnologie für die Historie', in S. Schomburg-Scherff et al. (eds), *Die offenen Grenzen der Ethnologie: Schlaglichter auf ein sich wandelndes Fach*, Frankfurt am Main: Lembeck, 291–309.

3. See: J. Rüsen and H. Laass (eds). 2009. *Interkultureller Humanismus*, Schwalbach/ Taunus: Wochenschau; J. Rüsen and H. Laass (eds). 2009. *Humanism in Intercultural Perspective*, Bielefeld: Transcript; J. Rüsen (ed.). 2010. *Perspektiven der Humanität*, Bielefeld: Transcript; M. Gieselmann and J. Straub (eds). 2012. *Humanismus in der Diskussion*, Bielefeld: Transcript.

4. J. Rüsen. 2011. 'Historik: Umriss einer Theorie der Geschichtswissenschaft', *Erwägen Wissen Ethik* 22(4), 477–490; idem. 2011. 'Diskursive Bewegungen in der Historik', ibid., 604–619.

Introduction

The basic principles of metahistory that I follow were developed in the 1970s. They are closely related to my attempt to conceptualize and systematically advance the foundations of Johann Gustav Droysen's own *Historik*.[5] Apart from one significant modification – contrary to Droysen, I explore the question of what history is first and the question of what historical method is second – I generally follow the structure of his *Historik*, as it unites all the essential elements of a theory of history in a coherent form.

The Development of Metahistory   Critical reflection on historical theory, as characterized in Droysen's *Historik*, was popular in the 1970s. History as a discipline was confronted with a fundamental critique of its traditional form and new theoretical and methodological approaches to re-form the discipline were considered.[6] Such fundamental crises in an academic field call for systematic reflection on its constitutive principles. At the time, my attempt to meet this demand was of course defined by the contemporary and traditional standards, contemporary challenges and general discourse. My aim was to seize the innovatory potential of socio-historical thought by adapting the ideas and propositions that originated from the social sciences, especially from sociology, and using them in historical theory and research methods. In doing so, it was important to defend the practical relevance of historical understanding as well as the claims of rationality in academic historical thought without losing sight of its practical political relevance.

Notes for this section begin on page 5.

Since then, the position of historical thought has changed dramatically. Analogous to the transformations that occurred in the field of social history in the 1960s and 1970s, a whole range of 'turns' has been proclaimed, reflected upon and established, though hardly in any consistently systematic way. If we summarize these turns in view of fundamental aspects and strategies of historical thinking, then we can now also speak of a cultural historical or cultural scientific turn on top of the earlier socio-historical turn. Today, critical new impulses for historical studies no longer come from the social sciences but rather from cultural anthropology.

In response to this 'turn' and its related questions of legitimacy and criticism, some have wondered whether the earlier theories of historical studies will be integrated or merely overtaken by the newer ones. I hope to address this controversy in its basic elements with my revised concept of metahistory, without contradicting the relevance of my original idea in its old context in any way. Even at that time I was not able to radically reject the historicist tradition in historical studies, especially its theoretical achievements. It was therefore more straightforward for me to tie post-historicist analytical concepts of social history to the neo-hermeneutic modes of thought that determine the recent developments in the field. By doing so I could simultaneously address and systematically incorporate the ideas on the role of memory and dealing with the past (*Erinnerungs-Diskurs*) that arose from cultural studies.

In the 1970s and early 1980s, historical scholarship was one of the most – if not *the* most – pivotal references for German historical culture (*Geschichtskultur*). It is questionable whether that is still the case today. The overwhelming power of new forms of media, the relentless success of historical museums and exhibits, the lively debates concerning monuments and memorials – all of this threatens to relegate historical scholarship to a minor role in doing what it is in fact, through research, most capable of doing.

Aesthetics, Post-modernism, Post-colonialism To formulate my point more precisely, we are faced with the fact that critical, methodological thinking in dealing with the past risks drowning in the sea of images available to us in the media everywhere and at all times. Aesthetics as a mode of perception has always been an essential element of historical thinking, also in its academic form. But this disciplinary form that is characterized by research with verifiable claims for truth, as well as by a critical handling of socially powerful historical orientations, is at risk of being pushed into the background. A critical attitude no longer appears to play an especially important role in historical culture. The call for transdisciplinary work, and the urge to escape the restrictions of a specific field of study for the sake of the supposed free creativity that all too often comes with it, has pushed aside the cognitive achievements that result from methodological standards of historical research.

Furthermore, post-modern trends in the cultural and social sciences have discredited the traditional standards of rationality in intellectual pursuits. Under the auspices of post-colonialism and the demands to respect non-Western traditions when dealing with the human past,[7] claims of universality in academic works are all too quickly discredited as ideological, as a sign of the growing obsolescence of Western hegemonic thought.

These developments contain legitimate criticisms, but advocates for these ideas tend to throw the baby out with the bath water. Metahistory as a theory of history remains committed to explaining explicitly the specific cognitive possibilities that historical thinking as an academic discipline has opened up. The question of truth thus remains relevant. When one demands that historical thinking and its disciplinary rationality be separated from all aspects of our cultural orientation, then historical studies, and metahistorical thinking itself, become conceptually misguided.

This being said, my aim here is to revise my study of metahistory, while remaining committed to the same agenda as expressed in my work twenty years ago under the title *Historische Vernunft*.

Interculturalism Context awareness and the logics of rationality claims within historical thinking help us to recognize the challenges presented in intercultural communication in the period of globalization. We can no longer continue to simply and indiscriminately perpetuate the Western academic tradition, that is, the powerful rationalizing impulse of historical thinking, and assume that it is transcultural. In recent decades, non-Western traditions have become something of a corrective tool, if not an outright alternative to occidental concepts,[8] by presenting other contextual frameworks of historical thinking that have hardly played any role in the established discussions of historical theory.

Two reactions to post-modern and post-colonial criticism are possible: to defend standards of rationality in critical academic thought with claims of universality in the field of history on the one hand, and to relativize the influence of cultural contexts on the other. Neither is plausible. Instead, it is important that the cultural context of historical thinking in the real world is taken seriously as our driving impulse. At the same time, we need to recognize cross-cultural criteria of truth, which allow the establishment of a transcultural methodological rationality. These criteria are simply based on the fact that even though we all live in different cultures, we as humans have our humanity in common, which we can agree on with good reason.

It is essential to include the fundaments of being human in our critical reconstruction of the logics of historical thinking and in its specifically academic ('scientific') claims of truth. Cultural difference should become an inspiration rather than a limitation to historical knowledge.

History as a Field of Study   Metahistory as a theory of history also faces another challenge, namely the academic status of 'historical studies' as a discipline. As the organizational structure of historical understanding, historical scholarship has a long tradition that can be traced back to the eighteenth century. The ways in which historical thought developed within this structure varied; the structure or form itself, however, has mostly remained consistent. This might soon change due to the more recent changes in history education at universities. The discipline of history has recently found itself shrinking to a mere component or even fragment of various constellations of knowledge and modes of thought; it is dwindling down to being just one part of a broader course, its cognitive status becoming downright precarious. The creation of curriculum conglomerates most often serves the interests of producing practical and applied competencies. This applied or practical standard does not guarantee any internal cognitive or methodological coherence in the respective contributions of different disciplines to a specific course of study. This lack of coherence carries over to the level of competence in students, blurring the expectations and goals they face in their studies. It especially affects effective and methodological rationality in academic research. This type of academic education severely limits students' critical thinking skills, as critical academic work is based on institutionalized and methodological processes of investigation. This basic inadequacy is cloaked and concealed by the proud language of interdisciplinary and transdisciplinary work. How could either of those things be possible if the original disciplines that they should be based on no longer exist?

Metahistory as a theory of history is a kind of reflexive legitimization of established forms of scholarship. It does not simply establish a status quo in an academic discipline. Rather, it develops standards for the organization of the processes of gaining knowledge based on the methods of cognitive investigation employed in those processes. It emphasizes the inner dynamic of this organization as well as its ability to change and develop. At the same time, though, it offers decisive arguments for the professional character of these standard research methods. It clarifies what it means to 'do history' as an academic field of study. It does so by revealing the necessary requirements for an academic education that claims to provide the fundamental capabilities for critical thinking.

Real World Setting   Professionalism is not everything. Without it, academic or scientific historical thinking does not exist. But in its academic form, historical thinking nonetheless refers to factors both in- and outside of its professional scope. Its relevance as an essential factor in cultural orientation is only apparent if we refer to its academic character, to its definable and methodological rationality, to the foundations and contexts that give it its specific identity, even its own logic. It is obvious that historical thinking bears both differences and similarities to other forms of thinking in the world of academia. What this means can only be explained when we examine the real world setting of historical thinking, which is not abandoned but rather enriched by academic historical thought.

Taking into account the real world setting of historical thinking, a whole new set of perspectives that determine all historical thinking come into view: its aesthetic structure, political function and didactic focus and their related forms, development and impact. Professional historians address the influence of such perspectives in their work. They are not, however, consistently reflected upon or established, but instead dealt with sporadically, or more often unsystematically. Metahistory is an attempt to conceptualize an overall context for such reflections in order to make them more coherent, more insightful and ultimately more effective. We will judge its success here by how far metahistory can go in strengthening the intellectual powers of historical thought that are combined and organized within its academic form.

Notes

5. J. Rüsen. 1969. *Begriffene Geschichte*, Paderborn: Schöningh.

6. J. Rüsen. 1976. *Für eine erneuerte Historik*, Stuttgart: Frommann-Holzboog. Also idem, 'Grundlagenreflexion und Paradigmenwechsel in der westdeutschen Geschichtswissenschaft', in idem, *Zeit und Sinn: Strategien historischen Denkens*, Frankfurt am Main: Fischer Taschenbuch, 50–76.

7. As an example, see S. Seth: 'Reason or Reasoning? Clio or Siva?', *Social Text* 22(1), 85–101. And the works of Vinay Lal, 'World History and its Politics', *Economic and Political Weekly* 46(46), 40–47; idem, 'The Politics of Culture and Knowledge after Postcolonialism', *Continuum: Journal of Media and Cultural Studies* 26(2), 191–205.

8. I refer here to only one example: C.-C. Huang. 2000. 'The Defining Character of Chinese Historical Thinking', *History and Theory* 46, 180–188. An intercultural debate subsequently took place. See 'Chinese and Western Historical Thinking'. 2007. Forum in *History & Theory* 46(2), 180–232. See also J. Rüsen. 1999. *Westliches Geschichtsdenken: eine interkulturelle Debatte*. Göttingen: Vandenhoeck & Ruprecht. (*Western Historical Thinking: An Intercultural Debate*. New York and Oxford: Berghahn Books, 2002.)

CHAPTER 1

What is Metahistory?

There is a simple answer to this question: the German term *Historik* (or metahistory) is a theory of historical studies. It is composed of three ele- ments: history, scholarship and theory. Let us begin with the latter term. Theories are forms of knowledge that employ a high degree of generaliza- tion to explain specific facts or phenomena. As such they are a fundamental part of every kind of academic thinking, including historical studies. But metahistory as a theory of history is something special. We do not apply it in order to read or comprehend the human past within the framework of academic thinking. It is a theory about this interpretation itself. It reflects his- torical thinking back onto itself. There is a term in philosophy for this type of thinking: metatheory. In German, following the classic work of Droysen, we call this historical thinking in its disciplinary and scientific form *Historik*.[9] In the English-speaking world we usually use the term 'metahistory'.[10] Less frequently used terms are historiology or historiography.

Reflexive Form   Metahistory also focuses on the academic field of history. It transcends the borders of disciplinary thinking in order to reflect upon it. We therefore need to clarify how this thinking relates to the work that professionals of historical studies do when reading, or interpreting, human history. Why should historians tread beyond their own practical field, or move beyond its borders? In so doing, they withdraw from the immediate area in which they are trained as specialists.

Notes for this section begin on page 11.

But then, what makes a person professionally or academically compe-
tent? Professional competence in scholarship or science is not just defined
by being well versed in the procedures of producing scholarly knowledge.
The ability to determine the expert handling of academic subject matter, or
in other words, the ability to say what competency is and how we acquire
it, is also important.

Metahistory, then, is also a theory about the practice of acquiring knowledge in historical studies. It makes explicit and systematizes the reflexive elements of academic competency. There are many reasons for such reflexive
theoretical work. They can be understood through the metaphor that one
must be able to see the forest despite the trees, if one wants to see the trees
in the forest.

Three Dimensions   Metahistory deals with three dimensions of reflexive
knowledge about historical studies: (a) disciplinary, (b) interdisciplinary and
(c) transdisciplinary.

(a) The *disciplinary* dimension of metahistory includes knowledge about
what the academic study of history is; that is, what makes this approach to
history different from other approaches in the handling of the human past.
The focus here is the question of what it means to be concerned with history
in a scholarly or (more modestly put) professional manner. The question is
significant because to answer it, we need to be clear on what we mean by
history and by 'academic' or 'scientific'. What makes this handling of that
distinctive matter we call history 'academic'? Both the uniqueness of history
and the academic character of thinking about it are anything but clear, and
in fact are topics of debate.

(b) In its form as knowledge about the questions and issues dealt with
in historical studies, metahistory has an *interdisciplinary* dimension as well.
It positions the academic discipline of history within the larger context of
other academic disciplines that use different methods for exploring similar or
related subject matter. The central question here is how the academic study
of history within the field of history relates to the academic study of the past
in other fields. Where are the borders between these various fields? What
makes them unique? What are the kinds of thinking and types of knowledge or methods borrowed from other fields that prove useful for historians
and how does the work of historians contribute to the work done in other
disciplines?

(c) In its *transdisciplinary* form, metahistory is concerned with the relation between the discipline of historical thinking and the real-world setting
of human beings. The key question here is what role historical knowledge as
an academic discipline actually plays in our cultural orientation: How does
the academic approach to history relate to other levels or strategies of cultural

interpretation among human beings and their life worlds? How does the unique role of academic historical knowledge relate to the role of historical culture and to the memory of history or the culture of remembrance?

Crossing Borders   In all three cases, our view of metahistory transcends the borders of the actual academic discipline of history. In order to define what it means to 'do history' in an academic manner, it is necessary to determine what is actually meant by 'history'. The phenomenon of history is not exclusive to the domain of academic institutions but rather is much older and much broader than a field of study. It is an essential element of every cultural orientation in the living world of human beings and occurs in highly variable forms in all cultures.

From the interdisciplinary point of view, it is important to determine exactly what the specific scientific claims of historical studies are. What does it have in common with other fields of study and what specific qualities make it different from other fields?

The transdisciplinary perspective focuses on the relation between the scholarly pursuit of knowledge and the approaches and rigour behind this pursuit and the various uses and functions of historical thinking in the real world.

By combining these research questions, metahistory integrates various specialized ways of thinking and areas of discussion. When addressing the question of what history is, metahistory becomes a philosophy of history. When addressing the question of the academic nature of historical thinking, metahistory becomes epistemology, methodology and theory of science. And finally, when addressing the question of how academia and living in the real world are connected in historical thinking, we turn to various disciplines that deal with the cultural orientation of human beings in the real world, such as the fields of ethics or politics. There is a particularly close relationship between metahistory and historical didactics, which focuses on the role of historical culture as a context and historical consciousness as a means to teach and learn history.

Themes   What is the common thread between all these different questions and ways of thinking in metahistory? Ultimately it is about two fundamental themes: history itself and how we deal with it as subject matter.[11] The key question of the first theme concerns the facts in 'history'. Are they objectively predetermined as more or less fixed objects of actual knowledge? Or are we simply dealing with retroactive interpretations of a past that is long since gone? The second topic has to do with the question of truth. Can historical thinking even be academic or scientific? Should historical thinking as an academic field of study be judged using the same criteria of truth that get their persuasiveness from other academic fields, especially the natural sciences? Or does a specific historical truth exist?

The two themes are closely connected to each other. History is not simply a collection of facts, objectively predetermined and then subjectively adjusted for human understanding. Of course history concerns the human past, which contains facts with an objective character. But history is much more than that: as an element and determinant of human culture, it has mental qualities that make it subjective as well. Historical thinking and its cultural function in everyday life are also determined by these 'mental' or 'subjective' elements (in ways that are to be analysed later in this volume).

Here we find the intersection of the practical function of historical thinking, or its life-serving purpose, and the academic way of thinking that gives historical studies its unique position in historical culture. The key concept that ties the two together is what I call 'sense', from the German *Sinn*, which is closer to the English word 'meaning', or the meaning behind the meaning. Metahistory deals with the meaning of history. However, it does not do so in the same broad terms as in philosophy of history. We who focus on metahistory are more interested in the question of what this meaning or sense is and what role it plays when trained specialists study the human past in a critical academic ('scientific') manner.

But the question of meaning is more fundamental than that. The question of academic or scientific status can only be addressed if we first resolve this question of meaning.

Functions With these themes and issues, metahistory claims its own intellectual niche in the area of historical studies. This niche is not as institutionalized as the specialized areas concerned with different historical epochs or regions such as medieval, eastern European or economic history. This has to do with the fact that metahistorical thinking is already present in all of these areas, encompassing yet circumventing them all. And since it cannot function without drawing systematically from other disciplines (such as philosophy), its metadisciplinary status is fundamentally uncertain. It does not fit into the standard repertoire of teaching and research in the field of history. And yet it has a wide range of functions that are difficult to ignore; I name four of these below.[12]

(1) In academic teaching, metahistory is indispensible for its didactic professionalism. The field of history is overwhelmingly, if not exclusively, presented to students as a multiplicity of specialized areas rather than something that can be studied in its entirety. At the same time, in all its diversity it wants to be recognized as a distinct entity. Metahistory, as well as the history of historical thinking, serves this purpose.

(2) Metahistory is also present in historical research, where it is characterized as 'reflexive clarification' (*reflexive Klärung*). Historical research is a core element of historical studies. It follows its own logic and is determined by the discourse and debate among its own experts. However, the most effective impulses in research do not come from within the discipline itself but from other areas of study. These impulses can emerge from scientific disciplines such as the social sciences or cultural anthropology, or from the challenges stemming from problems of cultural orientation in the societal context of historical studies. This 'openness' toward research topics in historical knowledge can lead to methodological problems that can only be resolved reflexively, through explicit analysis of the determining factors of the research methods. Here, metahistory takes on a relevant function for research.

(3) Historical thinking finds its expression in the writing of history, which, compared to research, has a unique position within the field. Writing does not follow the same line as research, but goes beyond research; or better yet, writing is a return to the production and reception of texts. Here, too, we are dealing with the interweaving of different dimensional aspects (aesthetic, rhetorical and political) of history and their role in human consciousness. Here the cognitive status of historical knowledge remains an ongoing theme, producing more uncertainty today than ever. What is the relation between literary forms and understanding in historical knowledge? This is not simply a question of retroactive reflection on historical work done in the past but rather a problem in the process of acquiring knowledge itself. Here, too, metahistory can offer reflexive clarification.

(4) Finally, we must clarify the role of academic historical knowledge in the processes involved in cultural orientation. Is the orientating function only an external factor of historical knowledge, or is this idea of the life-serving purpose of history also important for the forming of historical knowledge within its academic context? Metahistory can show that this is not a case of either/or. Without it, we cannot adequately explain what historical education is or why it is so essential.

Notes

9. This is also the case for Italy, Lithuania and other countries.

10. David Carr has criticized this term, which came from the German tradition. He suggested speaking of a philosophy of history, which I consider to be misleading. The philosophy of history is concerned with history itself (whether as facts or as a form of thinking) and is not interested in its unique way for gathering knowledge that became an established academic field. What is especially lacking in Carr's designation is the very crux of historical enquiry: its method of research. Admittedly, metahistory cannot deny the fundamental question of what

history is. In this respect, the philosophy of history is a fundamental element of history, but the one does not simply merge with the other (D. Carr. 2011. 'Which Way is East? Rüsen's *Historik*', *Erwägen Wissen Ethik* 22(4), 508).

11. Reinhart Koselleck limits the area of responsibility for metahistory to the first theme and develops it into a transcendental philosophy of history. 'Metahistory ... illuminates the conditions for possible history' (R. Koselleck. 1987. 'Historik und Hermeneutik', in R. Koselleck and H.-G. Gadamer, *Hermeneutik und Historik* (report from meeting of the Heidelberger Akademie der Wissenschaften, Phil.-hist. Klasse, Bericht 1). Heidelberg, 97–118; quote, 99). Koselleck does not include historical method in his definition – something key to the tradition of metahistory, let alone for the theoretical problems currently facing historiography today. According to Droysen's conceptualization of metahistory (or *Historik*, a term essentially defined in the German-speaking world), Koselleck deals only with the *Systematik*, issues of systematic order, and not with issues of methodology or subject matter.

12. A detailed explanation of the functions of metahistory can be found in *Grundzüge I*, 32 sqq.

CHAPTER 2

The Foundations of Historical Thinking

This chapter deals with the question of what history actually is. In order to answer this question, we need to shift our attention away from historical studies as an academic discipline for the moment. Before the past is researched and placed in a historiographical framework as an object of academic study, it is always already present in – and interrelated with – daily life. Outside of an academic context, a distinct and recognizable 'history' as such does not exist in the cultural realm. Rather, it first appears when specific attention is paid to the past, having nothing to do with methodological rationality and not being especially scientific at all.

History in General There is no human way of life in which a meaningful relation with the past does not play an important part in navigating and dealing with present-day action and suffering. Everywhere and at all times human beings draw on the past to understand the present and to anticipate and plan for the future. If we want to devise a single concept describing the mental processes of interpreting the past, understanding the present and anticipating the future, we have various terms available to us that can be used in an academic or specialized sense. In German we have the competing terms of, on the one hand, *historisches Gedächtnis* (historical recollection) and *historische Erinnerung* (historical memory) and, on the other, *Geschichtsbewusstsein* (historical consciousness). These are key concepts in highly advanced academic discourse that have essentially formed independently of one another and to this day remain unmediated.

The following considerations could be read as an attempt at such a mediation or synthesis. I aim to describe the common human characteristics of interpretive interaction with the past that underlie historical thinking in all cultural manifestations as well as in modern academia. One could call this approach cultural anthropological, as it deals with universalities of human cultural life, that is, dimensions, processes and factors involved in the interpretation of the human world. These are shared by all cultural manifestations and play an important role in them. (With such an approach, theoretical history can help us face present-day challenges of intercultural communication.)

Working from this foundation of culturally universal interpretation of and dealing with the past, we need to further examine the elements that define modern historical thinking, especially the cognitive capacities related to historical experience.

1. How Does History Come into the World?

Experiencing Time as Contingency   Humans interpret themselves and their world. Which interpretive capacities underlie historical thinking? There is one primal human experience in human daily life that describes the cultural coping mechanism of these interpretive capacities: the experience of contingency. Time is a universal dimension in human reality. It appears in human lives in a particular form that requires interpretation: as rupture, a disruption of the regular order of events that take place in human life. The basic human experience described here is found in all expressions of our cultural self-determination. A poetic expression of this experience appears, for instance, in Shakespeare's *Hamlet*:

> Time is out of joint; – O cursed spite,
> that ever I was born to set it right![13]

Elsewhere, Shakespeare describes the experience of time that humans need to navigate with the help of history in the following dialogue:

> King Henry:
> O God! That one might read the book of fate,
> And see the revolution of the times
> … how chances mock,
> And changes fill the cup of alternation
> With divers liquors! O, if this were seen,
> The happiest youth, viewing his progress through,
> What perils past, what crosses to ensue,

Would shut the book, and sit him down and die.

…

Warwick:

> There is history in all men's lives,
> Figuring the nature of the times deceased;
> The which observed, a man may prophesy
> With a near aim, the main change of things
> As yet not come to life, which in their seeds
> And weak beginnings lie intreasured.
> Such things become the hatch and brood of times;
>
> …

King Henry:

> Are these things then necessities?
> Then let us meet them like necessities …[14]

Disruption and Readjustment in Meaning   This brief dialogue makes our subject matter clear.[15] Something happens that disrupts the default temporal order of daily life. Those who face this disruption must interpret it so that it fits into a concept of time according to which they can orient their actions in a meaningful way. Such an experience of contingency could be a great historical event that calls into question all cultural patterns of interpreting history, such as the conquest of Rome in ad 410 or the French Revolution. However, we also encounter these experiences in our daily lives in the minor disruptions and catastrophes we face. In any case, a disruption in the way we act is caused by an experience of suffering that must be dealt with through interpretive efforts so that life can go on.

Shakespeare's dialogue also describes a disruption of meaning caused by the experience of a rupture or break in time and the recapturing of that meaning by re-interpreting time. The disruptions of meaning are perceived as something from the *outside* breaking in, as something that is unpredictable and definitely not wanted or intended. The re-forming of disrupted meaning, on the other hand, comes from *within* and is deliberate and intentional. I distinguish between two times here: a natural time that acts disruptively ('natural' meaning time that is independent of our interpretation of time, that is, time from 'outside'), and a human time that readjusts these disruptions, that comes from within, and that shows the common themes of human life and suffering.

These opposite concepts of time can help define the mental capacities that are of importance here: natural time must be transformed into human time so that human life can be lived in the flow of time, in outside and inside time simultaneously. An elementary and universal process of humanizing time (*Humanisierung von Zeit*) is the fundamental mental capacity for historical thinking in human culture.[16]

From Natural Time to Human Time   Of course, the differentiation between two kinds of time – natural time from without and human time from within – is artificial. But it refers to elementary qualities of the temporality of human existence (*Dasein*) that determine all human life through the flow of time in which, or rather, *as* it takes place. On the one hand, time can be irritating, in the form of rupture, dissonance, misfortune, pain and suffering, and, most radically, death.[17] On the other hand, time can mean reliability and constancy, the success of human living motifs and intentions, the accomplishments of goals, and, most radically, the idea of overcoming death, of a human life culminating in a fulfilled moment. The activity of forming meaning out of historical consciousness takes place between these two extremes.

The naturalness of time does not disappear in this forming of meaning, as contingency cannot simply be removed. Rather, natural time acquires meaning, thereby losing its irritating character. It becomes elevated through meaning. When people accomplish this meaning-making work they acquire a new self-confidence. The original helplessness against the challenge of time is transformed into the capability of integrating it into our interpretive world in such a way that we gain ourselves. It is like the expression 'what doesn't kill you makes you stronger'. Through coping with experiences of time that define life everywhere and at all times, the human self grows. The self gains subjectivity and temporal depth.

Thus, it is in this specific modus of the human mind interpreting the circumstances of its subject matter that history comes into the world. It does not spring forth from the human subject, but acquires its specific character through the pressing experience of time on its subject. In order to determine this specific character, that is, in order to understand what history actually is, we need to consider a more detailed analysis of the essential mental activities in human consciousness that are so significant to history.

2. The Elemental Forms in the Forming of Historical Meaning

a) What is Meaning?

Sense (*Sinn*), or meaning, is the central and fundamental category that defines culture in human life by determining the basis for all human cultural capacities.[18] It would be too much to attempt to present and analyse the many definitions of this category of meaning or to attempt to clarify its inner coherencies here.[19]

To clarify the mental processes involved in the forming of historical meaning, the following interpretations of the category of sense will suffice to illuminate its capacity in historical thinking. Sense is the capacity of the human mind to make sense of the world in which we live. Sense, or rather, meaning (as it will be referred to below), concerns human sensibility as a gateway to experience, a fusion of the human mind with its surroundings, as well as a tool to integrate the experience of this world with the context of mental significance in the face of human suffering and human action. Meaning is the fundamental criterion by which we as humans structure our relationships with ourselves and with other human beings, and that determines our intentions and the direction of our will. Meaning makes orientation possible. It places human life in an interpretive context. It makes it possible to understand the world and the people in it. It has an explanatory function; it forms human subjectivity in the coherent structure of a (personal or social) self. It makes suffering bearable and stimulates action through intentions. And finally, meaning allows communication as a process of interpersonal human understanding.

All of these capacities or capabilities must be performed in the human mind so that human beings can live in the context of time, both in time's internal and external form.

The Mental Processes Involved in Forming Meaning　All historical thinking is based on a specific capacity to form meaning grounded in the experience of time. In order to explicate this mental capacity as the basis for our historical consciousness, it is useful to divide the mental activity of meaning making

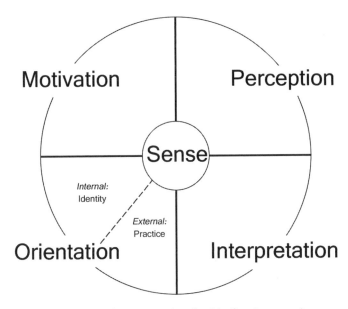

Figure 2.1 The four mental operations involved in forming meaning.

into four different, closely related and even overlapping activities: experience or perception, interpretation, orientation and motivation.

We can imagine these activities in a temporal order: the production of historical meaning is first set in motion through the *experience* of a temporal change. This change casts doubt on the human subject's way of life and thus demands a second step, an interpretation. This interpretation leads to a third step, the cultural orientation of human existence or the human way of life. In the framework of this orientation, the irritation that develops out of disruptive temporal changes is overcome. The interpreted experience of time allows the development of *motivations* for human action in that same framework.

Meaning is the link between these four activities. It brings them together as a unity of fundamental points of view in the human interpretation of the world and the self. It is in this unity that we find the capacity for culture in human beings.[20]

b) Meaning of Time

With this anthropological concept of meaning we can analyse the specific formation of meaning that constitutes the anthropological foundation of historical thinking. Historical thinking is the interpretive handling of the aforementioned experience of challenging contingency. This is not experience of time in and of itself, but rather the specific experience of a contingency that requires interpretation. Historical meaning is formed by integrating temporal changes as experienced by individual human beings with the temporal changes that occur in their world into an interpretive model. This model allows human beings to incorporate their lives into the context of temporal certainty. Using this model, a human being can overcome suffering and perform actions. We articulate meaning within a certain concept of the passing of time (*Zeitverlaufsvorstellung*). Moments of contingency become integrated into this conceptualization of time through interpretation in such a way that contingency, and its specific character, furthers our understanding of the human world and its temporal dimension.

What Makes an Event Historic?   In order to understand the character of historical thinking, it is important to examine more closely the status of events or occurrences over the passage of time in the human world. An event is an occurrence at a particular place and time that happens in a particular way for particular reasons. It is this concrete definitiveness – described as 'individual' in the traditional epistemology of historical thinking – that characterizes the historical event. As a pure fact, it is not yet historic. It only becomes historic when it is interpreted as an event or occurrence that is related to other events in time and part of a meaningful process, that is, when it can be integrated into a conceptualized course of time. This conceptualization gives meaning to the daily events or processes of human activity, making them accessible for all those affected by them. Crucially, this conceptualization does not efface the particular facts, or rather the factual particularity of events, nor does it render them meaningless. Rather, it preserves them, turning these events into the vessels that carry the meaning of history in the interpretive framework of conceptualized time.

Interpretation can also disperse with the concrete definitiveness of events, by emphasizing broad contextual meaning. Isolated or single events still bear meaning within a broad context, but they are no longer singled out for their particularity. Such contexts are, for example, the conceptualizing of time in a cosmic order in which the particularity of a concrete, temporally definable event disappears. The meaning of the whole consumes the singular entity. This precisely does not happen in historical thinking: the specifics of events are not lost but maintained. This is necessary because the concrete time-specific contexts of our ways of life are the things that have to be made understandable in historical thinking. We need a form of interpretation that does not allow the particularity of things to become lost in a general sense of meaning, but that interprets this particularity in combination with broad meanings in a meaningful way.

There are many ways in which something can be significant. It could be the individual character of a single event, such as an accession to the throne or a declaration of independence, or the specifics of a complex order of events such as a war or an entire epoch.

c) Historical Experience

Change is at the core of historical experience. This change is lived or, more commonly, suffered at a specific point or period of time in the multifaceted contingency of human living. Such a profound change can, for example, take place in power relationships. There is a rupture or a dismantling of time that creates a before and after, between which a transformation or alteration is experienced. The challenging character of such an experience touches upon the cultural need of human beings to navigate their daily lives with a concept of the passing of time that produces a consistent meaning through the chain of events as they transpire. This is a means to resolve this rupture in time.[21]

This experience of rupture is immediate and real. It is not what we would generally call 'historical'. It does not refer to a distinct thing that happened in the past that can be separated from the present. However, when we want to understand this 'thing' as past, as an event that is 'historical', then we must create a distance from the past in the present. It proceeds as follows: the distance we experience between the present and the past is seen and

understood against the background – or better yet, on the basis of our experience of a rupture in time. As mentioned previously, there are two times
in this rupture of time in the present: a before and an after. Here we touch
upon an essential element in historical experience: we deal with the experience of differences in time, with the disparity of time, with the own and the
other time (where the other time is experienced as anything but unessential
or unimportant; it was ours and became something other).

Difference in Time, Factuality and Meaning   I have emphasized the experience of a rupture or disruption in time and the meaning of this experience
because historical experience generally only refers to distant time periods;
that is, if we even speak in terms of experience at all. The fact that something
happened in the past is not something we experience as something past but
rather as something that is in some way still present. Such an experience
is, contrary to a current rupture in time, between a then and a now, not
especially meaningful. (It is here that many historical theorists arrive at the
highly problematic position that historical meaning exclusively originates in
the present, and the past in and of itself has no meaning.[22]) Traditionally,
this experience is understood as 'pure': it has no meaning in or of itself.[23]
This purity is emphasized in metahistory when it deals with the investigation
of the pure facts of past events (e.g., the simple fact that the Frankish king
Charlemagne was crowned Roman emperor on the evening of the 25th of
December, Christmas Day, ad 800 by Pope Leo III). The pure fact of this
occurrence exists beyond any meaning or significance, but it is rarely if ever
considered in its absolute 'pure' form. It is simply a derivative, a secondary modus in terms of difference in time. It is basically an experience in a
reduced or shrunken form. It has lost its evocative quality; or better said,
we have lost sight of it since it has been torn from the context in which it
is experienced as different and meaningful.[24] It is exactly this importance of
difference that motivates historical thinking to conceive of the connection
between the far-off past and the living present as comprehensive historical
context.

It would be too limiting to merely consider the historical experience
as a challenge that questions the cultural practices we have for dealing with
time in negative terms. There is another way of experiencing difference in
time. It is just as challenging as the one already discussed. This experience
does not represent a lack or deficit in meaning in the context of a given
cultural orientation, but rather the opposite. The 'other' time can inspire
historical interpretation as a source of meaning, even as a force of meaning.
Historical experiences as sources of meaning can illuminate absences of
meaning in the present. Historical experience is significant in addressing this
absence or deficit; it resolves the problem of deficiency by acquiring new

historical meaning. Such a difference in time is above all emphasized by those intellectuals (including historians) who recognize a lack of meaning in modern secular civil society and who seek to compensate for this absence by recovering meaning from the pre-modern past through remembrance.[25]

d) Historical Interpretation

The irritating character of this experienced difference in time asks for interpretation. It bothers human beings until they have dealt with the matter so that it fits within the organized structure of their lives. What form does this interpretation take? Difference in time is interpreted when it is integrated into a broad conceptualization of time that determines the cultural orientation of human activity.

This can happen in many ways, depending on the challenging character of the historical experience. In archaic societies, every temporal change that was experienced had to be interpreted in such a manner as to maintain an existing or established tradition. It was, in other words, immobilized. In modern societies, the rupture in time is integrated within a dynamic historical process, within an idea of history that makes change meaningful. We could also interpret beyond the particular time of historical change and understand what has occurred as a process that documents a general rule of human behaviour. In other words, we are provoked to formulate a general rule when something happens, and it is this rule in combination with the occurrence itself that makes meaning. The historical experience is then placed within an interpretive pattern that makes it understandable. When it becomes understandable it can then be accounted for, or registered, as a cultural asset. Historical experience thus strengthens the ability of those concerned to handle temporal change productively. By bridging the interpretive gap, historical experience can prove effective in the life-serving orientation of human existence.

e) Historical Orientation I: The World

Interpretation turns historical experience into historical knowledge. When certain methodological standards take effect in interpretation we can speak of knowledge. It enters into the cognitive landscape of the human world and can be used for the purpose of orientation. Not all interpretation is orientation. Orientation requires a direct relationship to the human way of life or a quality of life-serving purpose. This can mean different things to different people, depending on the various circumstances in which people live. For one thing, historical knowledge can strengthen the power of traditions. It can also do the opposite. It can weaken the power of tradition and enable a new orientation. Historical knowledge can strengthen and intensify the competency for ruling human life among the educated elite. It can be used to suggest the possibility of improving living standards (in

the interpretive framework of our concept of progress) and to mobilize the
necessary potential for action.

f) Historical Orientation II: The Self

Historical orientation does not only serve to extrapolate the temporality of
the world so that human beings may better adjust to that world. History
offers a means for human beings to find orientation about, or better yet,
in themselves. Historical orientation extends into a human's inner being,
the depths of a person, even as far as the dark corners of an individual's
subjectivity. 'The world' naturally includes the living, breathing human
beings who makes sense of the world around them. Historical knowledge also serves as a way for human beings to form their own inner time.
Here we find one of the most important functions of historical orientation:
its role in the cultivation (*Bildung*), negotiation, assertion and alteration of
identity.

Identity   Today, identity is considered a non-concept (*Un-Begriff*), unusable
in any halfway decent clear rational argumentation.[26] But together with the
concept, the matter it refers to is also in danger of becoming increasingly
blurred or descending into semantic randomness in which all is possible and
nothing excluded, where its meaning becomes so obscure that it makes discussion impossible. But when we understand the term 'identity' as something basic – as simple as the answer to the question 'who am I?' – then the
conceptual confusion can (hopefully) be curbed.

These questions – who am I? who are we? – are repeatedly asked on
both a personal and a social level. The answer always depends on a concept
of time concerning the 'I' and the 'we' that is grounded in experience and
in anticipation of the future. Historical orientation involves the human self
in a permanent state of questioning or self-questioning within the context
of a temporality. Through the course of time this orientation gives the
human self – as it moves through, takes on and interprets time – a life-
facilitating base. It helps the self find its proper footing in the temporal
world. This could be in the form of preserved tradition that legitimizes
fixed and assigned status roles. It could also be in the form of a formative
or educational process through which communities or individual human
beings understand themselves as representatives of the human species, establishing their personal and social status as humans. Some examples of this are
the different humanistic traditions, as well as the discord between modern
French and German national identities that have developed in different
ways through their contentious processes of foundation, but together intellectually refer to humanity.

g) Motivation

Cultural orientations generally extend into the dimensions of human mentality where motivations for action are formed as impulses of the will. Such motivations are also fuelled by the experience of suffering (which is overlooked in most action theories). Historical knowledge, which is transformed in these dimensions, obtains a thoroughly practical function here. For example, this can go as far as inspiring a willingness to kill other people for the sake of a historically articulated national identity, or to sacrifice one's life for the nation. The same is true for the possible results of particular actions committed in the name of certain (fundamentalist) historical interpretations of religious conviction.

Max Weber described the motivational effect of interpretive patterns (*Ideen*, or ideas) using the metaphor of a *Weichenstellung* (points on a railway track) to describe interests (as impulses for action).[27] In doing so he articulated a fundamental relationship between thinking and acting. We could link this to Nietzsche's popular concept of the *Willen zur Macht* (will to power). But in contrast to Nietzsche, who emphasized that this will is blind, we must consider the anthropological understanding of will as having a view, and thus it unfolds its power within the context of an interpreted world. Historical knowledge is an indispensable element of this interpretation of the world.

The power or strength of motivation that develops in humans in the processes of identity formation is fundamentally a matter of self-assertion of individuals and communities. Historical patterns for interpretation grounded in experience can motivate human beings to modify conventional ways of life and prompt a reflection on motivation aimed at feasible purposes. Historical knowledge can be used as a defence against unrealizable expectations or demands and with this knowledge human beings can motivate the will to change or transform.

In transforming historical knowledge with its capacity for orientation into motivation, emotions play a significant role.[28] Emotions negotiate between thinking and wanting. As such they represent an essential element in realizing the orientating function of historical thinking. Emotion concerns our 'motive' in thinking. It would be misguided not to recognize the role of emotions or to limit this role to merely the motivation behind action. This would misrepresent the role that emotions play in the initiation and 'direction' of historical knowledge.

h) The Narrative Logic in the Forming of Historical Meaning

What does it mean to form historical meaning and how should we understand historical studies as a specific way to form historical meaning about the past? In order to answer these questions, an insight into the logical structure of historical thinking is of central, if not decisive importance. It is the insight into the narrative structure in which interpretive dealing with historical experience takes place and in which historical knowledge as the result of this interpretation is represented in its particularity.[29]

Historical thinking acts as a bridge between time periods that are so different that they are experienced as irritating and need to be processed. This bridge is a 'history'. It represents the meaningful passage of time in which the experience of different time periods must be integrated through interpretation. This 'history' is a narrative.[30] Meaning gathers the events that are in need of interpretation and orders them in a sequence with other events. In this time-referential connection the historical experiences that need interpretation acquire meaning, which they need in order to be dealt with. This sequencing occurs in the narrative telling of history.

Narration is a fundamental and universal activity of the human mind. It is how we form the meaning of events. This is not to say that narrative is the only way to form meaning from events and experiences. We can, for example, also interpret experiences as single instances within a general pattern. However, in such an interpretation the concrete temporal particularity of an experience is lost, as it is precisely this particularity that must be disregarded in order to make something conform to a pattern. Narration usually also employs a concept of general coherence between events. This is, however, a very specific coherence based on a passing of time that moves by and through the events and carries them along rather than dispersing them.

Forming Meaning in the Experience of Time: Vusi Goes Back   Our theme here can be illustrated with a typical example of a simple historical interpretation.[31]

In 1981, a handbook for social work was published in the townships of Johannesburg. It included a comic that was supposed to serve as an explanation of the horrible conditions of the townships to the people who lived in them. The idea was that they should learn what led to this situation in the first place, and thanks to this explanation they would see the chance for future opportunities and be motivated to act to improve their situation.[32]

Vusi, the hero of the story, who lives in a township (and with whom township residents were supposed to identify), visits his grandfather in his homeland. The living conditions and suffering there provoke him to feel anguish. His grandfather then tells a story that explains why things have come to be so miserable. This story has a clear beginning, middle and end. It represents the changes in the living conditions of the black people of South Africa over a specific period of time (in a highly schematic and completely ideological way, a point that is however irrelevant for our purposes here).

By using a historical narrative to explain how the conditions of the present came to be, a perspective for the future and a call for action are

Figure 2.2 Vusi Goes Back. From: Cloete and Mason, *Vusi Goes Back: A Comic Book about the History of South Africa*, Prezanian Comix, E.D.A. Used with permission.

drafted. I am interested here in the structure of time and the form of representation presented in the speech bubbles. This time structure features a coherence of events that is presented in narrative form. The specific logic of historical thinking, in its elementary and fundamental form, is demonstrated. We can summarize this by way of theory: history is an event-based, temporal coherence between the past and the present (with an eye on the future) that creates meaning and the orientation needed in daily life through narrative.

At the same time, the comic illustrates another essential feature of the forming of historical meaning: its communicative character. Historical meaning making is not a monologue but always takes place within social contexts. It unfolds its life-serving purpose in these contexts. The fact that this life-serving purpose is not something of a purely extrinsic nature is crucial for understanding the particularity and capacity of historical thinking. It cannot be understood as merely something that can be used or applied and that has no influence on the thing itself, namely the interpreted experience of time. The meaning that historical experience gets through interpretation by historical thinking cannot be adequately unravelled or understood without a systematic consideration of this life-serving purpose. It does not arise from pure cognitive processes in the human mind but is ignited by experiences that provoke the human mind for a response. Such a response is only satisfying when it removes the barrier we face when confronted by changes in our lives that demand interpretation. This happens through the integration of this experience into a meaningful temporal coherence of past, present and future.

Narrative   Narration is a particular mental process in our capacity to form meaning. Within it we find a good amount of cognitive knowledge, but also a fundamental reference to an ethical standpoint that both determines action and handles suffering. It is empirical and normative at the same time. It also underlies the distinction between facts and norms or values that is so important for the philosophy of science and epistemology. (An attempt to unravel the particular cognitive capacity for historical knowledge with this distinction would be doomed to fail for purely logical reasons.)

In his brilliant analysis of the stories in 'A Thousand and One Nights', Volker Klotz clarified the fundamental rooting of narrative in the practical context of life, where telling a story takes place in a communicative way.[33] After invoking God as the source of all meaning in the human world, the story begins with an unsettling experience with deadly consequences. Scheherazade, the archetypal storyteller, heals the wounds inflicted by a troubling event (the sovereign's wife cheats on him) with her stories. Her listener, the enraged victim of the unfaithful wife, learns from her stories and transforms into the 'life-serving' and good ruler. The threat of death that is delayed for a thousand and one nights transforms into happiness. Scheherazade becomes the consort of the sovereign, who has returned to his political responsibilities thanks to her.

This paradigm of storytelling is not specifically historic but is nonetheless representative for the narrative form of historical interpretation. It represents its inner ethos, its vital reference to practical problems of orientation in the lives of human beings.

History as Narrative   When does a life-serving story become historic? This question can best be answered by differentiating between historical thinking and other (ideal-typical) forms of narrative production of meaning, that is, from myth, art and religion. These forms of cultural orientation also use narrative, address disruptions to the human experience of time, interpret them and integrate them in a meaningful temporal coherence. But there is an essential difference. The events told through myth are different from those in historical narrative: the former occur in a 'dream time' that differs from life as it is lived 'in the real world'. The events of history are, however, part of the real world. Events represented in artistic expression are not historic in the sense that they have a fictional quality that is essential in art. Regarding religion, the difference is more difficult, at least when religious faith depends on sources that have a historic character as well, such as the life of Buddha, the Jewish prophets, Jesus of Nazareth or Muhammad. As long as this reference exists, we can say that religious storytelling is also historical, and theoretically, religious narrative is not essentially different from historical narrative. However, in historical processes, in which a culture of historiography has developed, the standard conceptualizations of time have a secular character. It is important to remember that a narrative is historical when it refers to real occurrences in the past.

3. An Aside: Contingency and Freedom

The internal ethics of the historical narrative, its specific synthesis of experience and norms, touches upon a basic anthropological fact: human beings orientate their actions according to vantage points that go beyond the given circumstances to something different or better. The mental structure of our orientation towards action (and dealing with suffering) is characterized by a basic surplus of meaning, which extends beyond the given circumstances. It is not just the experience of shortcomings and suffering that motivates humans to change the conditions that create these experiences. The desire for meaning, the wish for happiness, and utopian pursuits all fundamentally transcend the realm of experience of our daily lives, too. It is this anthropological transcendence inherent in the intentionality of human consciousness that enables the irritating experiences of contingency and the ensuing push toward interpretation. Only when there is a fundamental discrepancy between the situation at hand and the existing framework of meaning can events lose their role in producing meaning within the existing interpretive context and provide an impulse to form meaning in a new way.

In this conflicting position between meaning-making consciousness and the pre-existing living conditions around us, we find the roots for what we commonly call 'freedom'. What is meant is the anthropologically fundamental fact that all human beings strive to form their living situations according to viewpoints that they deem meaningful. They want to know that their

lives are their own and organize them accordingly. There would be no experiences of contingency or the resulting need for interpretation without this
'obstinacy' in human culture.

Suffering at the Base of Interpretation   The activity of meaning-making historical consciousness is composed of two things: a constitutive moment of
suffering – things in our world are not happening as they should – and at the
same time a constitutive moment of freedom – we go against the flow of the
default meanings and interpretations and we set our own course according
to views that we consider our own.

Whether such a course can realistically be taken is debatable. But the
experience of suffering sparks the idea that things could be different. This is
less idealistic than it sounds and does not completely accurately reflect the
state of historical consciousness. Not all suffering can be transformed into
meaning. The worst kinds of experience, the traumas of meaninglessness and
absurdity, do not fit effortlessly into a concept of meaning in our cultural
orientation. It is part of the peculiar nature of our sense of direction in daily
life (including the narrative forming of meaning in historical consciousness)
that unresolved suffering is contained and concealed within these experiences. Within this concealment, whether it is in- or outside the borders
of the established interpretation, it proves to have a powerful effect on us.
These unresolved remains of historical orientation carry the limit of freedom
manifested in a culture's handling of history in daily life. At the same time
these remains create the constant unrest that pushes us to move beyond our
limitations.

4. Experiencing Crisis and the Forming of Historical Meaning: A Typology

Of course, the mental patterns involved in forming historical meaning (and
on which the specific processes involved in academic historical thinking are
based) are more complex than they seem in the aforementioned examples.
But we first need to consider the fundaments of historical thinking that can
be accepted as anthropologically universal across space and time. In the following I will outline a first step in distinguishing different possible ways to
translate the experience of time into knowledge-based historical orientation.

Historical thinking is fundamentally 'critical', meaning it is based on the
challenge of distinguishing different time periods in the process of changing
human circumstances. We can call this challenge a 'crisis' and understand
the forming of historical meaning as a solution to a crisis in the experience
of time. This solution can naturally take many different shapes, depending

on the character of the crisis at hand. We can distinguish three ideal types of time crises, as well as three ideal types of interpretive integration of these crises into a life-serving orientation for daily life in its temporal context. Crises can be categorized as (a) normal, (b) critical and (c) catastrophic. The varying interpretive patterns for the forming of historical meaning can be divided accordingly.[34]

(a) *Normal crises* are experiences of change that can be resolved in the framework of established historical interpretive patterns. This type of crisis concerns the challenge of an experience of contingency that can be addressed through existing methods of historical interpretation. Such 'normal' experiences of time are the most common. They preserve the effective interpretive patterns of an established historical culture and maintain it. The global financial crisis of the previous decade is an example in which a crisis was resolved historically by interpreting it in terms of the cyclical nature of the development of capitalism.

(b) *Critical crises* refer to experiences of time that cast doubt on the established interpretive patterns that now prove ineffective in dealing with them. These crises reshape the interpretive landscape; they inspire cultural efforts to change the patterns for historical interpretation. For example, the crisis of the onset of cultural modernity, termed *Sattelzeit* (saddle period) by Koselleck, brought on a new way of thinking about history. Historicism, which has represented this modern way of thinking about history for almost a century, is based on such a crisis experience and how contemporaries (mainly of the French Revolution) interpreted the events of that time period.[35]

(c) *Catastrophic crises* have a traumatic character. They destroy the interpretive potential of historical consciousness. They appear as meaningless or absurd, destroying the existing capacity for meaning making in historical thinking. Or we can say that the capacity for meaning making is not sufficient to resolve or overcome this meaninglessness or absurdity without concealing, deferring or repressing essential parts of the experience of temporal change first. An obvious example of this is the Holocaust. Such crises no longer allow for a conceptualization of time in which we can integrate these

Table 2.1 The three types of crises.

Type of Crisis	Reaction
Normal	Application of established patterns of interpretation
Critical	Change of established patterns of interpretation
Catastrophic	Destruction of established patterns of interpretation

events into a coherent and meaningful narrative. They destroy any attempt to establish genuine historical coherence in the sequence of events. In this case, the meaning of temporal change can only exist above all history, as apocalyptic, beyond the context of coherence between different times.[36]

The differentiation between these three types of crises is based on logical abstractions. In the actual processes of dealing with history the three blend together and complex and varying processes of historical thinking develop out of our experiences with the challenging nature of time.

Notes

13. W. Shakespeare. *Hamlet*, Act 1, Scene 5, line 189 sq.

14. W. Shakespeare. *Henry IV, Part 2*, Act 3, Scene 1, line 45 sqq.

15. Considering 'The which observed, a man may prophesy, ...' as a specific concept of history or interpretation, I will not go into here. See this volume 159sq.

16. It is important to emphasize that the concept of 'humanizing time' (*Humanisierung von Zeit*) is not necessarily an anthropological interpretive pattern but rather a quality of time that is compatible with the intentions and conceptions of meaning in the lives of human beings. Humanizing time in pre-modern societies is represented by a godlike figure who steers the course of human destiny, or by a divine entity of an impersonal nature (e.g., Dao in Chinese culture) who grants meaning to the temporal processes in the human world.

17. The constitutive meaning of death in interpreting the human experience of time, as in the narrative process, was impressively analysed by Walter Benjamin: 'Death is the sanction of everything that the storyteller can tell. He has borrowed his authority from death. In other words, it is natural history to which his stories refer back.' (W. Benjamin. 1969. 'The Storyteller', in idem, *Illuminations*, edited by H. Arendt, New York: Schocken Books, 369; W. Benjamin. 1977. 'Der Erzähler', in idem, *Gesammelte Schriften*, vol. II.2, edited by R. Tiedemann and H. Schweppenhäuser, Frankfurt am Main: Suhrkamp, 450).

18. More fundamentally, see E. Angehrn. 2010. *Sinn und Nicht-Sinn*, Tübingen: Mohr/Siebeck.

19. I attempted this in a joint project with Karl-Joachim Hölkeskamp: K.-J. Hölkeskamp, J. Rüsen, E. Stein-Hölkeskamp, and H.T. Grütter (eds). 2003. *Sinn (in) der Antike: Orientierungssysteme, Leitbilder und Wertkonzepte im Altertum*, Mainz: Philipp von Zabern, 1–16. Also see this volume, 68sqq., 'Das Sinnkonzept "Geschichte"'.

20. It is important to add that, with this definition of culture in terms of how human beings form meaning, we have attained a perspective with which we can distinguish culture as a dimension in the lives of human beings from other dimensions, such as regarding economics, society, politics and environment. At the same time it becomes clear that there is no area in which culture does not play a role in the lives of human beings. Such a definition counters the presiding vagueness in cultural categories that tend to describe everything in the lives of human beings as culture. Cognition fosters analytical selectivity with regards to basic concepts and prevents them from being forced into a schematic system.

21. Christian Meier has shown this in a practically paradigmatic interpretation of Herodotus. C. Meier. 1973. 'Die Entstehung der Historie', in R. Koselleck and W.-D. Stempel (eds), *Geschichte-Ereignis und Erzählung* (*Poetik und Hermeneutik*, vol. 5), Munich: Fink, 251–306. Hermann Kulke presented a similar argument in H. Kulke. 1998. 'Geschichtsschreibung als Heilung eines Traditionsbruchs?', in J. Rüsen, M. Gottlob and A. Mittag, *Die Vielfalt der Kulturen*, Frankfurt am Main: Suhrkamp, 422–440.

22. As, for example, in H. White. 1973. *Metahistory*, Baltimore: The Johns Hopkins University Press; or in H.-J. Goertz. 2001. *Unsichere Geschichte*, Stuttgart: Reclam. Also from the same author: H.-J. Goertz. 2009. 'Was können wir von der Vergangenheit wissen?', *GWU* 60(12), 692–706.

23. Max Weber speaks tellingly of a 'vast chaotic stream of events which flows away through time' ('*ungeheuren chaotischen Strom ... von Geschehnissen, der sich durch die Zeit dahinwälzt*'). M. Weber. 1968. *Gesammelte Aufsätze zur Wissenschaftslehre*, 3rd ed., edited by J. Winckelmann. Tübingen: Mohr/Siebeck, 213 f.

24. When Max Weber speaks of the humanities or social sciences as reality-based or objective sciences ('*Wirklichkeitswissenschaften*'), reality means facts that have already been shaped or filtered through our *Wertbeziehung* (reference to values), through the context of our own lives and ideas.

25. This explains the allure of the work on religious history by Mircea Eliade. The difference between our own time and that of another (which through interpretation becomes historical time) is experienced as loss. This helps explain the title of the work by Peter Laslett, *The World We Have Lost* (P. Laslett. 1965. *The World We Have Lost*, London: Methuen).

26. See L. Niethammer. 2000. *Kollektive Identität*, Reinbek: Rowohlt.

27. M. Weber. 1922. 'Die Wirtschaftsethik der Weltreligionen', vol. 1, Tübingen: Mohr/Siebeck, 252 (introduction).

28. See also J. Rüsen. 2013. 'Die Macht der Gefühle im Sinn der Geschichte', in J. Brauer and M. Lücke (eds), *Emotionen, Geschichte und historisches Lernen*, Göttingen: Vandenhoeck & Ruprecht.

29. For a fundamental and influential example, see P. Ricoeur. 1984. *Time and Narrative*, vol. 1, Chicago: University of Chicago Press.

30. A detailed analysis of the logic in historical narratives is found in this author's work: J. Rüsen. 2001. 'Historisches Erzählen', in idem, *Zerbrechende Zeit*, Cologne: Böhlau, 43–105.

31. See also ibid., 57 f.

32. D. Cloete and A. Mason. 1981. *Vusi Goes Back*, Johannesburg: Prezanian Comix in association with the Environmental and Development Agency (EDA) Trust, fig. 2.

33. V. Klotz. 1982. 'Erzählen als Enttöten', in E. Lämmert, *Erzählforschung: Ein Symposion*, Stuttgart: Metzler, 319–334.

34. With the following typology I am referring back to this author's work: J. Rüsen. 2001. 'Krise, Trauma, Identität', in idem, *Zerbrechende Zeit*, Cologne: Böhlau, 139–179, esp. 153.

35. Also cf. F. Jaeger and J. Rüsen. 1992. *Geschichte des Historismus*, Munich: C.H. Beck.

36. As a paradigm for this kind of transformation of history into something apocalyptic, see Walter Benjamin's *On the Concept of History*. Also see this volume, 105, n. 120.

CHAPTER 3

History as Academic Discipline

The Issue   Starting from a fundamentally anthropological basis for dealing historically with the past, I would like to address the question of what historical thinking as an academic study or science is. What exactly makes historical thinking academic or scientific? Following the considerations concerning the capacities of historical consciousness presented in Chapter 2, the answer to this question is: a specific mode of making sense of our experience of time by way of narrative. The following considerations are not concerned with the institutional realities that characterize the discipline in its academic structure. They are also not an exploration of the historical processes that have shaped the field of study. Rather, the following arguments focus on letting historical thinking 'unfold' from its anthropological basis in the sense of a systematic development rather than tracing its historical origins.

Metaphorically speaking, I want to construct a 'historical science' building on the foundation and groundwork of our mental processes in forming historical meaning. My argument focuses on the logical form, the cognitive core of historical thinking, by focusing on one key issue: the scientific validity of historical knowledge. At the same time my argument turns to the contextual relations in which this cognitive core – the specifically historical character of historical thinking – is connected to other mental processes and intellectual principles. Only in these contexts can we discover the uniqueness of historical thinking.

Notes for this section begin on page 64.

If we consider history only in terms of its scientific merit, this core looks problematic in comparison to other fields of study, especially when compared to scientific enquiry in the natural sciences. One could fundamentally dispute the scientific merit of historical thinking using arguments based on the specifically non-scientific (often aesthetic or poetic) aspects and approaches of historical thinking that necessarily and logically result from the context of historical practice. This perspective loses sight of the unique features of how research is organized in the field. We need to consider both the cognitive core and its inner contextual relationship to non-cognitive aspects and procedures in the human mind.

1. Historical Meaning and Academic Study

Academic study is a specific process of forming knowledge that distinguishes itself from other forms of intellectual endeavour through specific procedures involved in the generating and validating of this knowledge. Scientific knowledge is cognition and cognition is an especially distinctive form of knowledge. It can be characterized as follows: the propositions or, in terms of historical thinking, the specific structures of meaning in a 'history' or 'historical narrative' contain reasons or rationales that other renderings of the story do not. In the case of history, we can simply say that the scientific pursuit of knowledge is based on research, and research is a systematic process founded on generally accepted principles. This process forms empirically grounded data into temporal structures and gives them the form of a knowledge-based 'history' or 'historical narrative'. We call the principles on which this process is based the 'historical method'.

History as academic or scientific study gives methodical structure to historical thinking. With this structure, the academic study of history asserts its claims of validity for its research results and for the narratives that incorporate these results. The methodical structure in the academic or scientific pursuit of knowledge is grounded in the protection of validity claims. Scientific knowledge makes ambitious validity claims based on research and its treatment of evidence.

By referring to methodical research, the scientific study of history distinguishes itself from other ways of forming historical meaning, such as through art, myth, religion and – especially for the modern world – through ideological forms of knowledge, in which history plays an important role. The concept of method can be used in a different or metaphorical way, too. After all, there are specific methods in art and religion and the like. But these methods are fundamentally different from those used in academic study. However, method in the narrow sense of the word is the distinguishing criterion for the forming of scientific historical meaning.

2. Method and Truth

Why should we consider method? Historical research draws historical knowledge from empirical information or data left to us from the past, information that is generally available (before our eyes, so to speak). The methodical process of eliciting knowledge serves to strengthen the validity of this knowledge and to systematically establish its plausibility or soundness. Method substantiates knowledge by making its assertions verifiable. Plausibility, soundness, the possibility of verification: these concepts come together and form *truth*.

All cultural forms of meaning, in the communicative contexts of their effect, presentation and discursive negotiation, claim to be true. Regarding the peculiar nature of academic study, method and truth are closely related.[37] The cognition of scholarly study bases its truth claim on its method, or the methodical process, and this cognition in turn depends on methodical structures to acquire and substantiate knowledge.

Truth is a big word, and when we use it to characterize a certain way of thinking we must first explain what we mean by it. As mentioned before, the forming of meaning in all cultures is grounded in truth claims. But do these claims have the same intentions? We could answer this question with both a yes and a no: yes, in the sense that the aim is always to make meaning plausible, to present and accept it as plausible; no, in that there are many different kinds of grounds for plausibility.

The Complexity of Truth   Generally speaking, we can distinguish the following types of truth claims based on varying principles:

- *Scientific truth* is based on principles of empirical testability and theoretical consistency. Droysen called this truth '*Richtigkeit*' (rightness) in his *Historik*.
- *Practical truth* (that is, moral or ethical normative claims of validity) is based on principles of what is 'good': in the case of historical thinking, this is where its life-serving purpose comes in.
- *Political truth*, as the possibility of consensus in power relations, refers to their legitimacy.
- *Therapeutic truth* is a specific form of truth in dealing with the phenomenon of health and illness; its point of reference is healing. True is that which heals.
- The truth claim of *technical cognition* is based on feasibility or functionality.
- *Strategic truth* refers to the battles human beings wage with each other (we could also speak of a polemic truth[38]), and gains persuasiveness through victory. True is that which leads to victory.

- *Aesthetic truth* is based on judgements of taste. It refers to a very specific quality in the artistic forming of meaning that is generally called 'beauty'.
- *Rhetorical truth* is claimed in the process of verbal communication through the persuasiveness of statements. True is that which can convince others.
- We can also speak of a kind of *religious truth*, which is grounded in the desire of belief systems for plausibility. A specific set of criteria that we would call salvation or redemption is important for such plausibility. True is that which redeems or saves.

This list is by no means complete. It can be expanded further, considering the diverse dimensions and orientations of the ways in which humans make meaning in all its geographical and temporal contexts. As these dimensions and orientations represent, in their complex correlation, the span of human culture, constantly both distinguishing one culture from another and relating one culture to another, so too we see different 'truths' within a highly complex network of relationships. Truths never appear in isolated form, but rather almost always in mixed proportions. (This is of central importance for understanding the validity claims of historical thinking.) Determining what these proportions are also involves validity claims. In this case we deal with truth on another level, a meta-level. It is at this level that we also find conceptualizations of truth. A meta-concept can, for example, establish a hierarchy among truths, differentiating between lower or higher truths. The idea that underlies all of these truth concepts is of course that the different truth criteria should not contradict each other.

From the previous considerations (with due care and without further delving into the philosophical discourse on the subject), we can form a definition of truth for the following discussion of the scholarly nature of historical studies using this essential criterion: truth is a property of our capacity to form meaning that is based on a constellation of regulative principles that can be employed in asserting, discussing, accepting, discounting or changing claims of validity in discursive communication.

The sense, or meaning (*Sinn*), of culture that is necessary for the human way of life is the most important criterion in all matters of truth. Truth must make sense and have meaning; it only has meaning when it has a life-serving purpose. The life of a human being is more than just a biological process: as Aristotle emphasized, human beings always want a 'good' life. In terms of modern societies, we could borrow Thomas Jefferson's idea of the pursuit of happiness as laid out in the American Declaration of Independence. Thus cultural truth should, above all else, be based on that which makes human life 'good' or 'happy'.

3. The Criteria for Truth in Historical Thinking

The scientific character of historical studies comes down to its claims of truth. 'As long as there are enough historians who consider history as a legitimate field of study, so too will history maintain its grip on the truth.'[39] But which truth is meant here? In order to answer this question, we need to address the foundation of historical thinking in the real world, or in its anthropological roots. The validity claims that always come up when we deal with our experience of time and differences between past and present through narrative should be identified. It is this narrative that helps us to form meaning that provides orientation and allows us to bridge the gap between past and present.

All historical narratives claim to be true. They articulate these claims, too, in vastly different ways: one can, for example, refer to divine authority like Hesiod did in the opening of Theogony, or to witnesses who were there when it happened, and so forth. And since historical studies can only form narrative meaning in a specific way alongside other experiences of time it must also follow the criteria of truth for historical thinking in general. Historical thinking becomes academic when its validity is dependent on methodical processes; when it becomes methodical. Science is method: no discipline or field of study that wants to call itself scientific (or academic or scholarly) can ignore this fact.

In order, then, to understand what the critical historical method for history as science is, we first of all need to examine the fundamental validity claims of historical thinking. This is far from clear, as histories want to be plausible by a variety of different means.

Four Means of Plausibility   We can distinguish four such means. The difference between them is more or less artificial, as it is determined only by dismantling the unity and internal coherence of a narrative history in order to expose the varying logics in plausibility. We are concerned here with terms of (a) experience, (b) explanation, (c) interpretation and (d) meaning:

(a)   Histories want to be true in terms of what they claim about the past: that what is told in the present has in fact taken place in the past.
(b)   Histories want to be true in terms of how they *explain* the reported events of the past.
(c)   Histories want to be true in terms of what they claim about the meaning of the past for conceptualizations of time in the cultural orientations of the present.
Finally, (d) histories want to be true in terms of how they represent the interpretation of factual past events for the sake of the present through narrative.

To reveal the scholarly character of historical thinking, we need to identify the cognitive elements in these criteria of truth: the first is empirical
evidence, the second is theory. (a) Empirical evidence refers to the factuality
of reported events. (b) Theory refers to the inner factual coherence of these
events that explains the relation between the separate facts in a temporal
context. In a third instance, (c) norms and values come into play, that is the
normative points of reference in the practical orientation of daily life. The
cognitive form of these points of reference is a value judgement. Fourth
and finally, (d) a synthesis is formed out of evidence, theory and normative
standards through the narrative coherence of a story.

Academic study combines these four points of reference into a methodological form. They are merged in a discursive process of argumentation
through which they gain a specific character traditionally called 'objectivity'.
This concept has been discredited for some time now, as it suggests that
academic history deals with the enquiry and presentation of the pure facts of
past events in which the subjectivity of the people telling this history from
within their own cultural place and time plays no crucial role. This notion
may have been (and may still be) considered valid by some professional historians. But it is rarely found in in the prominent works in which historians
reflect on the study of history.[40] The opposite is actually the case: the insights
of perspectivism, of the dependency of historical knowledge on the standpoint of its subject regarding the events of the past, are a part of the origins
of modern historical studies.[41]

Then what other concept should we use here? Historical studies, with
all its reflective discourse, is remarkably silent when it comes to the cognitive uniqueness of scholarly historical thinking. Since the term 'objectivity' is misleading, as it assumes 'history' as a presentation of facts from
the events of the past, we should use a narrow interpretation. It should
only come into play when it really comes down to verifying the factual
nature of past events through methodical research. Regarding the means
of plausibility described above, we should instead speak of *intersubjectivity*,
as it concerns historical claims (histories) presented (or told) in such a way
that we can generally agree on them. 'Generally' here means notwithstand-
ing differences in context, interests, preconceived notions and practical
intentions.

Whether such a thing as the capacity for agreement or common ground
(*Zustimmungsfähigkeit*) exists is a point of discussion. Nonetheless, the academic status of historical studies as a professionalized discipline is based on
the claim that such agreement is possible through certain methodical processes.[42] That is, it is claimed within the framework of discursive practice in
which professional historical knowledge is produced and presented in historiographical form. If this claim did not exist then there would be no need to

discuss, i.e. to justify representations of history. This intersubjectivity can be summarized as follows.

Types of Plausibility in Historical Thinking   (a) *Empirical* plausibility in historical thinking increases the possibility of agreed-upon histories by referencing verifiable facts. In this case, the concept of 'objectivity' is appropriate. It is based on what has been called the '*Pathos des Dokumentarischen*' (the pathos of documentation).[43] Claims about what, when, where, how and why something happened in the past must be verified in the present with evidence from the past. The corresponding research method for this is the critical examination of source material (source criticism).[44]

(b) *Theoretical* plausibility in historical thinking increases the possibility of agreed-upon histories by explicitly and reflectively referring to generalized comprehensive statements that form, or at least enable, theory. Here, intersubjectivity refers to the explanatory value of historical statements. This explanatory value increases when the explanations are based in theory. (For that, however, it is necessary to determine what exactly theories constitute in the historical cognitive process and how they are used.[45]) The corresponding research method here is interpretation.[46]

(c) *Normative* plausibility in historical thinking becomes a criterion for intersubjectivity by way of reflecting on and explaining perspective. In this way, the relevant perspective, which brings the realized past into the present day, will be illuminated with respect to the prevailing problems regarding orientation in the context of the current day. Only through perspective does the past have any historical meaning for the present. These interpretive perspectives in historical thinking always involve norms. These norms, and the views on the past that are based on them, are not arbitrary. On the contrary, they are grounded in problems of orientation that develop from the context and standpoint of historical thinking in the present. In this regard, they must be seen as 'objective' (in the sense of 'predefined'). They become relevant in the interests of cognition (*Erkenntnisinteressen*). Such interests are of course subjective, though also explicable and not merely arbitrary.

We can explain them by turning to problems of orientation. All those dealing with problems of orientation are intersubjectively tied to history, or historical knowledge. Problems of orientation can lead to conflicting perspectives and different related interests in social life. So, too, can normative historical perspectives be different, even contradictory: history from below, history from outside, history from above, history from the perspective of victim or perpetrator, and so on. It appears as if there are clear limitations to cognitive validity claims. But norms, as previously mentioned, are based on reasonable grounds – a point that is also true for the different interest

Table 3.1 Schematic rendition for claims of truth in historical thinking.

Plausibility	Explanatory Source
Empirical plausibility	Reference to evidence/experience
Theoretical plausibility	Strength of explanation
Normative plausibility	Consideration of perspective
Narrative plausibility	Reference to life-serving purpose

groups that are conceived in a normative framework in historical thinking. The grounds that cover the scope or the depth of the historical perspective in question become specifically historic. Their validity depends on the extent to which they integrate interests or 'concerns' (*Betroffenheiten*) into the explanation (e.g., a perspective that encompasses the 'interests' or 'concerns' of the perpetrators and the victims).

(d) *Narrative* plausibility in historical thinking becomes a criterion of intersubjectivity by explicating agreed-upon, or common, meaning. In the final analysis, the validity claim of historical knowledge depends on the sense, or meaning, that this knowledge has in the cultural framework of daily human life. The claim is judged on its life-serving purpose. Explanations or rationales become a matter of practical reason. This becomes increasingly necessary because historical thinking, being fundamentally rooted in the orientation problems of the present, is prone to ideology and easily corrupted. When something is life serving, it can also serve those who struggle for power by providing them with the intellectual ammunition for their own self-justifying purposes.

Humanity at the Heart of Truth   Are there validity claims that are specific to academic study? What does it mean to claim that historical meaning is intersubjectively valid? Or, what does it mean to ascribe intersubjective validity within the discourses of historical meaning making? In order to clarify what 'intersubjective' means here we need to ask: For whom should these histories hold true? A concrete answer to this question is: everyone who is affected by these discourses. But isn't there more to the idea of truth? To figure out what else there is to it, it is important to consider what can motivate us to agree to histories or narratives. To agree to histories is to adopt them for the purpose of cultural orientation in our daily lives, that is, to make them 'our' histories, our narratives.

Such agreement can be reached in different ways and degrees. Histories are not generally accepted in their entirety or without further ado, but rather adopted through discursive production, or in other words, integrated into the horizon of interpretation of the recipients. Historical truth can be thought of as a gauge for measuring the ability to adopt, or better yet, transform historical knowledge. In this regard intersubjectivity ultimately has a universally human dimension.

When can histories become common sense? This occurs whenever the historical narrative offers a practical orientation and identity that is shared by those affected by the narrative. From this we can then conclude that histories with a universally human claim must have a high degree of acceptability. Such histories draw upon the elements of identity that refer to our humanity. Of course, this humanity is not based on somehow overcoming the differences among us – differences in understanding, in circumstances and context, as well as the fundamental difference between 'us' and 'them'. On the contrary, historical interpretations must be compatible with the uniqueness of all living situations and with the 'otherness' of others, which is a basic constitutive element of identity. They must merge into the broad horizon of living circumstances that have become history and into the humanity that is shared with others. *Truth would then be the capacity for accepting difference through others.* Truth gets its subjective depth and life-serving force from the mental power from which human beings (can) contend and (must) assert their uniqueness in relation to others while accepting the otherness of others.

4. Academia: Intercultural Validity or Culturally Specific Relativity?

Reflections on the 'scientific' nature of historical studies are often accused of being 'Western'. After all, history as an academic discipline did originate in the West and was only adopted by other cultures some time later. Due to this sequence of events, the academic discipline of history is often seen as only valid in and for the Western cultural context. Despite, or even because of the popularity of academic history, this charge or reproach deserves closer inspection. Empirically, the claim is sound. Yet, does the historical context of a form of knowledge or an epistemological process automatically limit its validity? Logically, a point of origin and a claim of validity are separate issues. But even empirically, limited validity is not an evident general axiom here. To give a contrary example: the mathematical concept of zero comes from India, though no one would suggest that this limits its mathematical usage or consider its use to be alienating.

Context-dependency and Validity Claims   However, things appear to be different in the humanities and social or cultural sciences. Here, cognition is more dependent on context and the use of these disciplines for political purposes is a generally known fact. Furthermore, these fields of study fundamentally stress the differences in human ways of life and their temporal transformations, that is, the uniqueness or individuality of human beings. But here we need to distinguish practical use from theoretical validity.

What is the issue here? Historical study, as stated above, is a matter of methodically extracting and securing knowledge of the past. The field is anthropologically based on the fundamental capacity of human beings to reflect on the validity of their own thinking. Science is a systematic intensification of this capacity; it has changed throughout history and continues to change. This anthropological core of scientific rationality is unshakeable. Naturally, it takes on various forms in different geographical and temporal contexts, and these differing manifestations are still active traditions of thought. The self-asserting tendencies of cultural ways of life play a large role in these traditions. And since self-assertion always means to differentiate between 'us' and 'them', there is a certain tension between the different traditions. In historical thinking, this uneasy relationship appears as politically effective and highly problematic ethnocentrism.

Does this mean that historical thinking can only be justified in terms of the reduced scope of its ethnocentric tendencies? The opposite is true: a critique of ethnocentrism should have become the standard in academic or scientific thought by now.[47] The capacity to even formulate this critique is the same capacity that enables its scholarly form. The concrete precondition for this capacity comes from the field of human sciences: the human sciences must interrelate (even explicitly) the vast array of traditions in human thought with regard to an overarching form of people's lives. This is exactly what happens in the process of globalization and in the ideas about modernizing rationality (even when we criticize this rationality or even attempt to overcome it). Cultural relativism as an intellectual attitude originated in the context of the universalizing rationality of modernity (as a reaction to it). The claim that knowledge generated by the human sciences is context-dependent stems from a concept of rationality as transcending or exceeding context. This dialectic should be pursued and not dismissed or avoided.

The Critique of Ethnocentrism in the Clash of Cultures   Is the clash of cultures the final word in the discourse on validity claims in historical thinking, and is the will to power the ultimate basis of its functional activity? Or should we stress the aim of peace and the will for truth when we discuss a common meaning for our experience of time? Science can be understood (and effectively realized) as a way of thinking that does not contest cultural differences but rather connects them through critical argumentation. Scholarly thought asserts an anthropological potential in the human intellect that does not dissolve in its culturally specific form but rather is committed to a concept of common humanity (*Humanum*). The interest in such humanity should reduce the importance of cultural relativism in validity claims in the human sciences. (As a matter of fact, every kind of relativism faces the logical verdict of performative self-contradiction as long as it assumes itself to be generally true.)

Despite this, arguments that question a scientific concept that cannot deny its origins in a culture that confronted other cultures with ethnocentric destruction should be taken seriously. The logical universality assumed for this concept of science is only legitimate if it is tempered not only by critical reflection on this form of ethnocentrism, but also by showing that it can rise above it, and how.

5. Disciplinary Matrix I: The Five Factor System

The remarks thus far have been very abstract and general. They had to be because we are dealing with the fundamental question of how history as an academic discipline relates to common human (and anthropologically universal) forms and practices of forming historical meaning. In other words: How can history in all its uniqueness be made plausible? We now need to consider more closely the scholarly cognitive process of historical thinking so that we can observe exactly what happens in the day-to-day operations (*werktätige*[48]) of history.

The Disciplinary Matrix as a Schema for Historical Studies   We can develop a schema of the intellectual procedures of historical thinking that clearly emphasizes the standard points of view in knowledge and at the same time reveals their differences as well as their inner coherence. I call this schema *the disciplinary matrix of historical studies*. I borrow this term from Thomas S. Kuhn, who introduced it into the history of science and theory of science to great effect.[49] This does not mean that I readily transplant his definition of a scientific paradigm to historical studies. On the contrary, my aim is to elucidate the uniqueness of historical studies in a structural and analytical manner. Therefore, practical relevance, for instance, plays a constitutive role in this matrix.

The matrix emphasizes the processual character of historical knowledge and underlines how dependent it is on a specific time and a specific historical context. At the same time, detaching historical thinking from the specific demands of practical orientation is crucial for the scholarly validity of historical studies. The active link between scientific historical thinking and the historical culture of its particular time should not be cut off on objectivist grounds or even disregarded when we consider the unique cognitive achievements of historical research and its historiography. On the contrary:

this link should be explicated precisely where historical thinking gains its own inherent academic dynamic and asserts itself against strong external influences. We could also speak of disciplinary autonomy as long as the word 'autonomy' is not equated with the false idea that historical thinking exclusively considers its own specific orientations when it forms its own specific cognitive structures and continually develops new interpretations.

Multi-dimensionality   The schema emphasizes the cognitive dimension of historical thinking while showing its systematic relationship to other dimensions, especially the aesthetic and political ones. If we were to lose sight of this relationship, we would not be able to recognize or structurally analyse the specific character of historical thinking and the real processes with which it operates.

The schema's potential has its limitations. They lie in the eventual need to refer to the multiple external conditions and contexts (especially those of an institutional nature) in order to understand the achievements of professional historical thinking.

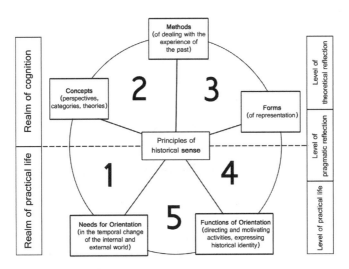

Figure 3.1 Matrix of historical thinking.

a) The Five Factors of Historical Knowledge

The schema presents five essential factors in historical thinking. Each separate factor is *necessary* for historical thinking but only the combination of all five is *sufficient* for an understanding of what historical thinking is and how it works as a cognitive process.

For me, one of the great advantages of the schema is how it reveals the fascinating dynamic of the relationship between academic study and practical living in the foundations of historical thinking. Academic study and the way we live in the real world are both tightly connected and clearly separate. On the one hand, all historical knowledge depends on the standpoint of its subjects in the discursive context of the historical culture of its time. Thus, there is no historical representation without an interpretive perspective that follows from this point of view. On the other hand, within the framework of its scientific or academic form, historical thinking is shaped by the methodical processes that ensure its validity, which grants every perspective intersubjectivity and positions it in a non-relativistic relation to other perspectives. One is the flipside of the other. They are closely connected in such a way that they are mutually dependent without being completely determined by each other.

When we imagine historical thinking as a linear process (which is of course a one-sided view, though it nevertheless characterizes its developmental dynamic), we can understand these five factors as sequential: the *need for orientation* initiates historical thinking. To satisfy this need, historical thinking transforms it into a perspective on the experience with the past. This process produces an *interpretive perspective*. This perspective incorporates concrete *elements of experience* in a methodical manner. The intended knowledge about what happened in the past becomes a representation of the past in *historiographic form*. In this form, the gained historical knowledge can become *effective* in the current processes of historical orientation.

Of course, the real processes in which historical knowledge is generated, formed and presented are much more complex. From the very beginning, all the factors are systematically interdependent. Nevertheless, this relationship can be thought of as temporally arranged, from a beginning (a historical question) to an end (the historiographic answer and its effect on practical living).

A look at this temporal dynamic clarifies why historical thinking finds itself in a constant flow, and why history must continually be written anew and can never be fixed in conclusive knowledge. New questions constantly emerge from the deep roots of historical thinking, embedded within the need for orientation in our day-to-day living, that must be dealt with or responded to by new and current approaches. Max Weber called this dynamic of knowledge in the human sciences 'eternally young' (*ewig jugendlich*).[50] (Correspondingly, we can interpret and understand academic and historiographic phenomena in a structurally analytic manner using the conceptual schema of the matrix.)

b) The Desire for Interpretation and the Need for Orientation

The need for orientation in the practical day-to-day living of human beings is at the core of the historical cognitive process. As described earlier, this need is caused by diverging temporal experiences that precede as well as underlie all academic work. Without realizing the full extent of how embedded academic study is in the context of historical culture, we cannot understand the type of historical thinking that shapes it. The fundamental questions about orientation and identity in a particular place and time and their answers develop from this context. Academic study is shaped by the point of view of the historian in his or her temporal context. However, this context-dependency in no way already precludes how academic study will deal with these needs for orientation, the needs which then lead to historical thinking. In addressing the need for orientation, academic study uses its own type of thinking, namely academic or scientific thinking. With this type of thinking, historical cognition detaches itself from the practical world of day-to-day living from which it originated and from which it takes the impulse for interpreting the past. In this process, this type of historical thinking transforms needs for historical orientation into interests in cognition. The scientific nature of historical thinking is grounded in this transformative process.

Practical Living and Academic Study History as academic study is a specific form of 'rationalization' of the historical thinking that occurs in daily life. It distinguishes and distances itself from common, day-to-day historical thinking and many other aspects of historical culture with its own forms and strategies. Nevertheless, history as academic study is still determined by the non-scientific impulses of cultural orientation. History can reflect these impulses, criticize them, distance itself from them or even reject them, but it still remains determined by them (even in negating them, history is still dependent on them).

A glance into the history of academic study clearly shows how contemporaries and contemporary settings (*Zeitgenossenschaft*) determine the prevailing questions that historians deal with. This is especially the case when the questions are advanced and innovative. An active contemporary setting indicates a greater chance for innovation in historical knowledge. These contemporaries are especially significant when the discipline of historical studies falls into a so-called foundational crisis. Such crises are triggered by experiences of time that, in a critical form, necessitate a change in established interpretive patterns.[51]

Of course, this constitutive dependency of academic historical thinking cannot hide its relative independence when steering the cognitive process. In many cases the field of historical studies has been criticized for distancing itself from the practical needs for orientation almost to the point of total disregard. In historians' professionalism it is not unusual to come across the idea that they produce knowledge for its own sake; it requires no reference to the context of historical culture from which it was obtained in order to explicate its meaning and significance or, in the event the knowledge is disputed, to justify it.

As much as history considers itself an enterprise that exists for its own sake, so can it little deny the fact that this enterprise would not exist if it were not for the need for orientation of its context.

c) Heuristic Assumptions

The historical cognitive process starts with a question. This obvious point is not commonly understood by professionals. For many, the process starts with the so-called 'source', the empirical evidence of what happened in the past. Of course such evidence plays an important role in historical thinking, but is not in itself already a 'source' or an origin for the process of historical thinking. Rather, the origin, the original push (that leads to the source material) is a question, a problem. Ultimately, this question or problem that drives the discourse among professionals in which sources play a vital role arises from the context of the need for historical orientation. This does not happen directly but is rather mediated through a process of rationalization that (as mentioned earlier) transforms the need for orientation into cognitive interests.

The Development of Perspectives   Hence, it is about generating cognition. In order to accomplish this, we must develop historical perspectives from questions. In these perspectives the past – mediated through the testimony of empirical evidence – is envisioned. Then we can speak of concepts, working hypotheses and assumptions that first guide our view to the data that must be researched. These should provide information about what we want to know. The actual pursuit of cognition begins with this forming of questions about the human past. Whether and how the heuristic concepts developed here follow a particular and methodological logic is debatable. It is easy to argue that we can only know something if we know what we want to know. Therefore, we must clarify what is meant by the word 'knowledge'. This must be clear before we turn to source materials to obtain the information that we need to attain the knowledge that we are hoping for. The debate on the cognitive factor of concepts is not about the question of whether we need such concepts. That can hardly be disputed. The issue pertains more to the form that the concepts must or can assume. Here the playing field of possibilities expands: from structuralized assumptions to explicit hypotheses.

It is important for our understanding of what academic work means in the realm of historical thinking to discern the fundamental role that these concepts play. They are our gateway into the world of historical research. When we grant them a theoretical status, this does not mean that they are closer to or further away from the empiricism of sources. On the contrary, they first draw attention to empirical material and thus make the past recognizable through what is left of it; namely, the sources of verifiable knowledge.

To state this more clearly: they are the guiding references into the human past, the concepts of historical thinking, their frame of reference, the prevailing interpretive pattern. They make what is left of the past the 'source' of cognition.

d) Methodical Processes

Within this framework the findings must then be incorporated by way of heuristic assumptions and working hypotheses, empirically tested, altered and finally made concrete. The process in which this occurs on an academic level is called research. The leading principle of research is method.

Method literally means 'way'. It is the way from a question to an answer. It is the way of research that gains historical knowledge with structured procedures. And it is these structured procedures that grant this knowledge its specific validity claim or rational verifiability and intersubjective plausibility.

What is Method? Before the concept of methodology attained its central importance in the scientific claims of historical thought (starting at the end of the eighteenth century), it meant something else, namely the ways and means of presenting historical knowledge in order to make it understandable. 'Understandable' meant that it was useful for the sake of orientation purposes. Method was the way historical thinking moved from the producer to the recipient. It ensured that the recipient's desire for reliable knowledge with normative standards for orienting one's actions was taken into account. Method meant impartiality and practical application of historical judgement. It was a matter of presentation. As such it required authors to stick to the facts and avoid any bias in their representation. At the same time, it regulated this objectivity, indeed lending it its historical meaning. In this way method could freely, even systematically, deduce practical rules for human action. This was expressed through the directive formulated by Cicero that history is life's teacher (*historia vitae magistra*).[52]

In modern historical thought method means something quite different. In his first work, Leopold von Ranke revealed as much with a formulation that became the worldwide slogan for professional history: 'To history has been given the function of judging the past, of instructing men for the profit of future years. The present attempt does not aspire to such a lofty undertaking. It merely wants to show how, essentially, things happened.'[53]

Methodology has been transformed from the application of historical knowledge to the agreed-upon intersubjective production of that knowledge.

As historical thought took on a scientific nature, the process of working with sources to discover reliable knowledge about the past developed into the standard for historical research. Adherence to this process and its productive use defined and still defines the professionalism of historians today. As such, the reflection on and practice of this process play an important role in education. Along with the so-called auxiliary sciences in history, there are now special areas in the field that develop especially complicated processes for the analysis of historical source material.[54]

Science through Method   The professional command of methodology forms the core of the scientific claim of historical studies. This emerged with the claim of being able to produce generally valid knowledge about history. Key concepts for these claims were 'objectivity' and 'value-freedom'. 'Objective' meant empirically verified, that is, attained and verified through experience. 'Value-freedom' meant that the validity of facts attained through historical research was independent from different standpoints in the historical culture of a given time and therefore also independent from value-determined perspectives in historical interpretation. These validity claims were often understood as the neutrality of scientifically obtained historical knowledge in the interpretive struggle within the historical culture of the time. Because of this, historians could see and present themselves as high priests of truth. They could label themselves as the voice of the historical processes that created contemporary living conditions and defined future perspectives. In such a way, the historical method became the guarantee for truth, which was not compatible with the dependency of historical knowledge on context-determined interpretive strategies and their criteria for what makes sense and what does not (*Sinnkriterien*).

Recognizing the incompatibility here has too often led to a denial of the real credibility that the methodological process unquestionably brings to historical research. The historical method, with its testing of knowledge by empirical evidence, does in fact represent a chance to introduce a critical point of view into the power struggles within historical culture, thus criticizing certain claims of validity that are ultimately based on a will for power.

Progress of Cognition   The methodical assessment of source material can lead to the assumption that acquiring knowledge is a linear, progressive movement consisting of steadily collecting data about the past and producing an ever-expanding body of knowledge about 'history'. However, such an assumption is misleading as it supposes that history is something tangible that can be distilled out of evidence of the past. This assumption disregards the essential role of perspective in any notion of history.

Of course our knowledge of the human past steadily and increasingly grows through historical research. We could call this 'progress' but that would mean ignoring how interpretation and meaning affect historical knowledge. Accordingly, the idea of progress is accompanied by a growing meaninglessness of the immense body of knowledge about the past.

Conversely, the reference to experience and the testing of evidence with regard to knowledge are not mere functions of historical interpretation. Working with historical source material can falsify the anticipation of meaning (*Sinnerwartung*), which is inherent in historical perspectives, and refute respective interpretive standards.

e) Narrative Forms

For a long time, the methodical processes of historical research dominated the scientific understanding of historical studies. On the other hand, the significance of presentation, of historiographic representation, in the process of acquiring knowledge, was underestimated. What makes knowledge specifically historical? It is not merely its factuality. The explanatory interpretation of facts about the past is not what makes the methodically attained knowledge historic either. Without an interpretive pattern (based on a temporal perspective), information about and explanations of past events are not yet historic. They first become so when they gain significance in the conceptualization of time that meaningfully connects the past to the present and future. They gain this significance only in the context of a 'history' or a historical representation.

'History' is known for being ambiguous. The concept means both events of the past as well as their representations in the present. If research with its methodical rules focuses on the past that is empirically present through sources, then the representation moves this past into the present, making the present more historical. In this respect, questions about historical representations play a part in the understanding of what historical thinking represents, also and especially in its academic form.

This is not to say that representation is merely a superficial aspect of historical knowledge. Rather, the representation is the clear manifestation of an essential form for historical knowledge. (With this form, historical knowledge distinguishes itself from knowledge in other academic fields.) This is the form of a 'history', a story. Historical knowledge is written as a narrative. This narrative character is an integral part of history.

Narrativity   This insight into the narrative form of historical thinking leads to many misunderstandings. These misunderstandings are based on the fact that storytelling is a mental process in the forming of meaning. Storytelling is not limited to the boundaries of the 'historical' but is also found in art as well as in the process of daily human communication. It is true that historical thinking extends to these areas, but always as something separate and particular. This particularity is not already presented in its narrative form.

A narrative form becomes historical when it expresses the temporal relationship that systematically connects the interpretation of the past to an understanding of the present and the expectations of the future.

Such a specifically historical representational form can be articulated in many different ways. It can freeze the temporal context of time that constitutes history into the image of one single time. Then no more histories can be told. It can describe an epoch; it can reflect on interpretations of time in essay form; it can focus on establishing complex facts or instances from the past, that is, unfurl research results in argumentative form. In short, it can help itself to a tremendous arsenal of representative forms that extends beyond the perimeters of storytelling. A decisive factor, of course, is that these representations refer to facts from the past, the significance of which for the present can only be expressed in the form of a story, a history (without having to explicate this form).

f) *Practical Functions*

What meaning shaped by narrative is can only be made clear if histories or stories are understood as an indispensable part of the cultural orientation of our daily lives. Ultimately, historical meaning, which carries the entire undertaking of scholarly historical knowledge, originates from our need for orientation in the temporal character of our lives, and it attains its particularity the moment when histories need to be told to interpret the time that defines our lives and sorrows.

Without this functional aspect, historical thinking cannot be sufficiently understood. This is where we find its place in human life. If we were to ignore this aspect, we would not understand exactly what the point of it is; by way of experience, we interpret time in such a way that it can be incorporated into the orienting perspective of our lives and our sufferings. For the purposes of metahistory, the practical functions of historical knowledge are a reference point for self-reflection in discerning the essential aspects of its cognitive form. The numerous questions that are often raised concerning the responsibility or ethics of historians[55] cannot be answered sufficiently if the significance of this practical function for the entire process of historical thinking and its specific scientific form is not systematically considered.

It is trivial to mention that historical thinking and politics are closely related. It is, however, anything but trivial to examine the logic of this relationship. Historical thinking, with its deep roots in the daily lives of human beings, cannot be done or conceived of as something apolitical. And yet politics and knowledge follow different rules in the forming of meaning. How are power and truth related and how are they different? Both questions must be dealt with and answered together if we want to understand how historical thinking functions and what role historical studies play in the historical culture of a given time.

6. Disciplinary Matrix II: The Schema of Five Practices

The principles of forming historical meaning discussed earlier are systematically related to each other. They are mutually dependent and can therefore only be discussed and understood with regard to one another. In this schematic representation, these principles are listed one after the other, but this does not mean they can be strictly sequentially separated. On the contrary, they continuously merge in the discursive processes of historical consciousness. These mergers can also be schematically listed, again in terms of abstract and one-sided ideal types, in the same order as the principles for forming meaning. Within such a schematic rendering and its unavoidable use of abstraction this sequential ordering or listing represents the temporal dynamic of the forming of historical meaning. It also demonstrates the mental operations in which the single principles of forming meaning are mediated and interconnected.

Historical meaning is always and fundamentally formed through communication. In the following I want to reveal this communicative/interactive dynamic in the process of historical cognition. I want to make clear that this communication follows varying directives and how it does so. I also want to illustrate the structural analysis of historical thinking as communication unfolds.

a) The Semantic Discourse of Symbolization

The process of transforming the temporal needs for orientation in the lives of human beings into concepts of historical thinking can be described and analysed as a *semantic discourse of symbolization*. In this discourse challenging temporal experiences and the cultural structures of meaning in dealing with the past are connected in such a way that these experiences can be interpreted and ordered within the relevant contexts of cultural orientation. In doing so, we mobilize the interpretive power of concepts of meaning, apply these concepts to experiences of temporal disruption, and in doing so, we assert their significance. A prevailing understanding of history for a particular way of life emerges in this discourse. It underlies the various manifestations of historical culture and characterizes their part in symbolizing a particular place and time. This is where the unconscious forming of archetypes as well as the powers of repression and distortion play a big role. This is where communicative memories transform into cultural memory.[56] This is where we find Foucault's 'archaeology of knowledge', the overwhelming force of anonymous powers over human thinking.[57] This is, however, also where chances for freedom and possibilities for critical thought that can be used to confront this superior power open up.

Here science (academic study) acts as an intellectual means to interpret time. Its methodical rationality and cognitive structure are mobilized and actualized as a necessary form of interpreting time. The endeavour of academic study draws on the potential of reasonable thinking inherent in human life and articulates its references and validity claims.

Interpreting Time through Academic Study   Whether and how the needs for orientation in daily life can be cognitively channelled is an important question in the context of this discourse. Is it possible to rationalize the powerful interests of identity politics in research questions to be discussed and answered? Or is science just a weapon in the power struggle over a historical interpretation of one's own way of life? Within the framework of a theory of history we tend to treat this as a rhetorical question with an obvious answer: of course rational argumentation in academic thinking is more than simply a means for justifying claims of power and control. It is an indispensable element in the legitimacy of claims that assert the cultural significance of knowledge.

But things are not that simple. The relationship between knowledge and power is evident in the realm of the human sciences. The champions of the Enlightenment expose themselves to the reproach that their knowledge is culturally specific – in other words, Western – and therefore not only inappropriate but also dangerous for all those who wish to assert their own cultural tradition and identity as non-Western.[58]

Academic Study in the Clash of Cultures   In light of the undeniable effect of ethnocentric viewpoints on our understanding of history as an orientating factor in everyday culture, we must take this problem of science in the clash of cultures seriously. Here we find powerful challenges for historical thinking (especially in its theoretical self-reflection) in the current processes of globalization and intercultural communication. Even (or especially) academic historical discourse is not free of hegemonic claims. These claims cannot simply be eliminated; they express the tendency for self-affirmation of all human beings and in all human ways of life. Nevertheless, these claims need to be controlled to tame the conflicts that result from them.[59]

We must ask, then, the urgent question of whether it is possible to humanize such unavoidable tendencies through rational argumentation within our discursive discussions about the meaning of history. Can we confront (or even enrich) historical knowledge used for cultural orientation with a cognitive awareness that can assert its validity across all different interests because of its objectivity and explanatory rigour?

Such a claim of scientific legitimacy can only be made when it can draw on elements, factors and processes in the forming of historical meaning that have a general human quality that has an anthropological basis and is plausible in historical-philosophical terms.[60] The anthropological basis must primarily be discerned and identified before any cultural difference. The historical-philosophical continuation of the anthropological argument must be able to show that and how the cultural potential of all human beings for forming meaning when dealing with time has manifested itself in many forms, without losing the anthropological commonality in the argument. In view of deep-seated cultural differences, it is important to present this common humanity in the different manifestations as a possibility for a discursive treatment of these differences.

b) The Cognitive Strategy of the Production of Historical Knowledge

If we look at the area of communication between the concepts of historical perspectivation and the methods of empirical research, we find another kind of communication; it is still a discourse, but its intellectual driving force is of a strategic kind. This communication is driven by viewpoints in the form of rules. In this context, 'strategy' means that the discussions of academic specialists as well as their research are goal-oriented. Here, the methodical processes are key. Interpretive perspectives and patterns are negotiated through communication. These negotiations are about the analytical or interpretive power based on empirical findings, as well as the capacity for explanatory interpretation of the information found in source material. The discourse gains professional features and forms. We see the importance of debate in determining what knowledge gains in acceptance through the interplay between interpretive patterns and experience.

c) The Aesthetic Strategy of Historical Representation

The following area of communication is also dominated by a strategy. This strategy is concerned with how historical knowledge is presented in a historiographical manner. In the field of historical studies the narrative substantiation of methodology is critical in the validation of historical knowledge. The goal of strategic considerations on historical representation is no longer primarily cognitive but rather aesthetic and rhetoric (it goes without saying that rhetoric and aesthetics are not strangers of or hostile towards cognition). Cognitive structures are translated into aesthetic structures that must (or should) lead to a rhetorical strategy for facing problems of cultural orientation.

Within the reflexive perspective of this area of communication, which is governed by the aesthetic strategy of historical representation, we find a series of exceptionally complex and difficult theoretical problems. They involve the interplay between empirical knowledge concerning the explanatory interpretation of past events on the one hand, and a textual formation with its own viewpoints of narrative coherence and plausibility on the other. The crucial point is that the inner rationality of historical knowledge does not disappear but rather is revealed in its narrative representation.[61]

Of course narrative concepts of historical representation play a role in discourses on the symbolization and strategy of the production of knowledge. We should consider the enormous role that narratives play in the symbolic ordering of the human world while also systematically taking account of the deep relationship between professional (academic) historical thinking and this symbolic ordering. We can then say that the academic professionalization of historical studies develops from this narrative character of the real-world experience of cultural orientation. And since the symbolic power of historical thinking in our daily lives manifests itself primarily in aesthetic forms, it makes sense to speak of science as developing from art.[62]

d) The Rhetorical Strategy of Historical Orientation

It would be a mistake to maintain that the aesthetic character of historical representation is crucial in both the processes of historical thinking and the cultural orientation of human beings in their daily lives. Aesthetic constructs do play an important role in cultural orientation, but not the only one. When we speak of the communicative dimension and dynamic of history we need to keep in mind a fundamental distinction: the difference between art and politics. They overlap and intersect – one cannot be thought of without the other – and yet they follow very different principles in the forming of meaning regarding the appropriation and interpretation of critical experiences for human beings in the temporal transformations of their world.

Functionality as the Determining Factor   The area of communication between the forms of historical representation and the orientating function that applies the historiographic presentation of historical knowledge to the daily world of human beings is also determined by other aspects beyond the aesthetic. History has its own means of communicating. It mediates between the *aesthetics of historical representations* and the *political role* of historical thinking in the practical discourse of collective memory. This gap is bridged by rhetoric. The area of communication between the forms and the functions of historical thinking is thus determined by a *rhetorical strategy of historical orientation*. This strategy aligns the direction of historiography with the political culture of the time in which it (intentionally or unintentionally) plays a role. Rhetoric bestows aesthetics with the capacity to be used in the power struggle between historical orientations in daily life, especially the struggles over the legitimacy of political and societal power relationships. We could say here that in its historiographic form, historical knowledge obtains 'utility value' through its rhetorical presentation.

Considering that historical thinking claims to be scientific, this utility value and its communicative use – or even, its political use – seems precarious. All too often, historical knowledge is used superficially for purposes that have little or nothing to do with the cognitive interests ascribed to historical knowledge and its historiographic representation. This notion is, however, misguided. It emanates from a *déformation professionelle* regarding historical expertise and academic professionalism. The real interest of historical thinking develops from the disputes in which a way of life is interpreted and culturally asserted. The rhetorical strategy of historical orientation connects the cognitive yield of historical research to our daily lives. Without this connection or mediation, historical knowledge would be essentially meaningless. This means that the communicative negotiations about historical cognitive processes cross over into the non-professional, the realm of transdisciplinarity.

e) The Political Discourse of Collective Memory

In the area of communication between practice-oriented historical knowledge and the need for orientation with the subsequent demand for knowledge in our daily lives, all activity is transdisciplinary. Here the guidelines for the strategic negotiations in and about historical thinking merge into the discourse of collective memory. This means that the rules and regulations or controllability essential to the rationality claim of historical thinking are transformed into disputes in which politics and the struggle for power play a special role as new components in the intersubjective dimension and communicative constitution of historical thinking.

Science and Politics The academic legitimacy of historical thinking does not necessarily disappear at this point. On the contrary, academic historical thinking must assert its legitimacy within this political discourse. And it does. (Consider the role of contemporary history in examining the roles of West German politicians in the Third Reich.[63]) Here, academic study becomes politically relevant. A critical question in theoretical reflection on historical thinking is whether and how historical thinking and its particular standards of rationality can and should be asserted politically. When we consider that these standards have grown out of historical knowledge from the anthropological basis of human culture, the answer to this first question is a definitive 'yes'. Historical knowledge can only play a political role when the relevant

criteria for validity and truth undergo a *practical turn*. This turn does not
come from without, but is rather an inherent part of historical thinking and
stems from its origins in the need for orientation in our daily lives. As a part
of historical culture, historical thinking acts to humanize this culture in the
political power struggles of its time.

In summary, these five areas, or forms, of communication as regards
historical thinking can be listed schematically as follows:[64]

7. Disciplinary Matrix III: The Three Levels of Forming Historical Meaning

a) Construction and Constructedness of History

Forming historical meaning is a process of human consciousness. When
understood in terms of its anthropological basis, historical thinking appears
to be a matter of subjective processes alone. The real temporal change in the
human world itself does not appear to play a part in the matter. The past only
acquires meaning when it is placed in a meaningful relation to the present
through historical thinking.

Constructivism   This view is called constructivism. It emphasizes the intellectual capacity of human beings to give the world the sense and meaning
that are necessary for life. This constructivism appears in the work of great
authorities on historical theory like Droysen and especially Max Weber. By
making a distinction between 'affairs' (*Geschäfte*) of the past and history for
the present, Droysen showed that the historical character of these 'affairs'
(meaning the actions and suffering of humans affected by time) is only
established through retrospective interpretation.[65] The past, in the distance,
only present as shadows in historical documents, is not history. It becomes
history outside of its own time, through historical understanding in a later
period. Max Weber, strongly influenced by Neo-Kantianism, emphatically
supported this view by pointing out that all cultural historical efforts to

Table 3.2   The five forms of communication in historical thinking.

Form	Content
Semantic discourse of symbolization	Concepts of meaning
Cognitive strategy of the production of knowledge	Concepts of research
Aesthetic strategy of representation	Concepts of representation
Rhetorical strategy of orientation	Concepts of pragmatic use
Political discourse in collective memory	Concepts of historical culture

understand the human world are based on the 'transcendental assumption' that 'we are cultural beings, endowed with the capacity and the will to have a conscious response to the world and to give it meaning'.[66] Finally, Karl Lamprecht expressed this view through a religious metaphor: 'The historian must be able to breathe life into the past, as did Ezekiel the prophet: he tread through a valley full of dry bones, while the sound of awakening life rustled behind him'.[67]

Is this how we understand history? Does historical experience merely provide something like material substance (or what could falsely be called 'objectivity'), in terms of what really happens or has really happened outside of ourselves, for interpreting subjects out of which historical thinking moulds history as if it were a lump of clay?[68]

Where Does Meaning Come From?   This idea of the historian as a metaphorically godlike creator of the world is certainly interesting for all those who submit themselves to the cognitive labour of forming historical meaning. But does historical meaning really only originate from a meaning-forming subjectivity? In other words: is the historical experience in itself meaningless? It is difficult to answer this question with a resounding 'yes' when we take the challenging character of the historical experience and its stimulating effect on the intellectual efforts of historians seriously. The only meaninglessness that we encounter in such a stimulating challenge is the unsettling senselessness that sinks in when we are confronted with crimes against humanity. But that is not what is meant here. Because in the case of this unsettling meaninglessness there is again something in the world around us that relates to the inner world of the interpretive subject and intrudes on the procedures of forming historical meaning.

Is the past really so meaningless as assumed in the constructivist interpretive pattern? The past is meaningless when we consider it as pure facts: something occurred in a particular place at a particular time in a particular way and for particular reasons. But this is not what determines the historical experience. The facts alone can only inspire the forming of meaning in historical consciousness when they contain meaningful features, even if these features are absurd or senseless. The past must already have entered the horizon of meaning of the present way of life before the interpreting intellect can ponder and understand it.

Historical thinking does not occur in a realm of pure subjective inwardness, but always in communicative and dynamic contexts. These contexts influence the direction of historical thinking – they can indeed determine it, even prefigure it and often affect it without us noticing. What do these concepts constitute in the temporality of our lives? Simply put: they are the results of temporal processes of the past that have entered into the present.

The past is already present in these contexts before we even regard it as 'the past' that is distant from us. To borrow Lamprecht's metaphor, the historian does not tread through the valley of dead bones but rather moves within the fields of the ever-present past, existing narrative, prescribed meaningfulness. The past is not dead but very much alive as part of the present circumstances and order of life. This of course does not mean that the temporal changes that enter into and affect our way of life already provide sufficient meaning. However, meaning is necessary in order to experience the difference in time between past and present. It is embedded within that space between the two. But is meaning conceivable without frames of reference that the flow of time carries from the past into the present (and its anticipation of the future)?

Contexts and Their Potentiality for Meaning   The communicative contexts and the conditioning circumstances of historical thinking are in themselves meaningful. The formation of historical meaning is not even conceivable without a link – however critical – to these presets. Such pregiven elements that carry meaning from the past into the present – the most powerful one being language – should not be understood as having

Table 3.3   Constructedness and construction of history.

Constructedness	
Through their actions and suffering, human beings create a world for themselves and their offspring	Past
⇓	⇓
Generational chain: fact-determined contexts, 'causality of fate'	'Objective' history
⇓	⇓
Human beings act and suffer under conditions and circumstances bequeathed from the past and interpret them according to their experience with the past	Present
Construction	
Forming meaning through memory and historical culture	Present
⇓	⇓
Generational chain: value-based attitudes	'Subjective' history
⇓	⇓
Human affairs become history: the interpretation of the past is determined by viewpoints that people of the present actively insert into the handling of the experience of the past	Past

predetermined the historical meaning of the past buried within them. On the contrary, the reason why we have unsettling experiences of time is that our cultural orientation does not provide us with sufficient meaning-making capabilities that would enable a satisfying interpretation of temporal change in our lives.

We can represent the constructedness and constructive character of historical thinking in schematic form as follows:

In summary, we should keep in mind that the insight into the constructed character of historical meaning must be supplemented with the insight that the agents, the constructors, are themselves constructed. Though the interpreters of history can and must make use of the potential freedom of forming cultural meaning, they have little control over the contexts, or pre-given elements, of meaning that construct it. In light of this relationship between the presets, the purpose and the performance, historians should bridle their self-confidence with a certain degree of modesty whenever they appeal to the creative quality of cultural innovation in the field of historical culture.

It is also worth noting here that this modesty takes account of the enormous influence of unconscious emotions on the processes of forming historical meaning. Even though these processes are rarely discussed, let alone researched within the framework of metahistory,[69] they cannot be denied. These processes quietly transport the past into the present actuality of historical thinking.

Forming Meaning out of the Preset Elements of Meaning   In the language of Martin Heidegger's existential ontology we can formulate these considerations as follows. The meaning-making subject of historical thinking is placed or thrown (Heidegger speaks of *Geworfenheit* or thrown-ness, as being thrown) in the *Lichtung des Seins*, in the clearing of being, or in the interpreted being-in-the-world. We might add here that this clearing contains shadows, empty spaces and open borders of meaninglessness and absurdity. These shadows do not simply disappear when lit up, but rather impel us to do the continuous work of forming cultural meaning. Is there any doubt about the creative quality of this work, that is, of the human capacity to move beyond the cleared meaning of one's world? A look at the history of historical thinking removes such doubts, unless we assume (like Heidegger) that there is another, higher history in which historical thinking develops meaning beyond the perception of the subject. But this would be a different history from the one told by historians.

The complex correlation between the construction of historical meaning and the constructedness of preset meaning in the contexts and conditional framework of historical thinking must be analysed. Otherwise it is not clear which modes of historical meaning occur in the complex interchange between the processes involved in the determining of meaning (*Sinnbestimmtheit*) in daily life and the mediation of historical meaning through the deliberate work of historians as they communicate with each other and with all those in their contemporary world who can and want to influence the historical culture of their time.

Three Levels of Historical Meaning   Apart from the functional level described above, the formation of historical meaning takes place on two more ideal-typical levels: the reflexive and the pragmatic levels.[70] The functional and reflexive levels can be presented as opposites, and the pragmatic as mediation between them.

We can then speak of three distinctive levels: (b) the functional, (c) the reflexive and (d) the pragmatic.

b) The Level of Functional Meaning Making

I use the term 'functional' to describe the formation of historical meaning that has always happened and that happens in the daily processes of cultural orientation. The best example of this is language. Of course, language is not specifically historical, but historical meaning happens in and with language. It can never be reflected on in such a way that the cultural activities of human beings control the semantics and the power of orientation of language.

Meaning as Happening   On this level, meaning is not 'constructed', but rather occurs or happens as part of the reality of human life. It operates in the institutions and processes of upbringing and education, in political culture and in many other areas of our daily lives. Here, history is *effective*. It is any-thing but the product of a mental activity like the construction of historical consciousness. Rather, it precedes historical consciousness. It is embedded in people, transcending all the possible mediations and media. This is not just the case in the sphere in which meaningfulness is articulated, manifest and visible, but also in the darker regions of our sub- and unconscious selves. Historical meaning operates from and in the foundations of our daily cul-tural activities, in the dispositions of our attitudes towards the past, and in the habits of human behaviour in all areas of life. Historical meaning, or our sense of history, inspires a specific way of dealing with historical experience for each generation. It is embedded in the concepts of historical identity, in and through which we impose (or, have imposed on us) our belonging to and our disassociation from other human beings.

The Roots of Transdisciplinarity   Without systematic consideration of this functional level of meaning we cannot properly understand what the academic study of history is. At this level, we find the source of meaningfulness in our world from which historical thinking develops in the creative character of historical thinking. Considering its roots at the functional level, we can say that the discipline of historical studies essentially has transdisciplinary features. Transdisciplinarity does not come from outside the field but has already established itself at the level of the principles of the interpretive purpose of historical studies. This is not an argument against the disciplinary or academic status of historical studies, but rather a more precise rendering of what academic status or disciplinarity means. When considering the constitutive, transdisciplinary roots of historical studies, we do not question its disciplinarity. Rather, the disciplinarity emerges as a cognitively important and indispensable aspect of historical knowledge.

Of course the description of this level of forming meaning is an abstraction. It ignores the activities of historical consciousness in order to focus on the happening of meaning that always precedes them. Only then can we avoid the false notion of historical knowledge as something autonomous and removed from daily human reality, and acknowledge its inherent correlations with the daily lives of human beings and their cultural orientation.

c) The Level of Reflexive Meaning Making

The reflexive level of forming meaning is the contrasting side of these effective, preset elements. It is based on them and reacts to them. It does not simply let them operate, but tempers them. It originates from a gap, a fundamental openness or incompleteness in historical elements of orientation in which and with which cultural human life takes place. It arises from the simple fact that as a guiding principle for orientation, meaning is always uncertain, precarious, questionable, contradictory and insufficient. The preset elements of meaning in culture are basically formed to provoke cultural meaning-forming activities, in order to become activated in them and through them in the dynamic of human culture.

Ultimately, the 'open' if not precarious character of its preset elements is not the only thing that motivates historical thinking. It is also determined by the simple and basic fact that meaninglessness and even absurdity operate in the underlying cultural context of meaning.[71]

Without these activities, the sense or meaning with which human culture is endowed would lose its effectiveness, become weak and dissolve altogether. Culture depends entirely on the activities of human consciousness. This does not necessarily mean that culture is completely subject to or fully controlled by this level of consciousness. The resources of meaning in culture are always limited and the human desire for meaning always tends to go beyond its actual realization. Also, the preset cultural elements of meaning are always and fundamentally contested in the lives of human beings. People fight over them, even when they in fact determine how the fight is waged.

Working on Meaning   Cultural meaning is always 'uneasy'; it requires care, criticism and discursive mediation. It can be rejected, negated and renewed, and of course it changes to the same extent that the circumstances of daily human life change. All of this applies fully to historical culture, and especially to historical studies. Its interpretive capacities are based on preset elements of meaning within historical culture at a given time. However, these capacities do not reproduce these presets, but rather deal with them through the communicative form of argumentation and handle them critically.

The particularity of academic historical thinking unfolds on this level. This is where the specific regulative character of historical methodology fully asserts itself. And this is where the creative power of an aesthetic and rhetorical form of historical knowledge manifests itself.

d) The Level of Pragmatic Meaning Making

The third level brings the other two together. In this level the preliminary decisions about standard criteria for meaning and the process of historical thinking as well as the creative handling of these preset elements take place. Here, constructedness and construction meet in a complex network of relationships. On this level the professionals influence political decisions and political realities affect the work of professionals. This is where historical knowledge is integrated in the contexts that conditioned that knowledge. But when this happens, these conditions are (or can be) altered. The preliminary decisions about what meaningful historical knowledge can be become embedded in the production of this knowledge. At the same time, this meaning is used in such a way that the preliminary decisions for the production of further knowledge are (or can be) altered.

Use of Meaning   The term 'use' is critical for this level. Use is already at least partly established in historical knowledge, but it can come from 'outside' as well, that is, from beyond the impersonal mode of academic professionalism. This is not just the case for political use but ultimately for any other use, such as for the sake of entertainment or artistic purposes. Its practical use cannot be completely strange, since the logic of historical thinking contains the traces of its practical usefulness, which, as discussed previously, are a basic element of historical thinking considering its origins in the need for orientation in daily life.

On the pragmatic level, the professionality of historical knowledge asserts itself as a measure of reliability or unreliability of its practical use. We see this when it is used for ideological purposes:[72] ideology distinguishes itself from academic study through its consistent formation according to a viewpoint based on a specific interest in orientation that serves as a weapon in the struggle for power, or alternatively – in the strict sense of the word 'ideology' – serves to alter our view of complex realities and to produce a concept of reality that is guided by desire rather than experience. Such a formation strategy contradicts the foundations of critical control in the production of knowledge in historical studies (which does not mean this contradiction is not always thwarted, skipped over or ignored). Knowledge produced in a scholarly fashion, based on a logic of methodically regulated reference to evidence, is fundamentally critical of ideology.

Its relationship to religion is similar. Many religions develop a history of salvation as a way of interpreting the world, and they make use of historical knowledge in doing so. However, the specific religious meaning can never be scientifically substantiated, as this meaning always stretches beyond the interpretive realm of scientific knowledge. Science is fundamentally secular. This does not necessarily rule out a religious use of secular knowledge, but it does set a clear limit regarding religious assumptions and claims.[73]

Professionality as a Critical Compass   The pragmatic nature of the formation of historical meaning demands that the professionality of academically produced historical knowledge and its historiographic presentation – in all the uses of this knowledge – can (and must) be used as a critical compass to examine the validity claims that are asserted in our cultural orientation. Criticism is an essential point of view that historical studies introduces into the pragmatism of the formation of historical meaning. It is not the only point of view; educational viewpoints, too, develop from the rationality of academic historical thinking. Finally, this rationality has a high educational value that makes it the stuff of didactic and educational endeavours.

A schematic summary of these points is useful here:

e) The 'Unprethinkability' (Unvordenklichkeit) of History in Historical Thinking

All three levels are closely entwined. The *relationship* of the three viewpoints discussed in the last three sections can be imagined as a temporal process

Table 3.4 The three levels of forming historical meaning.

Level	Meaning Forming
Functioning	Context-determining, dependency on cultural preset elements: 'objective' meaning
Reflexive	Constructive interpretive output, subjective meaning
Pragmatic	Mediation between preset elements of meaning and output in meaning for pragmatic intentions

of the 'happening' of historical meaning. In this process we find historical meaning in the pragmatic interrelationship between something already there (preset) and input, between constructedness and construction. Here, the past and the future, or the given and the yet-to-occur, effectively come together in the present; they are one in the *happening* of forming historical meaning. Only in retrospect do we perceive and interpret this process as historical. As it takes place, in the here and now, in its presence, it cannot be reflected upon or understood, and it can definitely not be shaped.

This conceptualization of meaning as 'happening' (*Sinngeschehen*) provides the basis for and enables any formation of historical meaning. It is in fact a process, extended in time, something we can (ambiguously) call (actual) 'history'. But this history takes place before all historical thinking. It is 'un-pre-thinkable', and yet is very real and of central importance for historical thinking. This sense of historical thinking depends on something real and temporal, something simply happening, without being in control of it. In this unprethinkable happening of meaning we find its own historicity (or to be more exact, its pre- or fundamental historicity), that of a total presence. Only in a process of subsequent reflection can we unfold its temporal features into the multi-dimensionality of past, present and future. The present is and will always be dominant in this happening. However, the present is not simply an intersection between the past and the future. Rather, it occurs as the prior cohesion, as facilitator, as source for the inner connection between knowledge of the past and interpretation of the future in the understanding of the present.

Notes

37. The influential work on philosophical hermeneutics by Hans-Georg Gadamer is entitled *Wahrheit und Methode* (*Truth and Method*). The title is extremely ambiguous since the entire argument arising from this hermeneutical form of understanding, so critical to thinking within the human sciences, denies the methodological character, contending that the capacity for truth in understanding comes from outside or even against methodology. The scientific claims of the human sciences, then, are not only unsubstantiated, but also fundamentally refuted. As to the question of methodology and the search for truth specific to the established disciplines in the human sciences, Gadamer does not broach the topic.

38. In Greek, '*polemos*' means war.

39. E. Flaig. 2007. 'Ohne Wahrheit keine Wissenschaft: Überlegungen zur Wendung nach den Wenden', in C. Kühberger et al. (eds), *Wahre Geschichte-Geschichte als Ware*, Rahden/Westf.: VML, Leidorf, 49–80, quote, 52.

40. A Marxist theory of historical thinking, rarely defended these days, did, however, work paradigmatically in a certain direction in historical materialism within the concept of reflectance (*Widerspiegelung*).

41. This has been paradigmatically documented as the theory of *Sehepunkte* (viewpoints) through Chladenius: J.M. Chladenius. 1985. *Allgemeine Geschichtswissenschaft, worinnen der*

Grund zu einer neuen Einsicht in allen Arten der Gelahrtheit geleget wird (*General Historical Studies, in Which the Basis Toward a New Perspective in All Types of Scholarship Will Be Put Forward*), Vienna: Böhlaus Nachf. Extracts taken from H.W. Blanke and D. Fleischer (eds). 1990. *Theoretiker der deutschen Aufklärungshistorie*, 2 vols, Stuttgart, Bad Cannstatt: Frommann Holzboog, 226–274.

42. The phrase from Max Weber has, within this context, become famous: 'Es ist und bleibt wahr, dass eine methodisch korrekte wissenschaftliche Beweisführung auf dem Gebiete der Sozialwissenschaften, wenn sie ihren Zweck erreicht haben will, auch von einem Chinesen als richtig erkannt warden muss.' ('It has been and remains true that a methodologically accurate, scientifically based argument put forth in the social sciences must, if it is to achieve its purpose, be recognized as accurate even by someone from China.' M. Weber, 'Die "Objektivität" sozialwissenschaftlicher und sozialpolitischer Erkenntnis', in idem, *Gesammelte Aufsätze zur Wissenschaftslehre*, 3rd ed., edited by J. Winckelmann, Tübingen: Mohr/Siebeck, 155).

43. W. Emrich. 1957. *Die Symbolik von Faust II: Sinn und Vorformen*, Bonn: Athenäum, 117 f. Reinhardt Koselleck limited this empirical plausibility in historical knowledge to the '*Veto-Recht der Quellen*' (veto right of the source material). The information sought in the present from the empirical material of the past can be used to refute any claims concerning what happened in that past. This is of course correct, but the research-motivated use of sources is not limited to a refuting function. Most important here is the gaining of reliable information from the source material over the events of the past. The veto right of the sources is dependent on this reliability. See footnote 79 in this volume.

44. See this volume, 181.

45. See also this volume, 135sqq.

46. See this volume, 138sqq.

47. See this volume, 207sqq.

48. The author borrows the term '*werktätig*' (in the original German) from Horst Walter Blanke.

49. T. Kuhn. 1967. *Die Struktur wissenschaftlicher Revolutionen*, Frankfurt am Main: Suhrkamp. (*The Structure of Scientific Revolutions*, Chicago: The University of Chicago, 1962.)

50. 'Es gibt Wissenschaften, denen ewige Jugendlichkeit beschieden ist, und das sind alle historischen Disziplinen, alle die, denen der ewig fortschreitende Fluss der Kultur stets neue Problemstellungen zuführt.' ('There are academic disciplines which are marked by an eternal youthfulness and these are all the historical disciplines, that is, all those in which the ever-flowing current of culture is forever creating new problems to confront.') Weber, 'Die "Objektivität" sozialwissenschaftlicher und sozialpolitischer Erkenntnis', 146–214, quote 206 ('"Objectivity" in Social Science', 104).

51. See this volume, 29.

52. Cicero, *De oratore* II, 36.

53. L. von Ranke. 1874. *Geschichten der romanischen und germanischen Völker von 1494–1514*, collected works, vol. 33, Leipzig: Duncker & Humblot, VIII. (*The Theory and Practice of History*, ed. by G.G. Iggers and K. von Moltke, Indianapolis: Bobbs-Merrill, 1973, 137.)

54. See this volume, 136sq.

55. F. Bédarida (ed.). 1995. *The Social Responsibility of the Historian*, Oxford: Berghahn Books; A. De Baets. 2009. *Responsible History*, Oxford: Berghahn Books; J. Rüsen. 2003. 'Geschichte verantworten', in idem, *Kann gestern besser werden?* Berlin: Kulturverlag Kadmos. ('Responsibility and Irresponsibility in Historical Studies', in D. Carr, T.R. Flynn and R.A. Makkreel (eds), *The Ethics of History*, Evanston, IL: Northwestern University Press, 2004.)

56. See this volume, 174.

57. See U. Brieler. 1998. *Die Unerbittlichkeit der Historizität*, Cologne: Böhlau.

58. As in, e.g., Seth: 'Reason or Reasoning? Clio or Siva?', 85–101; another example: W.-M. Tu. 2009. 'Confucian Humanism as a Spiritual Resource for Global Ethics', *Peace and Conflict* 16.1, 1–8.

59. J. Rüsen. 'How to Overcome Ethnocentrism: Approaches to a Culture of Recognition by History in the 21st Century', *History and Theory* 43, 118–129, theme issue 'Historians and Ethics', 2004.)

60. The author outlined such an anthropologically based history of philosophy in J. Rüsen. 2012. 'Humanism: Anthropology – Axial Times – Modernities', in O. Kozlarek, J. Rüsen and E. Wolff (eds), *Shaping a Human World*, Bielefeld: Transcript, 55–79.

61. See also the debate in *Internationales Archiv für Sozialgeschichte der deutschen Literatur* (IASL). 2011. 36(1).

62. D. Fulda. 1996. *Wissenschaft aus Kunst*, Berlin: de Gruyter.

63. Alternatively, academic study can betray its academic legitimacy for the sake of political opportunistic reasons, such as in the case of the stab-in-the-back legend in Germany after the First World War.

64. See this volume, 51sqq.

65. J.G. Droysen. 1977. *Historik*, vol. 1, edited by P. Leyh, Stuttgart, Bad Cannstatt: Frommann Holzboog, 204 passim.

66. Weber, 'Die "Objektivität" sozialwissenschaftlicher und sozialpolitischer Erkenntnis', 146–214, quote, 180. ('"Objectivity" in Social Science', 81.)

67. K. Lamprecht. 1910. *Paralipomena der Deutschen Geschichte*, Vienna: Verl. des 'Wissen für Alle', 7.

68. Also see Goertz, *Unsichere Geschichte*.

69. J. Rüsen and J. Straub (eds). 1998. *Die dunkle Spur der Vergangenheit: Psychoanalytische Zugänge zum Geschichtsbewußtsein* (*Erinnerung, Geschichte, Identität*, vol. 2), Frankfurt am Main: Suhrkamp. (*Dark Traces of the Past: Psychoanalysis and Historical Thinking*, New York: Berghahn Books, 2010.)

70. I am following the ideas of Paul Ricoeur. 1988. *Zeit und Erzählung*, vol. 1: *Zeit und historische Erzählung*, Munich: Fink, 88 ff.

71. Here also an example from the epoch of 'classical humanism': Leopold von Ranke, in his introduction to his lectures from the summer semester of 1847 on 'Neuere Geschichte, seit dem Westfälischen Frieden' ('Modern History since the Time of the Peace of Westphalia'), said the following: 'The mass of facts unavoidable, the impression inconsolable. We see always the same, the strong overpowering the weak until someone stronger appears and overcomes the once powerful, destroying him, until at last the forces of our time have come, only to go the same way … Nothing remains but the feeling of nothingness in all things and a distaste for so much that is vile, in how human beings tarnish themselves. We do not see to what end these things occur, to what end these men existed and lived. Even the inner connectedness is obscured.' (L. von Ranke. 1975. *Vorlesungseinleitungen*, edited by V. Dotterweich and W.P. Fuchs (= *Aus Werk und Nachlaß*, vol. 4), Munich: Oldenbourg, 185 f.; translated here.)

72. See also this volume, 187sq.

73. I have discussed this relationship of science and religion extensively in J. Rüsen. 2002. 'Historische Methode und religiöser Sinn: Dialektische Bewegungen in der Neuzeit' in idem, *Geschichte im Kulturprozeß*, Cologne: Böhlau, 9–41; see also from the same author: J. Rüsen. 2006. 'Faktizität und Fiktionalität: Sinnbewegungen des historischen Denkens in der Nachbarschaft zur Theologie', in idem, *Kultur macht Sinn: Orientierung zwischen Gestern und Morgen*, Cologne: Böhlau, 119–133.

CHAPTER 4

A Systematic Approach

Categories, Theories, Concepts

1. What Is the Issue?

In this chapter, we will concern ourselves more concretely with the question of what 'history' is within the cognitive scope of historical studies. In previous works of metahistory (like the work of Droysen), the question of how to define history was dealt with under such designations as 'encyclopaedia' or 'systematic classification'. Both meant the entire range of historical knowledge. Both were meant to cover all of the knowledge, experience and thinking that historians saw as the domain of history.

This is basically 'history' in and of itself: all that happened in the human past that historical knowledge is empirically based on. We could call this the *content* of historical knowledge. The question 'what is history?' was and still is[74] also a question of the philosophy of history. The historical understanding that provides the basis for the possibility of modern historical studies began to take shape in the philosophy of history in the late eighteenth and early nineteenth centuries.

The discipline of history has rejected this philosophical way of thinking. Those behind this rejection accused philosophy of history of not meeting the scientific criteria that connect historical knowledge to the methodical rationality of empirical research. This position, though, ignores the fact that this research presupposes a certain approach towards the body of knowledge and experience of things that happened in the past. This approach is anything but self-evident.

That fact that it was philosophy that recognized the specific quality of this knowledge and experience as a knowable 'history' has got lost in the polemics of historians against the philosophy of history. A trace of philosophical analysis in the subject area of 'history' was, however, adopted in the attempts of the earlier forms of metahistory to describe the body of knowledge that academic historical study claims. Any description of history cannot avoid the specific historical character of what could be known about the past. A metahistory without philosophy of history would leave historical studies without precisely the intellectual grounds on which it wishes to base itself.

The Turn in the Philosophy of History   But with the subject area of historical thinking, with the entire content of historical experience, we need more than a philosophical – or close to philosophical – definition. In forgoing the claims of historical studies regarding research methods in dealing with knowledge of the past, the philosophy of history has turned to form: it has become the epistemology of historical thinking. It is no longer concerned with the content of historical thinking, commonly called 'history', but with the specific *form* in which and with which it carries out its cognitive work. Form and content are of course two sides of the same coin, and the focus is now on the other side.

What do we find when we consider a coherent relationship between form and content that is central to our understanding of the work of historical studies? This question relates to the *functional* aspect of historical thinking. It refers to the real-life setting for historical thinking. Only a combination of these three aspects – the material, the formal and the functional – provides an acceptable understanding of the basis, the scope and the objective of historical studies. We can also say that the question 'What is history?' can only be sufficiently answered if the different concepts of meaning that are associated with the word 'history' are clear.

2. 'History' as Concept of Meaning: A Look at Content and Form

It should be obvious by now that meaning is the key concept in this theory of history. The framework presented here is an attempt to make history, historical thinking in general and history as academic study in particular, comprehensible in the framework of a theory of historical meaning. The general thesis is that history is a concept of meaning. But what is a concept of meaning (*Sinnkonzept*)?[75]

A concept of meaning is a concrete expression of human interpretation of the self and the world that becomes a way of life, a definable expanse of social groups. It appears as ideology, world view, religion and similar measures for orientation. It synthesizes varying cultural practices (such as art, religion and science). It extends throughout different cultural practices: from the implicitness of the order of life to the complex articulation and reflection of this order by specialists, whether they be shamans, priests, artists or professors. A concept of meaning can be defined as follows: *It is a plausible and reliably authenticated and reflected upon contextual meaning of experience in our world. It serves to explain the world, to provide orientation, to form identity and to guide action in a purposeful manner.*[76] As established and authenticated interpretation, a concept of meaning is accepted in practice and enables social and individual agency.

A Matter of Differences   This definition is similar to Jan Assmann's view. According to Assmann, meaning (the German *Sinn*) is a cultural factor that organizes the human 'concepts of time, destiny and history'. Also, 'by *Sinn*, we mean direction and context. The experience of meaninglessness is either based on the inability to recognize the direction something "wants to go" or "is going", or the inability to recognize the context that connects certain events or elements. Understanding means to create a context for isolated elements or to recognize the direction of something. "Meaningless" is that which is without direction or context.'[77] It is worth adding the elements of *space* and *identity* to this description. To be more precise, we should speak of 'space-time'. Human action is always directed by intentions; it is oriented by an interpretation of the world that emphasizes the coherence of things; it always takes place in a certain place at a certain time. This time and place have to be interpreted in terms of enabling action. Finally, action presupposes a subject who knows who they are, who is like them and who is different from them. The subject and their actions are always shaped by a mental activity of forming personal and collective identity. The 'I' and the self as agents are formed in the struggle for recognition between individuals and social units. Individuals live in and through the idea of belonging and distinguishing themselves from the 'other'. This cognitive life always takes place in concrete social space and in concrete social time. A space has a geographical basis and is always situated within the dynamics of time, while a time always has a chronological basis and is localized in space.

Concepts of meaning exist in contextual knowledge, in comprehensive explanations of the world, in normatively charged definitions of directions and objectives of actions in space and time, in the combination of explaining the world and intentional actions, and finally, in the formation of identity and difference, of belonging and dissociation. These concepts have a specific medial dimension. They occur in and function through specific practices. They appear in different modes. They serve the orientation, motivation and justification of human agency and make suffering bearable. They are characterized by a minimum level of coherency and consistency. They can be combined with other concepts of meaning and can be integrated into overarching systems of interpretation.

Concepts of meaning have a practical effect, which means they are purposeful and future-oriented. They underlie socially accepted forms of perception and interpretation, the dominant norms of perception and coping mechanisms in dealing with what is perceived. They inextricably connect action and suffering as integral parts of human life – be it on an individual or collective level – with the substantiation and reflection of intention and interpretation and therefore with a constant legitimation of action and suffering.

Functional Differences   Concepts of meaning can function in the following ways:

- In their *hermeneutic* function, concepts of meaning provide conceptual systems that enable an understanding and explanation of the world we live in and experience.
- In their *communicative* function, they serve to create understanding among individual members of a group or a society. This concerns the make-up of the group and the value of group membership. With this establishment of value, meaning is a scarce and valuable resource, and in the interest of its societal value it must remain scarce.
- In their function of *guiding action*, concepts of meaning substantiate and legitimize the concepts and measures of value and their systematic connection with a 'behavioural code' and collective ethos.
- Finally, in their function of *forming a subject*, meaning and concepts of meaning serve the development, production and reproduction of collective 'identity' that must be formed and then permanently affirmed

Table 4.1 Schematic presentation of the concept of meaning.

Content	– Contextual knowledge
	– Determining direction and defining objectives in space and time
	– Forming identity and difference
Functions	– Orientation
	– Motivation
	– Legitimation
Modes of Effect	– Hermeneutic
	– Communicative
	– Action guiding
	– Subject forming

and reproduced. This always involves (a) concrete belonging, including and excluding as well as establishing rank and status of individuals; (b) self-assertion as the stabilization and self-reproduction of a group formed by these individuals, or a 'polity'; and finally, (c) overcoming crises and fending off external but also and especially internal destabilizing and disintegrating forces, which includes the channelling of change.

We can now analyse the phenomenon of 'history' within this framework of a theoretical concept of meaning.

The word 'history' has almost a double meaning: it refers to what happened in the past as well as the account of these events (*res gestae* and *narratio rerum gestarum*). One can emphasize either side of the double meaning to define history. For example, at the beginning of modern historical thinking, 'history' was understood as temporal facts, as a temporalized notion of humankind.

History – An Entity? Many have criticized this notion of history[78] as nothing more than an ideological construct that was used to substantiate claims of authority in the struggle for power. Should we then avoid using this concept and the idea of the temporal movement of humankind as an entity? Certainly, some use this construct when they use 'history' to justify political action – we could even speak of acting 'in the name' of history. 'History' is also used to judge political action. Since this kind of 'history' encompasses all temporal movements in the human world, it can easily turn into totalitarian thinking and have fatal consequences.

The notion of a 'whole' history works as an ideological motor for political action. This becomes especially clear when we consider our own identity and therefore the relationship of the self to the other. We place ourselves, our own people or our social formations (that determine who belongs to our group and who does not) at the core of history. We see our own interests and intentions as the reason for everything that happened in history. This necessarily means that the position of the 'other' in human history is diminished and subservient. For example, national identity (in its modern form) is laden with the notion that the own nation in its historical particularity represents the most advanced stage of development (or the most promising future) of humankind.

We can avoid the criticism of this definition of history when we view 'history' as simply a formal way of thinking and disregard its contents. History then becomes a product of interpretation instead of an interpretation of facts. With this turn to form, the unity of history as an encompassing temporal form of humanity disintegrates into an abundance of separate and individual histories. As a result, we escape the danger of a modern ideology of history but now face the problem of relativism. When the validity claims of historical interpretations can no longer be substantiated by references to empirical data, then these claims inevitably shift to the realm of political decisions. Historical thinking then encourages an ideologically laden decisionism in the process of forming historical identity. Truth claims are replaced with power relations. We fall from one ideology into another.

This counterplay of content and form does not simply favour one side over another. What is more relevant is the complex relationship between both, and how that can be revealed. The importance of political identity becomes apparent in this context.

3. Teleology and Reconstruction

What is at the core of the problem of defining history and understanding it as scientific study? *That core is found where the visions for the future of societal practice are connected to directions of temporal processes from the past that are relevant for life in the present.* There are two ways to conceptualize this connection of the past and the future in the present. They correspond to the two different meanings of 'history': history as teleology or history as construction.

Teleological Thinking   Teleology means that the temporal direction of current human action and the understanding of the present world of this action is based on a temporal process in the past. Daily life is part of the continuity of a long-term development. Its meaning is defined by a point of origin that across time determines the different shapes or forms of the world. This origin is a predisposition of the future. Within a teleological framework, the past dominates the future. In a teleological view, the present is aligned with an established and set principle of time based on long-term and future-directed developments.

The ultimate 'aim' (*telos*) of history, conceived by a teleology that makes the past the guide of the present to safeguard the future, was and is often identified with the origin of present living conditions and circumstances, their directive beginnings and an essential 'formation' or 'creation'. This is especially clear in origin myths and creation narratives, but it has also taken a secular form (otherwise we would not have a series of national holidays). However, teleology is not limited to such a reference to origins. This is especially the case when the future potentials of the origin can no longer be understood through supernatural powers, that is, in purely worldly conceptions of historical understanding. In such cases, the temporal sequences with which our own world has been connected to its current circumstances from the beginning present a direction and can therefore be understood as capable of providing guidelines for present-day action. In teleological terms, this can even be seen as surpassing the past for the sake of a better future. (This is clear in the notion that we can realize things that our ancestors could only have dreamed of.)

The power of teleological thinking in history is immense. It especially appears in intercultural discourse: we assert own cultural identity in contrast to others with strong arguments. China is a good example of this. We often hear of the unbroken continuity of Chinese culture over thousands of years, unlike that of other cultures. And when it comes to the particularity and power of 'the West' we often hear (not only in relation to others but also regarding itself) references to antiquity and Christianity as standard argumentation for cultural continuity. These examples show that teleological thinking brings tension and conflict into cultural differences. Teleology and ethnocentrism are closely related.

Constructivist Thinking   Constructive thinking, on the other hand, gives the future authority over the past. The criteria for meaning in the 'construction' of the past as history can only originate from the potential of meaning of human action that is oriented towards the future. The teleological narrow view on the past is opened up. This uncovers a wider range of historical perspectives that emerge from the multitude of competing interests in the power struggles of the present. A multitude of possibilities for the construction of history surmounts the unity of teleology. But it comes at a price: the secure basis on which present action is prefigured according to its origins in the past becomes unsteady in a pluralistic world. The need for coherence for the sake of forming cultural identity is no longer met. Clear indications of who we are as opposed to others are lost in the hybridity of multiple affiliations. The past becomes a playground of references to the present that cannot be mediated or decided on with arguments based on historical knowledge. We go from bad to worse, from teleological definiteness to relativistic ambiguity.

How do we solve this dilemma? Attempts to synthesize teleology and constructionism must mediate the dichotomy of the respective logics of historical thinking. In doing this it is useful to firmly base constructivist references to the past on historical experience. This takes account of the level of realism that teleology brings to the table when it comes to the historical orientation of present-day life. At the same time, however, we should not betray the multitude of perspectives of this orientation.

Not Construction but Reconstruction   In other words, this means that construction must gain objectivity through *reconstruction*. In this little prefix we find the weight of historical evidence.[79] Anticipated meanings and hopes, which shape the historical signature of the human past, are critically examined to check whether or under what conditions they can be reconciled with experience. Reconstruction means that we think of the past as a temporal chain of possibilities for shaping the human world to which we add expectations for the future. Experiences of the past are always 'historic' when they occur in a meaningful correlation with the present. In this correlation the past is projected into the present in a meaningful way. This is evident in the case of tradition, but is also true for the other patterns for forming meaning within historical thinking. With this empirical relevance for the present, a valid element of teleology is taken into account. Admittedly, this *telos* is not a determined objective (*Zielbestimmung*), but rather a certain conditionality of historical thinking that it can and must deal with in a critical and impersonal way. *Telos* is no longer a determined objective, but an open reference to the future.

What Happens with the Past?   This does not mean that the range of possibilities for the creative and cultural forming of meaning in dealing with the human past is closed off. Rather, these possibilities are structured in reference to the past. Every human formation of meaning – including historical meaning – is determined by preset elements or structures, the cultural conditions that shape our personal circumstances. This does not mean that the creators of meaning are prisoners of these conditions but rather that they (have to) refer to these preset elements of meaning in their cultural context. In doing so, they must demonstrate the plausibility of their constructed meaning in reference to these conditions and their foundations traced back over time. What makes teleology so plausible? Apart from the objectives of our present-day conceptual notions of time that are drawn from the depths of the past, its plausibility has to do with these depths and the connection between the present and the distant past. The further we reach back into the past, the more certain the foundations of our temporal orientations in the here and now appear. This reference to the past should not disappear when we replace teleology with reconstruction. It does not have to, since the past has already entered into the preset elements that are available to every reconstruction, and in the abundance of the developments on which current living conditions are built.

The Scope of Possibilities   The past can no longer be understood in the teleological sense of developing in a meaningful direction. Rather, any development is historically understood against the backdrop of multiple possibilities. In doing so, the range of possibilities is placed directly within historical experience itself, taking away its presentist arbitrariness. A great many histories based on the heterogenic nature of action in the present day then become possible. Each of these histories can then develop into a historical perspective. These different perspectives appear in varying histories. These histories can become discursive: we can compare them in a structurally analytical manner and position them in a relationship of mutual validation and criticism. Dealing with the multitude of historical perspectives in a structurally analytical manner means making them plausible in light of historical processes that have actually taken place. The processes of the past are interpreted taking into consideration the following question: Under what conditions could these processes occur, or how are they based on the preset elements of the past without being determined by them? The entirety of history is not lost in these many 'steps back', but is maintained on the level of internal reference to various perspectives.

We can also understand the contrast between teleology and construction as an alternative to causality and contingency. 'Causality' in teleological thinking denotes the distinction between actual developments and possible alternatives. It identifies the processes of the past that fit within a concept of meaning that goes way back in time. In contrast, reconstruction emphasizes contingencies and not fixed designations. In this case, meaning is not causally determined but rather left open in view of the range of possibilities in every historical action situation. The meaningfulness of reconstruction emphasizes this range as a chance for human beings to intentionally move beyond their own life circumstances, thereby influencing the circumstances and contingencies of their lives. Teleology gives historical development the appearance of necessity that does not know any real or effective contingency; reconstruction, on the other hand, takes the contingent character of historical events into account.

Because it opens historical meaning up to a range of possibilities and the experience of contingency, reconstructive thinking tempers the harshness of ethnocentric divisions and makes it possible to recognize differences in the processes involved in the forming of historical identity.[80]

4. A Problem Unresolved: The Natural World

The aforementioned definition of history as a tangible, temporal process of forming human existence has a weakness: the power of the natural world over

Table 4.2 Schematic presentation of teleology versus reconstruction.

Teleology	Reconstruction
Focused on origins	Future-oriented
Unilinear, mono-perspective	Multilinear, multi-perspective
Controlled by necessity	Open to contingency
Causality of meaning	Causality of conditions

the world of humans. The specifically human history can only be understood when it is not regarded as a purely natural occurrence. Rather, any understanding should take into account the anthropological and fundamental fact that humans are cultural beings who can only live if they form meaning in reference to their nature and the natural world around them, that is, when they are something more than their nature. At the same time, human beings remain natural beings who live in the realm of the natural world as well as in the cultural world they shape. The classical philosophy of history in its modernity, especially the work of Johann Gottfried Herder, has dealt with this correlation of nature and history in that it reveals and describes a driving force in both of these realms in human existence.[81] The discourse is of a 'cultivating force' (*Bildungstrieb*) that runs through all of nature and has led to the emergence of the human species. Nature culminated in human beings; it transformed itself into culture. Kant expressed this in his philosophy of history, referring to human history as a 'plan of nature' that assigned human beings their place in the overall processes of the world, bringing together the starry sky and the moral law.[82]

The Forgotten Connection Between Culture and Nature   This relationship is clear to me. However, it has become lost in attempts to perceive the meanings of culture and nature themselves as the essential components of the historical character of the temporal occurrences of human existence. On the level of universal historical representations, this problem can be circumvented by simply representing the history of the origins of the human species as part of natural history. As such, the historical development of the human species and its cultural products is explained as 'cultural' history ('cultural' meaning 'not natural') with a specific temporal perspective.[83] Of course such histories make sense, but it is incredibly difficult to clarify this sense and make it plausible in respect to its own principles. This is mainly because two ways of academic thinking that cannot easily be combined for epistemological reasons collide here: the natural sciences as a study of the natural world on the one hand and the cultural sciences as a study of culture on the other. A critical aspect of this incompatibility is the fact that the concepts of meaning of the cultural sciences are meaningless to the natural sciences.

The Discord of Sciences   The success of the natural sciences is based on the Copernican turn, in which we no longer perceive an inner meaning in nature. Rather, meaning is ascribed to nature 'from outside' and under the epistemological premise of fundamental meaninglessness through the use of mathematics and experimentation (according to explainability and technical controllability). In contrast, the history of human beings is characterized by determining the meaning of human action and suffering. Historical knowledge is built on this. Nature, and its vital role in the lives of human beings, takes on this inner meaning (through creation myths or – in rationalistic form – in the framework of a physico-theology). But under the cultural dominance of the natural sciences, we do not find a ready link to this idea today.

In any case, the environmental problems caused by the power of technology in a world in which nature is void of meaning represents an intellectual challenge that requires (at least according to cultural scientists) a new category of meaning that ties human beings and the natural world together. One starting point here is the fact that both nature and culture must be understood as temporal process and that they must be interpreted historically, both separately and together. The natural world has become so closely entwined with human culture that it is difficult to understand without considering the effects of human action against nature. The natural history of the planet has entered the 'Anthropocene' period, in which culture and nature are related in a way that demands a completely new ecological way of thinking.[84] Together they form a historical epoch of development of the earth. But what is the meaning of this history, when it goes way beyond humans and their concepts of meaning? Historical theory has not yet found an adequate answer to this question.

There have of course been attempts at a response.[85] They replace the contrasting difference between human beings and nature with a comprehensive process of development in which biological evolution merges with a cultural evolution. The effects of such a merger for our understanding of nature has yet to be revealed. In any case, the idea of meaning in nature can no longer be disputed, meaning that is created by those beings who form meaning to begin with: human beings.[86]

5. Means of Access I: The Categorical Dimensions of the Historical

The previous considerations about what determines or defines history, what constitutes the content and form of historical thinking and its academic cognition, resulted in a clear conclusion: this 'history' can be regarded by way of three categorical means of access or interpretations.

Categorical means of access,[87] or gateways of analysis, are means of accessing something but also of restricting something else, a means of admitting access while denying access, if you will. Designating what we should be looking at involves dismissing or concealing what we should not be looking at. The categorical means of access to what we call history always include a distinction between what history is and what it is not. These days, the usual distinction is the one between history and nature. But considering the entanglement of environmental problems and the lives of human beings, this distinction has become highly problematic. A distinction between the historical and the non-historical would of course be more logically convincing. But this is also vague; it does not reach the specific quality of the meaning-forming dimension of the historical. It is therefore better to explore this further and differentiate between the categorical distinctions of content, form and function of historical knowledge.

The Three Dimensions of History   There are three dimensions of cognitive access to history.

(1) The first is the *empirical dimension*. It concerns what happened in the human past, or the *res gestae*. The events of the past as such are not history. For them to become history, all that happened in the past needs to be integrated in a temporal perspective that meaningfully connects the past to the present and the future. Categorically, this dimension of events in time is made accessible as history through an actual and meaningful temporal context. Hans Michael Baumgartner called this category 'continuity', by which he meant that there is an inherent connection between temporal occurrences.[88] However, the word 'continuity' is misleading, as it indicates a particular quality of the temporal occurrences of history in contrast to others, such as discontinuity, disruptions in temporal patterns and so on. In this respect, it is more useful to speak of 'a concept of the course of time'. This categorical dimension manifests itself in the determinations of the course of events in human existence in all its forms and appearances in space and time. These are historical universals. Traditionally, this dimension is explicated in the philosophy of history.

(2) The second dimension is the *formal dimension*, which concerns the specific forms of thinking and expression used to focus on the special character of the past and the connections between temporal occurrences in that past, and to analyse and represent this special character. The prevailing categorical principle here is storytelling, or *narrativity*. Here, too, it is necessary to avoid certain misunderstandings regarding the distinction made by professional historians between traditional 'narrative' historiography and modern 'analytical' historical representations.[89] We could also speak of a mimetic versus a constructive historical representation. This distinction in fact reveals their common feature: both views concern (a) history that represents the specific temporal character of past occurrences. The prevailing mental process involved in this representation is narration. The aforementioned distinction can only be understood as being embedded within narration itself. It is a distinction between different modes of narrative, but not between narrative and something else.

This categorical dimension concretely manifests itself in the specific forms of historical thinking and knowledge that are found in all the variety and diversity of historical representations. In historical scholarship, professionals treat them as types of historical representation. Before the narrative turn, this dimension was the subject matter of epistemology and analytical theory of science; afterwards, it entered the fields of linguistics and literary theory.

(3) The third dimension is the *functional dimension*, or the 'real-life setting' in which historical thinking occurs. It is within this setting that we must define the particularity of historical thinking. In the unity of form and content, historical thinking has a specific function in human culture: it serves to create internal and external orientation for human beings within the temporal framework of their lives.

Internal and External Orientation   An external orientation connects the future-oriented direction of human action with past-oriented experience of human action (and human suffering). Human beings interpret the external passing of time in a meaningful way and transform it into an internal orientation. This, in turn, directs the time-related intentionality of human action. The subjectivity of every acting and suffering human being, which constitutes our cultural orientation in daily life, is critical for this temporal direction. In this subjectivity, in the depth of the human self (whether personal or social), we decide what must be seen as meaningful.

The acting and suffering subject perseveres and asserts his- or herself in an ever-changing temporal human world. The dominant viewpoint in historical thinking is the temporal consistency and coherence of the human self, often called '*identity*'.[90] In order to live, human beings must interpret the world in which they live. This essential act of interpretation involves a distinctly articulated consciousness of self. The need for meaning that makes humans cultural beings always includes the question: who am I (once again, whether personal or social)? The answer to this question often takes the form of a history. The dominant conceptualization of the course of time includes the experience of who and what we are, as well as the expectation of what we will be, what we want to be and what we can be. Both experience and expectation unite in a temporal orientation of meaning in human life.

How do we see this in a real-life setting? Where is the past alive in the present (without having been interpreted) with mediated content and form? This functional determination in historical thinking on a categorical level originates in *memory*. In an elaborate form, memory appears as cultural memory, as a product of historical consciousness in the orientation of daily human life. This product fundamentally influences the cultivation of human identity and the process of becoming an autonomous person (*Bildung*) that helps to adequately position our lives in a world marked by temporal change.[91]

We can summarize the categorical foundations and orientations of historical thinking in the following schema:[92]

6. Means of Access II: The Realm of Experience Revealed

In the following we examine the experience of the historical on three cognitive perspectives.

(a) *The temporal dynamic of human life.* The issue here is the dynamic forces that keep our world in a state of temporal movement through human beings and in human beings. This is about the fact that the world is fundamentally changing and that it also appears changeable to human beings.

(b) *Temporality as source of meaning.* This dynamic also produces the starting point or source of meaning for these changes. The meaning of these changes cannot simply be ascribed from outside (or after the fact) but can only arise and develop from within an inner connection to these changes. The human world is basically meaningfully formed. Meaning emerges from past forms of life. (This does not contradict the fact that this meaning also always includes absurdity.) Time and meaning in the human world must be viewed together.

Because it is about the human world, such a fundamental theory or philosophy of history can only be developed by going back to the (anthropological) basic humanity of human beings. Such a retreat to our humanity is necessary in order to take the intercultural orientation of metahistory seriously.

Jacob Burckhardt's Historical Anthropology   Burckhardt famously described this anthropological basis of historical thinking as follows: 'We ... shall start out from one point accessible to us, the one eternal centre of all things

Table 4.3 Dimensions within the philosophy of history.

The Historical	Relevant Determinants	Forms
Experience (facts and circumstances)	Conceptualization of the course of time ('continuity')	Material philosophy of history
Forms of knowledge	Narrativity	Formal philosophy of history
Practical functions	Cultural memory	Functional philosophy of history
	Identity, '*Bildung*'	

– man, suffering, striving, doing as he is and was and ever shall be. Hence our study will, in a certain sense, be pathological in kind. The philosophers of history regard the past as a contrast to and preliminary stage of our time as the full development. We shall study the recurrent, constant and typical as echoing in us and intelligible through us.'[93] This anthropology contrasts sharply with classical philosophy of history, as it points out that which perseveres in all historical transformations lending the historical world its human signature: the acting and suffering human being. The philosophy of history, on the other hand, has specifically referred to the changing of human forms of life and thus emphasized temporal changes rather than continuity. It is important to offset this contradistinction, as history can only move into anthropology if a fundamental de-historicization occurs. (And anthropology can only be called 'historic' if we understand it in terms of the principles of change.)

Burckhardt understood the inner bond that pulls the happenings of the past together, as part of the *humanum* (our humanity). This inner bond perseveres throughout all transformations and manifests itself in the diversity of human cultures. If we consider this *humanum* historically, we begin to understand something 'resounding and understandable in us all'. *The source of meaning for historical thinking lies within this* humanum. At the same time, Burckhardt provided an exceptionally important indication of what meaning is and how it is formed: it does not just come from human action and human intentions (or 'aspirations'), but also from human 'enduring' or suffering. This refers to an essential feature of human life that has mostly been ignored in historical theory until now: suffering. We can say that Burckhardt anthropologically re-evaluated the determining factor of suffering in human life to the point that historical thinking, when it wants to understand human beings in terms of our humanity, could be called 'pathological'.

First of all, we must determine what it is that remains constant in the human forms of life throughout all temporal changes. Within this constancy we need to determine the factors and elements that cause its temporal changes. After all, we do not intend to develop an ahistorical anthropology in which changes in the lives of human beings are seen as unimportant. We need to fundamentally examine this 'constancy' and permanence while grasping the full extent of how things change.

(c) *The source of meaning for temporality as a factor in historical thinking.* In this continuity of change we can discern the source of meaning that the suffering and acting human being uses in order to overcome suffering and to act intentionally. *This meaning, drawn from every respective culture, must be addressed in such a way that historical thinking, in its empirical orientation, can draw on it.* This meaning (or absurdity) initiates the understanding of the temporal change in the human world as history. The essential category for this is *development*.

In view of the above, I would like to sketch out an anthropologically based philosophy of history. It is tied to the ideas of Reinhart Koselleck and his 'conditions of all possible history' that account for the constancy in the historical movement of the human world.[94] I would like to add to his list of universals and clarify their specific historical meaningfulness and historicity.

The Human World as Realm of Tension and Conflict   All human lives occur in a very complex and uneasy realm of contrasts and extremes that present a constant challenge for the cultural formation of meaning. These contrasts produce the temporal dynamics in human forms of life. They constitute Kant's '*ungesellige Geselligkeit*' (unsocial sociability), which positions the human world in the movement of history.[95] Every human being and every human social group faces the following conflicts or tensions:

- The tension between nature and culture: this is where the human world attains its specifically uncertain form, its contingency and instability, its fundamental challenge of self-assertion.
- The tension between upper and lower: this is where social hierarchies are established.
- The tension between centre and periphery: this is where differences form in the spatial organization of human life that carry more than just social meaning.
- The tension between inclusion and exclusion, or belonging and not belonging: this is about personal and social identity.
- The tension between men and women: this is where gender becomes a fundamental social category.
- The tension between old and young: this tension goes beyond just biological differences. Positions of social status and approaches towards upbringing are based on these differences.
- The tension between power and powerlessness: here it is decided who gives the orders and who must obey.
- The tension between action and suffering: this is where life-determining ideas of a successful way of life and the fundamental ideas concerning happiness are formed.
- The tension between having to die and being able to kill: this is where power relations between human beings are formed.
- The tension between friend and enemy: this is where power relationships (and their transition to violence) are organized and thus the political realm is established.

- The tension between master and servant: this is where the social differences in acquiring and using economic resources are defined, power relations organized and the course of life established.
- The tension between rich and poor: this is where availability of goods among human beings is determined.
- The tension between individuality and sociality (collectivity): this is where human subjectivity takes shape.
- The tension between consciousness and unconsciousness in the mechanisms that drive human action: this is where the mental lives of individuals and communities are formed.
- The tension between worldliness and transcendence: this is where the basic structures of the interpretation of human beings and the world and the differences between religious and secular dimensions in our understanding of the world are formed.
- The tension between human and non-human in determining the real conditions of daily life: this is where the concept of what it is to be a human being is formed.
- The tension between good and evil: this is where ethical and moral rules of human coexistence are formed. This is also where the relationships between humans and non-humans and transcendent beings are shaped.

We could add even more. This list can help to categorize the realm of historical thinking. All possible historical processes can be classified in the complex relational network of these differences and contrasts. The contrasting elements are ideal types, interconnected in many conditioned and conditioning ways. They have a hierarchical order. In such an order, the contrast between acting and suffering is fundamentally essential.

An extension and alteration of the list depends on the heuristics of historical thinking, that is, on the questions whose answers demand a universal historical perspective. This network of historical universals categorically brings the past into the present and the future, as the living conditions of a given time in which historical thinking involving interpretation and orientation takes place are also determined by these universals.

The lives of human beings unfold within these fields of tension. Human beings must contend with them and construct their lives within them. This always (also) occurs in a meaning-forming activity that determines human action and inaction. It is clear why human action cannot be understood without a constant reference to suffering: the listed tensions turn into experiences of suffering in human beings and this suffering must be overcome.[96] If we understand culture as the epitome of this overcoming, then it is easy to comprehend that, as well as how culture is imbued with suffering and not just determined by human agency.

The Temporal Movement of the Human Way of Life In light of the aforementioned polarity of the anthropological universal factors that determine the lives of human beings, the temporal movement of human lives becomes clear. In their anthropological basis, human lives are fundamentally temporal; they take place in the constant possibility of change. The network of anthropological universals in which history is constituted is anything but static. In terms of philosophy of history, we could call it an 'anthropological generator of temporality' (*anthropologischer Zeitlichkeitsgenerator*).[97] This has to do with the fact that the specific contrasting elements present a painful challenge for every affected person. This challenge must constantly be overcome. Human beings cannot simply let things be. They must always position themselves in relation to themselves and other people, cope with suffering through the pursuit of happiness and assert themselves.

The temporality of human life is of course primarily based on natural (calendric or chronological) time, in which the things of the world come into being and pass away, in which we are born and in which we die. This natural time alone poses a continuous challenge to how humans form their lives. In addition, there is an inner temporality of human life. Human beings deal with nature, with their own world and with their own time. This time distinguishes our cultural 'nature'. The unease that follows, characterized by the need or demand for meaning, lies in the fact that in their pursuits and purposes, human beings fundamentally strive to go beyond the given circumstances of their lives, because these circumstances make them suffer. We can never completely resign ourselves to these hardships. Instead, we use our energy to overcome hardship and pursue our own happiness, which leads us beyond the given circumstances and conditions of our lives. The reason for this has to do with the fact that the resources available to us for satisfying our needs (whether materialistic, emotional or spiritual) are never enough. Human beings must live within a fundamental asymmetry between their needs and the opportunities to satisfy these needs. This is not only true in the economic sense of dealing with a surplus of demands over resources for satisfying these demands. All aspects of life deal with a similar asymmetry between demand and reward. For instance, the social constitution of human lives, whether on an individual or a social level, is shaped by a need for recognition. The individual or the social group always demands more recognition from others than they are willing to bestow.

This is evident in the internal and external structure of human needs: in contrast to animals, human beings develop new needs from satisfying their old needs. We cannot find or give any criterion for the distinction between 'natural' and 'artificial' needs in order to problematize the latter. The specifically human unease with time, then, lies in the Faustian nature of human beings: 'Und im Genuß verschmacht ich nach Begierde' ('and in enjoyment I pine to feel desire').[98]

The specific historical temporality as related to the realm of experience and to the horizon of expectations in daily life also lies in this dissatisfaction of the human mind with the world. The concrete form this dissatisfaction takes is not anthropologically predefined. But that it must develop (even under varying circumstances and in different forms) with the essential involvement of the human mind is true for all times.

Action and Suffering   The relationship between acting and suffering in human life ingrained in the conditions of human life is just as anthropologically universal. To be born into the network of tension-filled living conditions constitutes a suffering that must be seen as specifically human. Here we find the difference between the suffering described above and the suffering as a natural part of life that we share with all other creatures on the planet. What is particularly human is the consciousness of suffering we are subject to that forces us to deal with life through the forming of meaning.

One could say that human beings have to suffer due to their own intellectual capacity for transcending their particular living conditions. What follows from this suffering is the structure of the drive and intention to go beyond these conditions. Within this structure lies the meaning that guides human action and that does not allow action to be understood as mere behaviour. Suffering triggers the development of qualities of meaning arising from action that we overlook in a historical analysis if we only focus on action and dismiss suffering. Granted, there is no lack of emphasis on suffering in the area of historical experience (especially in religion and art). However, how this suffering enters into or is excluded from the retrospective formation of historical meaning is an important question for historical theory that has yet to be answered in a convincing way.

Forming Meaning within the Network of Universals   What does the human way of life look like in view of historical theory, with the formation of meaning embedded in the network of tension-filled universals that produce suffering and motivate action? Is the change that results from and is carried by the temporality of our lives already historical in and of itself? Or must we first find something meaningful in changes to qualify them as historical? If we were to answer no to the latter question, that would mean that the temporal changes that historical thinking is concerned with are haphazard or random. In that case, meaning can be assigned randomly, too. This, however, contradicts the analysis of the formation of historical meaning as based on preset elements. In these elements the past pops up (or rather, has already popped up) when we try to understand it 'historically'.

These presets, this pre-historical character of the past, must be considered in view of the anthropology of human historicity. Every interpretive reaction of people to the tensions in their lives provides the occurrences of their daily lives with a meaningful *directionality*. Every occurrence in time is directed in the sense that it takes place in relation to the past, present and future and can be positioned within a relevant chronological timeline. This chronological directionality is extrinsic to the occurrences. What is particularly human here is the consciousness that we are subject to time, to the occurrences of the past, to temporality. There is an internal temporal factor at play, too, as meaning is temporal. Human beings react to the contradictions in their lives by forming meaning in such a manner that they can live in and with these contradictions. And in this meaningful arrangement, in this 'residing in the world', there is something beyond the presets, something that fundamentally transcends them. In a historical view of the past, this transcendence carries the sense of time of something unfulfilled, or a hope, a longing. To connect with this sense of time and to interpret it historically (which can of course be done critically), is to make the temporal changes of the past historical. In terms of historical theory, we can say the following: *the changes in the past are only historical when they are developments.*[99]

Concepts of Direction of Temporal Changes   How do we determine direction within the framework of historical anthropology as outlined earlier?

In an anthropological sense, every fundamental and universal dichotomy concerning the organization of our lives demands an overarching concept of meaning. Only with such a concept can we as human beings endure the tension of the contradictions, be content and even (even if only partially) become happy. Such temporal direction can be found in the meaningful ways we have to deal with the dichotomies of daily life:

- In the dichotomy between nature and culture there must be a balance between the appropriation and preservation of resources. The idea of balance – which cannot be static but should develop dynamically – must comprise an intersection between the contrary poles for the sake of creating an overall unified entity. In this idea nature and culture are synthesized (e.g., in the concept of 'benign nature' or the ecological responsibility of human beings). In a temporalized form, this concept provides a direction for historical change. This is not an inner teleology but rather as a hypothesis of historical meaning, which is not simply imposed on experience but instead can be made plausible with this experience.
- In the dichotomy between top and bottom there must be a viewpoint of acceptance that legitimizes social differences. The proper term for

this legitimacy is justice. Regardless of circumstances, there is no human way of life that does not have this reference to legitimacy. When seen as extended over time, this legitimacy also determines direction, which makes temporal changes historical.

- The tension between centre and periphery creates highly conflictual relationships between different communities, ethnic groups, states, cultures, even individual places and regions. If we do not want to reduce these relationships simply to the natural condition of the fight of all against all, and if we do not want war to be the default state of things, then we need to create a viewpoint of compromise, of negotiability of contrasting poles, of exchange and recognition. An example of this is seen in the many cultural forms of hospitality toward guests. The transformation of enemy into guest, as the Latin term '*hostis*' expresses, represents a chance of survival for different communities, as a coming together of different groups in a clear relationship. These forms of hospitality might be amicable or leery, but at the same time they guarantee survival through togetherness. The historical direction here would be the tendency to move from monocentrism to polycentric diversification. This tendency would fall within Immanuel Kant's concept, formulated in modern terms, of an 'eternal peace'. That this does not represent a backward-looking projection is evident in the numerous visions of utopia formulated in pre-modern times.[100]
- The tension between insider and outsider characterizes the concepts of belonging and not belonging, of inclusion and exclusion, of personal and social identity. This tension is reduced through efforts and strategies involving the acceptance of differences.
- The tension and dichotomy between men and women has been seen and accepted as something natural for a long time. However, this dichotomy requires a culturally interpreted legitimacy in which fundamental views of reciprocity play an essential role.[101] From this anthropologically universal reciprocal relationship a temporal direction towards equality can be developed.[102] Even in times of patriarchal gender roles we find tendencies to reach beyond this inequality. For example, according to the canon of Christianity, the New Testament, differences based on sex are irrelevant as compared to the equality of all human beings in the belief of the 'son of man', Jesus Christ.
- The tension between young and old is interpreted as life-serving with reference to (temporally shifted) care. This perpetuates empathy between humans and provides a universal movement through time.
- The tension between power and powerlessness demands mutually accepted criteria of legitimacy in order to be sustainable. In this mutual relationship there is a temporal direction towards political reciprocity.

- The dichotomy between action and suffering is mediated as human beings transform the experiences of hardship into opportunities for action. The powerful longing for happiness in this transformation transcends the existing conditions under which and in which human beings act. These transcendental qualities can be interpreted as temporal directions of historical changes (or 'developments').
- The tension between having to die and being able to kill can be understood as a specific form of the dichotomy between action and suffering. It is livable by a conceptualization of life that grants it special value and thereby limits the killing of others to specific circumstances. The temporal directedness of this life-value concept becomes imperative when it is universalized, that is, when it is not limited to our own way of life.
- The dichotomy between friend and enemy demands a perspective of peace when the will to live is not limited by the idea of a natural state of war of all against all. Since such a limitation is fundamentally compromised by others' will to live, a temporal direction can be found in the political regulating of this dichotomy that secures peace (which can also be understood in terms of Kant's 'eternal peace').
- The tension between master and servant demands a social balancing, which leads to the temporal direction towards equality.
- The dichotomy between rich and poor can be endured with the notion of a fair distribution of economic goods. We could say that this is based on the meaning criterion of sufficiency. The temporal direction that follows is one of equality according to criteria for social justice.
- The dichotomy between individuality and sociality is mediated by a notion of human subjectivity, in which the relationships between human beings are based on and governed by the concept of reciprocal acknowledgement. This concept can be seen as an overarching perspective of historical development.
- The tension between conscious and unconscious factors in the human way of life demands a balanced relationship to the self as a form of subjectivity. It demands an inner coherence of human drives and a corresponding subliming subject formation that enables feelings of empathy, justice and acceptance. The temporal movement of life thus forms a direction towards human subjectivity accordingly.
- The tension between worldliness and transcendence in the interpretation of our place in the world is dealt with in an all-encompassing notion of universal order. The relevant perspectives can be seen as temporally directed since they move beyond a given world order toward a meaningfully determined order that is considered good.
- The tension between human and non-human in the perception and interpretation of life-defining conditions of human existence is mediated

by the idea that humans must live under non-human conditions. The principle of self-transcendence plays a fundamental role in this tension. This self-transcendence can be interpreted as a temporal direction.

- And finally, in the organization of human life, the tension between good and evil demands ethical and moral rules in which reciprocity plays a decisive role. This reciprocity gives a fundamentally temporal direction to the cultural orientation of human life (as seen from the present). It goes beyond the given contrariness in human beings, beyond the '*ungesellige Geselligkeit*' (unsocial sociability) in dealing with each other and with ourselves. It is directed toward a notion of the human world in which good triumphs over evil. This necessary counterfactual viewpoint provides ethics and morality with a direction that is not a given and that is interpreted over time.

This diverse temporal direction of cultural meaning making that human beings use to endure the contradictory conditions of life is not merely a retrospective construction. It already exists in the cultural tools for negotiating and overcoming the tensions described above. Through this overcoming meaning extends beyond the boundaries of our actual lives, thus expressing the importance of a time other than our own. Through historical thinking, the present reclaims this other time for itself, a time as conceived in the past.

This time context is based on the intergenerational connection between the past and the present. There has always been an intergenerational mediation between the past and the present. The cultural formations of meaning from the past are dealt with through this mediation (which has still to be elucidated). They must be dealt with in a deliberate and reflective (and of course critical) way. In this process of forming meaning, that now becomes genuinely *historic*, its pre-given possibility is realized as being temporally directed into the present.

Development as Historical Meaning   For a long time, the surplus of meaning that the human mind uses to deal with the conditions of the world was not articulated within the framework of a category of time, as presented in modern culture. But it has steadily appeared in the form of a clear notion of different time periods. Examples of this include the differentiation between 'primordial time' in the mythically envisioned creation of meaning of archaic life forms on the one hand, and inner-worldly concepts of time in daily life on the other. We only need think of all the utopian, eschatological, apocalyptic or other notions of time, whose meaning creates a sense of time stretching way beyond real time, as it is lived day-to-day.[103] The formation of historical meaning in the present can be linked to this 'other' time as a powerful tradition, for one, in the preset cultural elements of historical thinking. How we can or should address this is open-ended, organized along the lines of criteria of meaning that are critical for historical thinking about the present (e.g., along the lines of an asymmetry between our experience of the past and our expectations of the future). This '*Eigen-sinn*' (which can mean both 'stubbornness' and 'individual meaning' in German) of the present is especially important for the methodical rationality of historical thinking in academia. We must recapture this rationality in the philosophical-historical justification of historical thinking, including its reference to experience, its categorical ordering of the realm of experience. Otherwise, everything is in limbo and scholarship separates itself from the essential sources of meaning for acquiring knowledge.

Humanization as the Integration of Developments   By determining the direction of temporal movement in human ways of life, the anthropological foundation of historical thinking primarily takes on a historical form on a categorical level: directed developments emanate from changes. Anthropology therefore becomes philosophy of history.

In its material form, this philosophy of history explicates the directions of temporal changes that occur in the human world. It systematically summarizes these directions and orders them according to hierarchical aspects of their reciprocal relationships and internal entanglements. Balance, justice, polycentrism, peace, equality, care, legitimacy, happiness, a 'good' life, social equality, recognition, coherent subjectivity, self-transcendence, morality – how do we summarize these directions in the temporal changes of the human world? How do we systematically order their relationships? The relevant factor is obvious: it is always a matter of making the tensions in the conditioning of human life manageable, that is, human. *Humanity in the intergenerational temporal extension of ways of life is the principal perspective, according to which the historical realm of experience is developed (or can be developed) into a material direction through philosophy of history.*

This does not mean that, for theoretical purposes in historical thinking, our approach to the past must always be 'humanizing'. Such a normative quality of the principal perspective on the historical ordering of the past would only distort our view on 'how it really was' (of course, only with the best intentions). In order to avoid such humanizing blindness, we must differentiate our argumentation.

For a start, the past is human to the extent that it has to do with the doings and sufferings of human beings who live under non-human circumstances. Since this doing and suffering contends with (or must contend with) these conditions in a meaningful manner, it permeates our ways of life with normative definitions of humanity. The present can see them as being directed to it. In light of this normativity, we can and must speak of inhumanity when trying to understand concrete ways of life and their changes in historical terms. Such an approach would stop the traditional marginalization of suffering in historical thinking. The view of history would become more realistic than ever. The highest maxim of meaning of humanity inspires a way of viewing the experience of the past that then follows the maxim: it has to be able to be shown how it actually must have been.[104]

7. Means of Access III: The Realm of Interpretation Revealed

Formal Versus Material Philosophy of History? When the philosophy of history turns to the realm of interpretation of historical thinking, it ignores that which happened in the past. It turns instead to the viewpoints that are relevant for the historical interpretation of what happened. It becomes a *formal philosophy of history*. As an epistemology of historical thinking, it comes from a rich tradition that includes works by Rickert,[105] Dilthey,[106] Simmel,[107] Danto[108] and Ricoeur.[109] It developed as a critical turn against the so-called *material* philosophy of history and formed its own logic. This logic, however, formed a dilemma for historical thinking: the determining factors for this thinking are no longer coherently mediated with historical experience. In contrast, they are established outside of that which extends from the past into present cultural ways of life. Heinrich Rickert, for example, fully separates the sphere of values, which determines and distinguishes the historical character of work based on evidence from the past, from this evidence. Max Weber expressed this schizophrenia of epistemological philosophy of history in no uncertain terms: he quite rightly called the humanities and social sciences (*Kulturwissenschaften*) 'sciences of reality' (*Wirklichkeitswissenschaftern*), although he considered the prevailing cognitive forms of historical thinking to be pure constructions. He used the striking image of value ideas as a spotlight that lends historical meaning to history and illuminates the dark chaotic storm of happenings in the past.[110]

The following considerations attempt to circumvent the schism between subject and object in historical thinking. These considerations should highlight their inner connection without ignoring their differences. The aim is not to develop the formal philosophy of history as an alternative to content. Rather, I want to emphasize the limitation of both ways of thinking on the categorical level of historical thinking.

The Temporal Directionality of Events   The temporal directionality of events in the past is not sufficiently predetermined in the present. It is rather a surplus transcending the time of the past. References to the present from the past are derived from the present. A formal philosophy of history reflects on precisely this: it presents the perspective from which a guideline of the past for the forming of historical meaning in the present is exposed and above all transformed into historical meaning.

This inner relationship between matter and form is philosophically conceptualized as a notion of the course of time that connects the past to the present and the future, thus primarily enabling historical thinking. In other words, the formal philosophy of history gains the right to form what is created from empirical 'materiality'. The events of the past are not meaningless givens or mere facts ('refuse' – *Müll* – as Egon Flaig called it),[111] but carry the traces of formation of meaning that human beings must once have created in order to be able to live.

The notion of the course of time is inconceivable without the material philosophy of history, though this dimension alone in the philosophy of history does not suffice in truly realizing this notion. It must be compatible with evidence from the past, but does not entirely follow from the empirically given events of the past. It must provide a temporal directionality toward the present and the future to the residue, the remains of meaning of past ways of life. This notion of the course of time is therefore a *construction*. It cannot be sufficiently drawn or deduced from meaning predetermined by the past. In this respect, it extends into the dimension of the formal philosophy of history and joins both dimensions into a coherent whole.

The Principles of the Interpreting Construct   The formal philosophy of history examines the principles behind such an interpreting 'construct'. What kind of principles are these? The basic form of historical thinking is a history, a narrative. The relevant principles are therefore *principles that produce a historical meaning of the past made present through narration and allow it to manifest itself as representation in and through narration*. This happens when the events of the past are temporally strung together according to the blueprint of the notion of the course of time, and this 'temporal series' of historical processes is formed into a coherent history. The notion of the course of time must be conceived and used as structuralizing principle of narration in its categorical meaning for the (narrative) form.

Formal philosophy of history is a theory of the fundamental principles that underlie the narrative formation of meaning in the specifically historical coherence between past and present and their extension into the future. It develops the realm of interpretation of historical thinking, traditionally understood as the epistemology of this thinking, as a theory of the narrative form of historical knowledge for some time. Formal philosophy of history has become a *theory of historical narrative*.

As a result, the manner of historical meaning (or better said, creating historical meaning) – still effective today – is presented as a necessary condition for the understanding of the potentials and limitations of historical thinking. Narrative theory has become an indispensable part of metahistory. But this theory does not resolve what is at issue here in view of the categorical foundations of historical thinking. This theory does not sufficiently explain what the relevant perspectives of the (narratively presented) interpretation of the coherence of past events called 'history' look like. The mere form of historical thinking does not say anything about its content. When we consider how the given facts within the field of knowledge known as 'history' can and must be interpreted as historical, a formal philosophy of history, whether it is epistemology or narrative theory, is stuck for an answer. Narrative makes sense of time, but the form of narrative alone does not determine the relevant perspectives for doing so.

Metahistory thus demands a philosophy of history that adopts these perspectives and explicates them as categorical requirements for the gathering of knowledge in the field of history. The status of this philosophy of history must be specifically clarified. This philosophy of history assumes a narrative-theoretical understanding of historical thinking,[112] and addresses the relevant principles of historical interpretation for this (and in this) form of thinking. What is historical meaning? Metahistory answers this question by transforming the material philosophy of history into an interpretive framework that configures historical narrative. It is this narration that lends a structure of meaningfulness to what is narrated and in this sense produces the shape of meaning of a history. Formal philosophy of history as a theory of such an interpretive framework seamlessly transitions into a theory of historiography. The theory of historiography (or 'topics', topical theory[113]) explores the narrative forms of the formation of historical meaning and attempts to conceptualize the scope of these forms. Formal philosophy of history examines the relevant criteria of meaning for the narrative form of the formation of historical meaning.

Formal and Material Philosophy of History are Connected   The traditional (modern) philosophy of history has long suffered under a disastrous dialectic between objectivism and subjectivism that arose between its material and formal forms. It emerged at the end of the eighteenth or beginning of the nineteenth century as an attempt to order the accumulating knowledge about human beings and their world in a temporal perspective, or in the words of Schlözer, to progress from an 'aggregate to a system'.[114] Philosophy of history acted as an ordering system of empirical findings. In comparison, formal philosophy of history developed as an ordering system from interpretations of empirical findings. For the material philosophy of history, historical knowledge was a cognitive processing of given temporal facts. This could lead to the point of a theory of reflectance in the framework of Marxist-Leninist historical thinking. The understanding of the 'material' character of history justified the claim of objectivity in historical knowledge. This thinking was then to proceed by way of a sufficient level of facts, which mean to prove the temporal occurrences with their historical character that underlies and precedes historical knowledge.

The formal philosophy of history, on the other hand, emphasizes the cognitive functions that are applied to empirical facts (events in the past) and makes these facts historical in doing so. Decisive for the narrative character of historical knowledge (in the older, pre-narrative form) was a 'value-reference' of the perceiving subject to the objective facts of his or her external world.[115] There was no longer a given value determining the meaning of historical knowledge or its interpretation. According to this subjectivism, we could say that the phenomenon of 'history' emerges in the subjective operation of forming meaning through narrative. There is no such thing as history *an sich,* that is, as an empirical given.

This dichotomy between an 'objective' material philosophy of history and a 'subjective' formal philosophy of history is based on an epistemological premise that depends on a clear distinction between the subject and the object of knowledge. The idea of a pre-existing inner coherence is often dismissed when it comes to determining and defining true knowledge as a relationship between subject and object. Because of the dominant position of this epistemological premise, this relationship is overlooked in the philosophy of history.

Overcoming the Epistemological Subject-Object Dichotomy This dichotomy must be circumvented in order to escape this narrowing of the philosophy of history. This happens when the material philosophy of history can discern a pre-given quality to the forming of meaning in historical experience that the formal philosophy of history can take up. This is decidedly the case in the philosophy of history developed in the previous paragraph. The detailed list of human ways of life and their anthropological foundations provides perspectives for historical interpretation.

Furthermore, the human activity of cultural formation of meaning plays an essential role in the temporal movement of human living circumstances as condition for the possibility of history. This formation of meaning becomes a crucial point in historical-philosophical thinking when we try to explicate the developmental character of temporal movements in the human world. In the comprehensive conceptualization of the course of time that incorporates all developments into a unifying concept of the historical and empirical world, the 'material' temporal course of events in the past changes into a new interpretive framework. This framework is empirical, but it requires a cognitive realization that surpasses the limits of a material philosophy of history and enters into the realm of a formal philosophy of history.

This constitutive connection between the material and the formal character of historical–philosophical thinking is not something new. On the contrary, this link played a significant role in the first articulations of the philosophy of history. For Kant, for example, this link gives the philosophy of history a 'chiliastic' character, making it a determinant in the actual course of history.[116] For Humboldt, the same human spirit that constructs the historical character of the human world also determines the historical knowledge that shapes this character. He speaks of an 'original, antecedent congruity between subject and object'.[117] The course of history attains a reflexive form in historical cognition. And in this form, historical cognition becomes a determinant in the passing of time itself, as it is realized.

We can draw on this way of thinking if we want to overcome the false dichotomy between objectivity and subjectivity in historical thinking. This dichotomy does not exist in the anthropological foundations of human temporality. These foundations are the same for the interpreted past and the interpreting present. The present and the past share the prevailing intentions in cultural life to deal with the antagonisms and tensions that set this temporality in motion and continue to drive it. Of course, concrete formations of meaning may differ completely in time and place; their fundamental intention to make life 'humane' (or, in the Aristotelian sense, 'good') is essentially the same throughout time.

This commonality between past and present is ahistoric (or better: prehistoric). It systematically ignores the different forms and constant changes that determine the historical character of historical experience. In this respect, with recourse to the conditions shaping the possibility of not just every history but also all historical cognition, this commonality in itself is not enough to understand this cognition within the framework of a philosophy of history. The decisive argumentative step must be to temporalize the anthropological sameness of past and present, to span the period of time between both temporal dimensions where we find the categorical realm of historical experience made accessible by the material philosophy of history.

The Dual Arch of Time between Past and Present   In this timespan, past and present are linked in all their differences and changes in the human ways of life between then and now in two ways: (a) firstly, they are connected in the form of a temporally extended chain of conditions and circumstances (commonly referred to as a 'causal chain'). The course of time carries the potential of meaning in historical thinking along with it but remains external to this potential. There is, however, (b) an internal connection between different time periods, in which this potential of meaning is exposed and asserted. This connection concerns the transformation of cultural orientations across generations. It edges the past into the interpretive world of the present without appearing particular or distant – that is, genuinely 'historic'. This transformation of meaning through time is most apparent in the deep psychological processes that constitute human subjectivity on an intergenerational level.[118]

These meaningful courses of time are necessary conditions for human beings in the present to use the past for historical orientation and to come to intellectual terms with the temporality of their own living conditions. We must always take the objective preset elements of meaning and transcribe them for our own place and time, making them, as it were, subjective. These elements undergo a fundamental change. As causal conditions they are mute. But they are brought to life, are heard, in the discourse of historical orientation. They then acquire a completely different significance and become more than simply a condition or precondition. They come to life, are set in motion and become changeable (in principle). Historical thinking does not simply move backwards across the chain of internal and external links with the past. Of course it faces backwards and is bound by the temporal direction of chronology. But historical thinking does not pass consistently over the entire temporal chain that connects the present to the past. Rather, it picks out parts that are especially important in the context of perceived present-day problems that have turned into a need for orientation. The temporal chain is not fragmented but turned into a sequence, collected in our consciousness in the form of separate histories. (That these histories in turn have been prefigured by a philosophy of history in which a temporal whole for the human world is categorized, is another story altogether.)

Contexts of Meaning   In the objective overlapping of past and present, criteria of meaning in historical thinking are sustained in two respects.

(a) To repeat: the past and present merge together in the basic intention of the cultural interpretation of human life to endure the anthropologically given tensions and contradictions in the conditions of human life. Of course these intentions take on forms that are specific to a given time and place. Nevertheless, any later time always refers back to an earlier period in a critical manner in regarding the potential of meaning that comes, pre-given, from the past. The present is fundamentally based on this potential from the past, but must be dealt with, even mastered, through active interpretation in our own time.

For the *formal philosophy of history* this means that it provides human culture in its varying temporal and spatial forms with a time index that refers all these forms to the present, as if human beings in the past had already prepared their own interpretations for a later time period.

(b) This is, at first, nothing more than a merely formal temporal quality of past formations of meaning, meaning that is then reworked for present-day culture. This formal time is not completely without substance, as it is characterized by an underlying intention to endure the fundamental tensions and contradictions. The *material philosophy of history* describes this focus in detail. The intentions behind making life livable are of course very different for every time and place. But in their temporal connection these intentions bear universal historical meaning. History is essentially the history of humanity. As an overarching developmental process it can be interpreted as a comprehensive humanization of human beings. It must be understood as 'humane' (in the sense of a new understanding of 'humanistic').[119]

Historical thinking tapers this universally historical perspective to concrete and therefore specific circumstances of our lives in the present. As such, the formation of historical meaning of a given time follows the temporal presets that the humanizing efforts of culture have brought forth, neglected and brought forth again from the past. These presets are passed on to the future (and therefore, the present) through the transcendence of cultural meaning found in the circumstances in which human beings lived and live their lives. Without this tradition there is no history. And yet, history is much more than simply an unfolding of tradition.

Characteristics of Historical Interpretation Following the points made above, the interpretive capacity of historical thinking acquires its own cognitive character, which can be broken down in *formal characteristics of historical narrative*.[120]

(a) All historical interpretations are *retrospective*. The past becomes part of the present through narration in a way that does not cancel out its 'pastness' or make it disappear as a quality of time in the narrative. Rather, past is made present through the vividness of its presentation *as* something past. The fascination with the historical lies precisely in this presence of the past through narration. Historical narrative lends the present temporal depth.

(b) All historical interpretations are a matter of *perspective*. They do not simply reproduce, but rather offer a temporal contour to the past, delineating it from and yet referring it to the present. The narrative organization spins a temporal thread along which the happenings of the past are made present through narrative. This temporal thread follows the chronological order of the course of time, though this alone does not give it a sufficiently complete shape. It serves to uncover and emphasize a sequence out of the plethora of happenings that can be combined into a unified history. This unity develops in a dual temporal movement: (1) it proceeds from the past into the present. Only the happenings of the past that in fact lead into the present – in so far as they have produced the living conditions of the present – are made present through narration. (2) At the same time, the unity of a history or narrative is acquired through a temporal movement from present to past: only that which the present needs for its own self-conception is made present through narration. Simply put, only the things that we consider to be interesting, important or relevant in the present and for the present become part of the narrative.

Perspective and Temporal Directionality   The two temporal directions are closely connected. When interest in the past bypasses what in fact comes from the past in the context of occurrences or happenings filtering into the present, then this interest is empty and misses in this real happening the historical experience, which is needed to understand the present in its own temporality. Conversely, the basic character of the present as resulting from past happenings (its *Resultatscharakter*) must be explicated when these happenings are narrated. The narrative perspective of historiography establishes present living conditions in this conditionality of past developments. A genuinely historical perspective is a synthesis of both directions in time.

(c) All historical interpretations are *selective*, which is a necessary consequence of their perspectivist character. Only those happenings that fit within a given perspective are made present through narrative. Every narrative is also always a story not told. Every actualized occurrence obscures another. The selection of what is told and what is not depends on considerations of importance. In these considerations, the pressure of experience with which the past forces (or tempts, if you will) interpretation in the present converges with the present's interest in a sustainable future. Here we see historical thinking react to the wishes, hopes and fears that the anticipation of the future brings into the interpretation of the past.

(d) All historical interpretations are *sequential*. They always present the past as part of an overarching course of time that includes the past, present and future in a temporal whole. Historical narratives cover spans of time, from their beginning to their ending, that appear as part of an overarching course of time and can only be understood in this framework. The time of the narrated past is always more than what a historical narrative in fact relates. Before every beginning there is another history. And every ending can be a beginning of another one. In the medium of historical narrative, the unity of time can only be conceived as a multitude of narratives. Historiography is faced with the difficult task of referring to the possibility of many other untold narratives in every specific sequence in the uniqueness of every narrative. These other narratives, in turn, create the unity of the overarching course of time together with the narrative being told, connecting the past to the present and moving toward the future.

(e) Every historical interpretation is *particular*. It can only recover the experience of the past within the fundamentally limited referential framework of its historical relevance. Since human beings do not simply subject themselves to historically shaped conditions and circumstances but rather must deal with these conditions and circumstances through action and suffering, the past appears different depending on what impulses and intentions these actions and sufferings follow. It is a fundamental anthropological fact that human beings must relate to themselves and their world in their own way. From this it follows that analysing the past for the sake of historical orientation will vary among human beings. There is no one single narrative that we must tell to make sense of world. There are many.

(f) All historical interpretations are ultimately *communicative*. This does not just mean that narrative is always a communicative act between the narrator and the recipient. It means that this narrative itself is constituted communicatively in that it directly or indirectly refers to other narratives. It preserves culturally predetermined narratives, alters them, rejects them, replaces them with others and so on. Only as such can we understand them, and can they acquire meaning.

(g) Historical interpretation acquires a particular formal principle when it follows academic standards. This historiography develops an *argumentative* form. It does not just use the results of research, but specifically refers to them and explicitly takes part in the discussions in which this research unfolds. This can occur in various forms and degrees, depending on the chosen form of representation. A scholarly monograph (e.g., a dissertation) is defined by its participation in scholarly discussion, while a presentation geared towards a wider audience favours suggestion and allusion over argumentative reasoning to back factual information.

Table 4.4 The characteristics of historical interpretations.

Retrospective	The past is actualized as the past.
Perspectivist	The past acquires a temporal contour through narrative.
Selective	Narratives are told according to judgements of importance or meaning; all other happenings are omitted.
Sequential	The narrated time appears as part of an overarching course of time.
Particular	The narrated history is only one of many (possible) and therefore neither exhaustive nor final.
Communicative	Every narrative refers (implicitly or explicitly) to other narratives.
Argumentative	Scientific or academic narratives refer to research as justification for specific claims.

A Necessary Synthesis of Formal and Material Philosophy of History   The relationship between the material and formal philosophy of history is characterized by tension. Historical scholarship, with its undeniable research expertise, has adopted the claim that it objectively judges its own 'material'. Fundamental philosophical (or categorical) questions have thus been relegated to the area of speculation and their relevance for historical knowledge has been fundamentally questioned. Philosophy conformed to the historian's exclusion from the empirical world and took a formal turn as a result. Today, the formal turn dominates the reflections on the principles of historical thinking with its narrative-theoretical explication of the particularity of this thinking, neglecting its relation to reality. In its most pronounced form, the narrative theory that has taken the place of formal philosophy of history deduces the factual side of 'history' from the narrative style that describes the real happenings of the past. There is no such thing as history *an sich*, only past occurrences that acquire a specific historical character through their narrative representation.[121]

With this, the task of a material philosophy of history appears obsolete. However, the question of what actually makes past occurrences narratable – and of how it relates to experience from the past, without which historical narrative becomes meaningless – keeps the material philosophy of history on the agenda of historical theoretical thought.

With regard to the third dimension of this kind of thinking that unfolds its function for establishing practical orientation, the distinction between material and formal interpretations of history is secondary, even artificial. In the temporal orientations in which human lives occur, the past with its experienced factuality is already effectively interpreted. Here, practical reality and interpretive form are one. They form a foregoing synthesis that is all too easily overlooked in the reflexive view of historical thinking. We need to take a closer look at this synthesis. Only then will it be clear that these two distinct ways of thinking are not contradictory, but rather two sides of the same coin.

8. Means of Access IV: The Realm of Orientation Revealed

In order to really understand what history is, we need more than an analysis of content and form in historical thinking. We also need to consider its function in a systematic way. Without conceptualizing the place that historical thinking has in our lives, we cannot understand its specific cultural service. And we will be far from establishing the role that the discipline of historical scholarship plays in the cultural orientation of the present. It is an undeniable fact that scholarly historical thinking has become removed from the need for a practical orientation of its political and social context in order to expand its historical knowledge, elevate its particular assertions and make them plausible. But it is just as undeniable that the discipline is intrinsically interwoven with this need for orientation and cannot be understood without reference to its contemporaneity.

Both its distance and proximity to practical orientation in the lives of human beings define scholarly historical thinking. Its distance was always the point of criticism for those who faulted its self-sufficiency and disparaged its intellectual sterility and remoteness from practical living. The most prominent example of such criticism came from Friedrich Nietzsche and his second 'untimely consideration', '*Über den Nutzen und Nachteil der Historie für das Leben*' ('On the Use and Abuse of History for Life').[122] In the recent debates on the temporal orientation of human ways of life, the topic of 'memory' and 'remembering' dominated the discourse. Its extremely important role in culture was played out against established historical studies. Orientation was no longer the domain of historical studies; it was incompatible with the objectifying practices of methodical thinking and the associated demands of objectivity. This contrast between living memory and dead knowledge[123] cannot be maintained when we consider the functional conditionality of historical thinking in general and its scientific shape in particular.

Functional or Practical Philosophy of History: The Theory of Historical 'Bildung'
This opens up the intellectual possibility of a functional or practical philosophy of history, a pragmatic form of historical thinking. Classical philosophy of history dealt with this pragmatic concept,[124] though it never became a distinct area of study within the philosophy of history. This has led to an underexposure of the fundamental meaning behind the place of historical thinking in practical living. However, considered as a distinct part of the philosophy of history, this place acquires a special character besides the material and formal philosophy of history. This character then is a *theory of historical culture or theory of historical orientation*. In a special manner it represents a theory of historical *Bildung*.

We can identify relevant paradigms in the history of historical thinking in the work of Humboldt and Herder and in their ideas on the *Bildung* of human beings as the process of the individualization of humanity. In his concept of the 'didactic representation', Johann Gustav Droysen took up this theory of *Bildung* as the proper, even highest form of historiography and made it an essential element of specifically scholarly historical thinking.[125] In the Marxist philosophy of history, this pragmatism played an essential role: it conceived of historical thinking as an insight into the inner legitimacy of historical development, equipping the ideological actors or players in political action (the Communist Party) with the self-awareness that they were agents of real historical development.

A Categorical Imperative of Historical Thinking   Such a focus in historical thinking toward goal-directed action (mostly in the political realm) belongs to the classical concept of history as institutionalized academic discipline. This can be easily demonstrated by looking at the representatives of historicism. This pertains not only to explicitly political historians such as Gervinus, Sybel, Treitschke and others, but also to a characteristic of classical historicism that maintains a clear distance from the political demands for historical orientation. None other than Leopold von Ranke held this notion.[126] Only sporadically did he explicate the philosophical-historical premises of his historiography so they remained implicit in their nevertheless explicable systematic structure. However, in his work we find an astonishing statement that takes the issue of a practical philosophy of history and expresses it as essential guideline in his own historical thinking: '*In der Herbeiziehung der verschiedenen Nationen und der Individuen zur Idee der Menschheit und der Kultur ist der Fortschritt ein unbedingter*' ('in the attraction of varying nations and individuals to the idea of humanity and culture, progress is an unconditional').[127]

I consider this statement to be a useful example of how a theory of historical orientation or historical culture can be conceptualized. In this statement lies a principle for practical reasoning in historical thinking. From it we can extrapolate a categorical imperative of historical thinking that remains valid today. Ranke gave a historical turn to Kant's categorical imperative with his well-known statement that every epoch is immediately [linked] to God ('*jede Epoche sei unmittelbar zu Gott*').[128] We need only take up Kant's imperative that all human beings are always more than the means to an end for other human beings. They have purpose of their own and this grants each human being a fundamental and unconditional dignity.[129] It is this dignity that Ranke (and others before him – especially Herder) and historicism, as a paradigm for modern historical thinking, attribute to human beings in their historically different ways of life with the fundamental statement that the value of every epoch lies 'within its own existence'. On the basis of such 'dignity over time' in the diversity and differences found in human cultures, we can interpret Ranke's statement on unconditional progress for the idea of humanity as a categorical imperative of historical thinking. We can understand it as an expression of practical historical reasoning: think historically so that the purposefulness (or dignity) of human beings, in all their varying ways of life, can be identified and integrated into a comprehensive temporal context with all other ways of life over space and time. This context then appears as a general intellectual orientation in a particular present and its anticipation of the future.

The 'idea of humanity and culture' has both an empirical and a normative meaning. In its empirical understanding, it is the entire range of temporal movements in human ways of life. In its normative understanding, it determines this range with the regulative principle of human dignity as the leading concept in historical understanding.[130]

The Philosophy of History as Theory of 'Bildung'   In the classical theory of *Bildung* in German humanism, the historical-philosophical concept of a temporalized humanity as an idea of universal history has a fundamental and practical bearing on the upbringing and education of human beings. Every single human should be formed into a representative of humanity and all educational institutions should be structured according to this highest purpose of human subjectivity (or 'personality'). In this concept of *Bildung*, historical thinking, with its essential practical relevance, plays a decisive role.

This practical philosophy of history of humanistic *Bildung* has been criticized as being nothing more than an ideological soundtrack to middle-class emancipation. Its effectiveness in the cultural processes of a modern society that endure and develop through generational change has been disputed. However, if we consider that the temporal dynamic of modern living conditions and the capability to agree upon goals in living together must be connected in this generational change, then a philosophy of history remains practically necessary in a theory of *Bildung*. Without it, the anticipation of the future in the present ways of life cannot be attained. This anticipation of the future contains a dynamic link between past and present that material and formal philosophy of history expound in their specific manner.

But the philosophy of history does not just play its practical role in the development of the individual into an active subject in the context of the modern way of life. The field is also called upon to introduce and communicate general future perspectives to human beings, either as they act with or against each other, in all other contexts of action. In this respect, every philosophy of history is political in its functional dimension.[131]

Scholarship as Orientation?   What does this mean for the status of scholarship in the historical orientation of life in society? Historical scholarship sees itself as a field of study and not as the supplier of politically opportunistic knowledge (although it is constantly exposed to playing such a role, often succumbing to it, too). The discipline has this unique status as an agent of historical orientation because this status is tied to the condition that historians must rationally substantiate their work or claims. In order to do this, historical scholarship must translate the need for orientation of its societal context into an interest in cognition. 'Cognition' means here that the past is not made present according to a perspective of desirability. Instead, it should be represented in the form of methodically acquired and argumentatively verified knowledge in light of its relevance to the present.

The inner coherence between material and formal philosophy of history on the one hand and practical philosophy of history on the other is shaped by a structural asymmetry in the relationship between cognition and action. The determining of purpose of action cannot be adequately conceived of as a historical realization of the past, as 'grasped history'. In the real processes of human ways of life the future always transcends the past. However, the future remains underdetermined without a direction based on history.

What is the issue then in the practical functioning of historical thinking? We need to bridge the gaps between past and present, and present and future. Only then can we reveal the experience of the past through the activities of the present and establish a perspective for the future in which the purposes of human action are (or can be) determined and directed. This is an abstract formulation, but abstractions are unavoidable in the categorical determinations of historical thought. Nevertheless, these links in time created by human action must refer to real problems that can actually be described. The reality of these problems lies in the practical meaning of the course of time that is developed by historical thinking. The power of the historical experience is mediated in the dynamic of intentional action. We are made aware of the guiding purposes and intentions behind action. They become visible and tangible. Depending on the type of historical meaning that is formed, they can be traditional certainties, rules governing action based on experience, intentions of change and even a distancing from the demands of historical experience.

Historical Thinking and the Question of Identity   This direction of time in the lives of human beings that develops through historical thinking is only effective when it is *anchored in the depths of human subjectivity*. This concerns the inner temporality of human beings as individuals and as members of a community. We must mediate what we used to be with what we want to be in such a way that the gap between past and future is bridged in the self-perception and self-interpretation of the subject. We usually call this 'bridge' identity.[132] This concept is highly controversial, and yet it pertains to a fundamental fact in the lives of human beings. Perhaps it is better to speak not of the fact of our lives but rather of the 'act' of our lives, since it refers to the mental processes that must be set in motion in order to answer the question of who we are (again, both as individuals and as members of a community). This question is inevitably posed in light of the constant and constantly new experiences of contingency that human beings face internally and externally. It is hardly self-evident that I always remain myself or we always remain ourselves through the course of time within the reality of human life. Rather, our lives are much more a constant form of work done by the human mind within the cultural circumstances and internal conditions of life.

The question of identity is a fundamental fact of human culture. It demands a response. Historical thinking is an essential medium for that response. The question of inner coherence and the individual and the inclusion and exclusion of others is of course dealt with in different ways at different times. Presently, the question urgently arises on a categorical level in historical thinking as a question of humanity in inhumane times and as a hope for humanity. Identity is a question of humanity, because it is a fundamental benchmark for the concept of inclusion and exclusion in the modern living conditions of a globalized world. I share my humanity with all other human beings, yet I am different from all other human beings at the same time. In a broader sense, the necessary self-assessment of people and the inclusion and exclusion of social groups develop within the tension between commonality and difference.

For a long time, the historical experience was used to boost self-assessment and inclusion with positive values that were taken from the past and used to determine action. The otherness of the other was perceived as a lack of these values. The quality of their humanity appeared lesser or even as an opposite. This ethnocentrism is a critically important and highly influential determinant of historical consciousness.[133] It is a determining factor in the 'great narratives' of the past that inform human beings of their cultural identity.

The End of the Great Narratives? In the time of globalization, traditional ethnocentrically structured historical presentations of identity have become problematic. Because of this, in the intellectual exuberance of self-criticism regarding the attribution of the paradigm of humanity to our own (Western) culture, there has been a call for the end of the great narratives.[134] There is good reason for this: there is a predominant problematic asymmetry that (can) generate an inhumane response in the normative quality of how we define ourselves and the strangeness of others, in which the normative concept of humanity plays a significant part.

Abandoning the great narratives of the past does not solve this problem, as there is no human subjectivity without a coherence in self-reference and the social realm of our lives. This coherence must be articulated, in its temporal dimension, through narrative. Within the logic of historical thinking we can react to the question of identity by examining the experience of inhumanity among human beings, by understanding the world of the present shaped by the traumatic experience of inhumaneness. Eelco Runia found an impressive way to formulate the question of identity: *Who are we that this could have happened?*[135] Depending on our involvement in this historical experience – whether as perpetrator, victim, profiteer, observer, helper, contemporary or opponent – this question of identity leads to a variety of

responses. And these responses are not isolated. They are always interconnected with the communicative context of humankind at a given time as
a factor of the first order in cultural orientation. We need to discuss and
answer these responses with those people who have been placed outside of
us in our historical self-allocation.

On the logical level of a practical philosophy of history, the question of
identity is irrefutable. Just as irrefutable is the effectiveness of the responses to
this question that assert an asymmetrical relationship between the self and the
other. Also irrefutable is the ensuing problem that comes with such responses
and the necessity to overcome this asymmetry. This is possible when we
consider a response on a humanistic level: every human being has inherent value by being human, and each shares this value with all other human
beings. Within this commonality there is a place for the cultural diversity and
differences that shape the mental processes forming our identity as a necessity of our lives. In order to live, everyone must come to terms with being
other in his or her own otherness as individual self and as social being. We
must come to terms with others in such a way that common survival is possible. This is in fact the 'chiliasm' of the philosophy of history in its practical
cosmopolitan form that Immanuel Kant spoke of.

9. Interpretation in Context: Historical Theories

Historical categories open up the domains of historical consciousness and
the area of historical thinking. The content of this area remains undefined.
Its phenomena are only recognized as historical material, though not yet
fully grasped in a concrete manner. (This is the reason why categorical
considerations do not appear in the cognitive work of professional historians very often.) In order to approach the concrete manifestations of the
past (in their categorically developed historicity), it is necessary to take an
intellectual step that brings the historical experience closer to us. This step
is one from categorical considerations to theoretical concepts in historical
interpretation.

The transition from fundamental and general considerations on what
we call 'history' to the work on concrete historical phenomena is gradual.
We can, however, distinguish the logical dimensions or levels of cognitive
analysis in the historical realm of experience. *Categories* open up the area of
experience as a whole, while *theories* organize the area from within. *Concepts*,
finally, make it possible to identify the particularities in this organization. All
three ways of thinking are closely related but are nevertheless distinguishable
through logical abstraction.

Can Historical Thinking be Theoretical? Can historical knowledge produce theory? This question has been debated from the time of antiquity up until the present day. Aristotle claimed that poetry is 'more philosophic and of graver import than historical writing, since poetry speaks more of the universal, whereas history more of the particular. The universal is to present the things and the quality of things that people say or do according to a certain appropriateness or necessity; the endeavours of poetry are to give these things their proper names. The particular is to report [for example] on what Alcibiades did or experienced.'[136]

The epistemological analysis of historical thinking has adopted and confirmed this distinction, denying historical knowledge a theoretical status. The narrative turn in historical theory recognized the particularity of historical thinking as following a completely different logic (that of forming meaning through narrative) to that of theoretically sound academic fields. The cognitive aim of these fields is to uncover law principles in the context of observable phenomena (with the practical consequence of their technical controllability). As tempting as it was for historical studies to adapt to this type of cognition, it did not work out due to the particular form of historical phenomena and of historical thinking.

The narrative structure of historical knowledge strongly suggests that this knowledge is not as theoretical as research that aims for regularity (and therefore predictability and technical applicability) or measurability. But does this mean that historical thinking is fundamentally incapable of producing theory? Must historical studies abandon a basic characteristic of scholarship? Only if by 'theory' we mean the type of thinking that belongs to scientific laws or principles. But what do we achieve with such a fixed definition? It illuminates the differences between the logical forms of academic disciplines. But at the same time such a definition of theory obscures the idea that academic historical thinking also works with generalizations and does not simply realize the temporal sequences of concrete and separate events through narrative.

No one can deny that such generalizations exist within historical thinking or that historical studies cannot do without them. This is clear through the example of periodization.

a) The Concept of Periodization

Dividing time into different periods is a necessary step in ordering the realm of experience in history in general. Periodization gives historical experience temporal contours and makes the happenings of the past specifically historic on a general intellectual level in the first place. As emphasized above, events of the past are not in themselves historic, but become historic when they become part of a temporal context in which present and past are distinguished from one another and their difference mediated at the same time. Periodization provides the conceptualization of a course of time that is relevant for historical thinking with the contours in which the happenings of the past gain their specific meaning for the sake of understanding the present.

Periodization gives historical depth to present-day living conditions and therefore also a far-reaching perspective for the future. It cannot simply be deduced from past occurrences. Rather, it emerges from meanings that are assigned to these occurrences and that appear in an overarching and temporal context that related to the present. Periodization emphasizes the fact that the organization of life in the present is an outcome of the past. Without this reference to the past an experience-based anticipation of the future is not possible.

This is not the place to deal with the problem of periodization in historical thinking in detail. The point is simply that and how generalizations with a specific historical character are possible and even necessary in order to carry out the business of history. This is clear through two examples: a periodization of the history of humanity and a periodization of the media involved in forming cultural meaning.

Two Examples: Humanity and the Formation of Cultural Meaning   Being human is an important source and reference for the formation of cultural meaning in all ways of life and at all times. Contrary to natural and transcendental dimensions of the world, the particular character of being human is anthropologically universal.[137] Therefore, there is a perspective for a universal history of humanity that presents the commonalities and differences in cultures.[138] This universal history can be periodized according to the perspective of who is considered human (and in what way) and who is not. A first epoch in the cultural development of human beings can be characterized by the instance that the quality of being human is preferred, even if only for the members of one's own group. Humanity becomes particular and exclusive. A second epoch follows, in which this quality is universalized for all members of the biological species in principle, admittedly with a clear distinction between one's own humanity and the other's humanity, which is usually seen as a lesser version. Humanity becomes universal and exclusive. Following Karl Jaspers, this epoch can be characterized as '*Achsenzeit*' (the Axial Age).[139] The third epoch, which includes the present one, is characterized by overcoming this asymmetry and making humanity the benchmark for intercultural communication guided by the principle of critical recognition. Humanity becomes universal and inclusive. In the framework of such a periodization, we could see this time period as a second Axial Age.

A universal historical periodization in view of the development of the medium for cultural communication is clear: the Belgian historian Albert

D'Haenens coined the catchphrase '*Oralité, Scribalité, Electronalité*' to describe it.[140] This periodization is in fact universal. It can be applied to all phenomena in the human world, since everything that concerns the actions and sufferings of human beings occurs through interaction and communication with others, with the impact of such communication determined by the media involved. In my opinion, this periodization is convincing because it can be derived from everyday experiences. We could teach this universal historical way of thinking paradigmatically to children in history education. With this example it is clear that the succession of one epoch into another does not mean they change from one into the other. Rather, it is a transition in which the older period does not simply disappear but continues to exist under the dominance of the younger one. In this respect, contrasts between time periods such as the modern and pre-modern are not completely false but confusing, as they obscure the continuing presence of the older period into the new (of course in an altered form). Different time periods do not dissolve over time but rather overlap and therefore (tend to) occur at the same time.

Such periodizations characterize large stretches of time in the past. If we explore these further in order to tackle further differences and specifications, *theory* is the appropriate cognitive means to do so. Theories emphasize structures and developments, making the specifics of the past recognizable.

b) What are Historical Theories?

Jürgen Kocka gave a convincing answer to this question: historical theories are 'an explicit and consistent set of related concepts, which can be used to structure and explain historical data but which cannot be developed from the study of the source materials alone'.[141] He emphasizes their constructive character but also indirectly their reference to evidence through which the past (as described earlier) asserts itself as a factor of meaning in the subsequent interpretation of its historical context within the present. In terms of narrative theory, historical theories are *plots* (that is, structures that produce meaning) in historical narratives. They are to narrative details what a theory is to empirical facts. On the one hand, this means that historical theories have their basis in the narrative process. On the other hand, not all narrative is as 'theoretical' as academic or scientific study. Real theories only become *plots* when they are conceptually explicated as such and maintain a level of methodical feasibility. As such, the narrative gains a cognitive-constructive element. It presents something particular and belongs to the features of specifically scholarly historical thinking.

There are many examples of this.[142] From the era of classical historicism, Ranke's essay on 'The Great Powers' ('*Die großen Mächte*') should be mentioned. It is an essay in which he presents his interpretive concept for the formation of the modern state.[143] Ranke himself did not shy away from speaking of 'laws' without addressing the form of theory in the natural sciences as a paradigm for historical studies. Similar concepts of theory that also use the conceptualization of scientific principles are found in the work of Ranke's challenger, Gottfried Gervinus. Other (more recent) examples present the theory of medieval agricultural cycles. In modern history, we can mention the theory of modernization in its specific forms, as well as its generalization, and tapering into a theory of globalization. The history of historiography can also be empirically substantiated with theoretical concepts.[144]

Particularly instructive examples to help understand the specific form of historical theory can easily be found in the work of Max Weber. For example, his concept of 'three types of legitimate domination', which has universally historical implications, can be applied to interpret and understand very different kinds of power relations or structures.[145] A more recent example is Hans-Ulrich Wehler's *Deutsche Gesellschaftsgeschichte* (*Societal History of Germany*). In the introduction to this imposing work, Wehler explains his general interpretive concept and thus demonstrates his theory.[146]

The Theoretical Problem of Historical Comparison   Historical comparisons present a unique theoretical problem. What parameter do we use for comparisons? It would be a case of methodological ethnocentrism to take up one case and measure it against another. In fact, we need a parameter that can be set for both cases together in order to illuminate their differences as specific manifestations of a general phenomenon. The need for such a comprehensive parameter is especially evident for intercultural comparisons. For a long time, Western development was taken as the standard measure and the weight of non-Western developments only considered conditionally or in a fractured way against the Western example.

Finding a proper parameter for comparison that applies equally to the compared cases is a theoretical problem of the first order. It is therefore necessary to develop conceptual interpretive frameworks that are not culture-specific. Intercultural comparisons on a large scale require a theoretically informed explication of anthropological universals. Specific comparisons demand complex theoretical constructs that isolate and display the separate components of the historical information on the level of anthropologically substantiated commonalities and make their particular elements understandable as specific constellations. Weber's typology of legitimate authority, which includes basically all forms of legitimation of domination, is capable of demonstrating this type of construct. All three types occur in completely different manifestations, severity and constellations in all forms of human authority over other human beings. The historically specific form can be identified in its manifestation, degree of emphasis and particular constellation.[147]

We can compare cases synchronically or diachronically. Diachronic comparisons require a standard measure through general theoretically conceived (and methodically applicable) developmental processes. This means that specific developments should not be used to determine the standard measure, making it then difficult to construct such a measure. But we can resolve these issues when we develop a general dynamic of development of historical processes from anthropological universals and make it the starting point for the construction of such a standard measure.

10. Comprehending the Matter: Historical Concepts

Categories and theories demand a terminology of clearly defined concepts. Even the empirical identification of categorically developed and theoretically interpreted facts in methodical research is impossible without concepts. But what are *historical concepts*? These concepts must not disregard the particularity of events in the past but they put these events into view. How can they do this when concepts must identify information across all temporal differences without being able to express the specifics of a given time?

Concepts are terms used to designate facts and circumstances and differentiate them from other facts and circumstances. *Historical* concepts must provide information from the past (events and combinations of events) with a temporal qualification that reveals this information to be much more than mere happenings or occurrences. This means that we fit this information into historical theories and thereby express it within a specific historical temporality.

It is clear that the concepts we use to address phenomena of present living conditions cannot acquire this temporal qualification. It is just as clear that the terms used by people in the past to describe the phenomena of their own time cannot either. Historic concepts lie somewhere in between these two poles. They link the two poles in time, which creates a conceptual link between the information from a specific past and earlier or later time periods. These are narrative constructions.

The constructionist character of historical concepts is commonly described as 'ideal type'. The construction, or the result of a cognitive operation of the interpreters, is 'typical'. The 'ideal' refers to the unique focus of the specific historical character of that which is conceptually determined. It is not easy to describe this specific character of phenomena precisely. Any description must include the empirical reference to phenomena from the past as well as the interpretive meaning of the past for the present. Nowadays it is assumed that the present grants the past meaning. This view overlooks the starting points for this interpretation that stretch from the past into the present. The language of meaning from the past is silenced, or rather; it is drowned out by the language of meaning from the present. But the 'ideal' with which the present relates the past to itself and the inner referencing of meaning formed in the past to the present are both relevant. Only when they are combined can we speak, as described above, of 'history' as a development or directed time in the dynamic of human living conditions.

Ideal Types   In this respect, Weber's definition for historical concepts as ideal types must be re-interpreted. According to Weber, the ideal type becomes a historical concept 'by the one-sided accentuation of one or more points of view and by the synthesis of a great many diffuse, discrete, more or less present and occasionally absent concrete individual phenomena, which are arranged according to those one-sidedly emphasized viewpoints into a unified analytical construct (*Gedankenbild*). In its conceptual purity, this mental construct (*Gedankenbild*) cannot be found empirically anywhere in reality. It is a utopia. Historical research faces the task of determining in each individual case, the extent to which this ideal-construct approximates to or diverges from reality.'[148]

In this view, the entire decisive cognitive process of understanding the past takes place within the present. The past is to conform or comply, as if it has no influence on its meaning for the present. On the other hand, this meaning cannot simply be deduced from the empirical evidence from the past, nor can it be determined without the language of meaning of culturally defined ways of life from the past. Using the language of Weber, we can say that the 'utopian' character of past historical meanings is truly historic when we (retrospectively) bring the 'utopian' elements of past meanings, with which with the ways of life from that past rose above the here and now of concrete circumstances and conditions, into an inner temporal relationship with the interpretive operations of the present. Weber pits the reality of past events against the 'ideal' (constructionist) character of their present-day meaning, contrasts them and thereby manoeuvres himself into an epistemological dead end. He can no longer make the historical meaning of the past itself empirically plausible. (Here an epistemological subject-object divide that ignores the limitations of historical construction and narrative constructedness rears its ugly head.)

It is important to remember that ideal types are narrative concepts that must follow the logic of the narrative relationship between past and present. (Max Weber called ideal types 'genetic' and was thus on the trail of their narrative character. However, the Neo-Kantian epistemology that separated meaning from fact before their inner connection could be seen blocked his way.)

The term 'construction' should not be misunderstood as constructivist, as this construction removes the self-designations of the past, or the elements of the so-called 'language of the sources'. It is obvious that the 'language of the sources' is not enough to present the historical meaning of its content. We cannot conceive of this meaning without recourse to the later periods that the sources could not have known about.

The Role of Historical Semantics   The history of concepts, or more generally, *historical semantics*, is essential to the formation of a reconstructive conceptual language for historical knowledge. The content of meaning of historical concepts must include their own history. Indeed, the history of concepts needs concepts, too, and this leads to the unavoidable question of their historicity. We cannot answer this question with a conceptual history of the history of concepts, as that would lead to a never-ending reflexive chain reaction that would mean less and less and lead to semantic meaninglessness. We can avoid this when we acquire the concepts for conceptual history from the key concepts used to interpret the world in the present with the knowledge that past developments are embedded in their semantics. In a methodical reconstruction we explicate these developments as a part of their meaning. The present becomes the starting point, and the past develops out of the present as a development then moving again toward the present.

Functions of Historical Concepts   Historical concepts are narrative constructs that we develop and use for the sake of methodical rationality in the pursuit of historical cognition. Their function is primarily cognitive. However, historical cognition is presented in historiography, that is, in presentations in which non-cognitive and pre-cognitive factors are essential for the formation of meaning. Historiography mediates historical cognition, but in order to do so it transcends the cognitive dimension of historical knowledge and moves into the aesthetic and rhetorical aspects of historical representation. Then what happens to the concepts? Of course they do not disappear, but they become elements of a narrative style that merges the interpretation of the past with the vividness of its representation. This coming to life is expressed through language, giving concepts a meaning that expands beyond the limits of cognition.

We could speak of a 'return' to the language of history in the dynamic of narrative before its conceptual specification as found in the historical culture of any given time. The conceptual constructions of historical cognition occur under the pretexts of constructedness: they are dependent on the preset elements of meaning. These preset elements are constructively rationalized in the cognitive process with its methodical operations. Historical writing asserts these narrative, non-cognitive elements (aesthetic, imaginative, rhetoric) that operate in the preset elements of meaning. In fact, they constantly permeate the cognitive process but they do not explicitly influence this process. They manifest themselves in writing, in the presentation. Only then is the cognitive process complete.

What did we gain from the efforts of cognitive construction? In the cognitive process, the procedural, non-cognitive elements of historical meaning are not simply reproduced but rather crystallized through the process of methodical research. Historical meaning gains descriptive rationality. We could speak of a benefit of orientation acquired through the growth of argumentative intersubjectivity.

This can be shown in specific instances when historical thinking is related to and distinguished from the processes of remembering and the structures of memory.[149] By thinking we do not just formalize remembering, but we also modify it and criticize it, too, through critical analysis. We could only call this a loss of meaning if we believe it is necessary to abandon reason in order to glorify the past for the effects produced on the culture of the present.

The Conceptual Framework of Historical Knowledge   The language of historical knowledge is not conceivable without the element of conceptualization. It provides historiography with semantic precision and explanatory power. This conceptualization appears in varying forms and functions, which have

Table 4.5 Historical conceptuality.

Cognitive Form	Operation	Examples
Categories	Describe anthropological fundamentals, 'culture' in temporal movement, realms of historical experience	'Anthropological time-generators';[150] 'cultural history' in its entirety; economic tension between rich and poor (in analogy to other realms of experience and tension)[151]
Types	Delineate specific areas of experience in the realms of experience and place them in a temporal order	Periodization; (in the economic realm): subsistence economy, market economy, planned economy, capitalism, mercantilism
Concepts	Describe large constellations of events	Defined epochs; (in the economic realm): modern European capitalism, medieval agricultural cycles
Names	Describe concrete happenings	The French Revolution; (in the economic realm): the 'take-off' of modern capitalism in Germany

only been covered schematically in this chapter. This schematic presentation only allows for a distinction between two levels of using concepts: categories as basic concepts and concepts as descriptions of individual historical facts. Theories (as discussed earlier) are constellations of concepts and develop their own higher (more abstract) conceptuality. This differentiation between categories and concepts of a simpler and higher order is much too simplified to analyse the conceptual framework of historical knowledge. We need to add two further kinds of concepts: types and names. Together they form the following schema of historical conceptuality:

The boundaries between these distinctions are fluid.

In this schema, the ascription of meaning by concepts – and the normativity that always influences historical conceptuality – is not defined separately. This ascription is incorporated into all four forms.

The schema can only suggest that there is a (more or less highly) differentiated historical conceptuality. At the same time, it is obvious how insufficient this schematic representation is and what kind of work must be done to approach conceptually theoretical and methodologically correct historical representations, true to the language of science, that make their cognitive substance sufficiently clear. It is obvious that there is such a substance. We can only underestimate this substance if we cannot or will not recognize the traces of the cognitive achievements that historical scholarship is capable of in the language of historiography.

11. What is Historical Explanation?

a) The Rationality of Explanation

The formation of theories and concepts gives historical thinking a rational character. This character gives historical thinking an explanatory power that it does not have without such cognitive constructions. But what does it mean to explain something historically?[152] This question turns the rationality potential and the claim of scientificity of historical thinking into the object of an extensive debate within the analytic philosophy of history.

This debate was based on a notion of scientific rationality that came from the paradigm of those natural sciences that aimed to find knowledge that follows a general and possibly mathematical law or principle. To explain meant to relate observable processes to general principles, such as explaining the breaking of a thread by specifying its tear strength. The charm of such an explanatory model lies in the fact that its logic enables predictions. An explanation strengthened by laws or principles is therefore readily labelled 'rational'. This label differentiates it from all other forms of thinking that deal with why-questions.

This model of explanation can be applied to historical thinking. It does not contradict historical thinking. But it is not suitable to expose the particularity of historical thinking that distinguishes it from knowledge based on principles or laws. The vigorous discussion about this topic took place among philosophers rather than practising historians. For the historian, it is a 'glass bead game' with no end that does little to elucidate the logic of historical thinking. An attempt was made to identify this particularity with other models of explanation. This finally led to a fundamental notion for the formal philosophy of history that telling a story has an explanatory character in itself. With the introduction of the narrative argument in historical theory the debate on explanation in history came to an end. At the same time, the question of rationality in historical thinking faded away. This is unfortunate, as this narrative turn has not resolved the problem of rationality but suppressed it.

We need to consider this question of explanation and rationality in historical thinking – and of its scientific legitimacy – without abandoning the notion of a narrative structure of historical explanation. A clear distinction between varying types of explanation and their relationship to one another would be useful at this point.

b) Three Types of Explanation

Depending on the why-question and what it refers to, the answers could vary in terms of structure. We can distinguish three types of explanations as answers to why-questions. (I do not claim that there are no other forms, but these are the three types that played a prominent role in the debate on explanations in analytic philosophy and theory of science.) These types can help do some justice to the complexity of explanations in historical thinking. This complexity lies in the fact that all three types occur in the work of historians and that the particularity of a specific historical explanation can most likely be found delimitating it from the other two types.[153]

Nomological Explanation   The first type is a nomological explanation. A general principle is essential for this type of explanation. It explicates the – often causal – connection between two temporally different processes or facts ('cause' and 'effect') in a highly generalized (in the classical case of the natural sciences, mathematical) form. Historical thinking does not use these principles to explain historical developments, as such developments must prove to be specific instances of a general principle for this to work. However, then the particularity that defines the specifically historical character of the temporal process in question would be lost.

This does not mean that historical thinking abandons nomological knowledge. On the contrary, it makes use of this knowledge, even develops theories that emphasize uniformities, whether in general or in specific temporal contexts (e.g., agricultural cycles and conjunctures in economic history). But these uniformities are not what historical developmental processes are about. Theories of revolution, for example, could draw attention to the similarities between processes in different revolutions in different time periods and help to explain these processes. But such explanations ignore what makes these revolutions in themselves belong to a specific time. And it is exactly this specific quality that historical thinking must highlight in order to argue the meaning of such processes for the present. This also helps to answer the fundamental question of identity, found enmeshed in this meaning, as a why-question: why are we the way we are in our specific way of life? The historical dimension of human culture is not concerned with the human way of life as such, but with how this way of life evolves in different ways and changes in temporal developmental processes. Therefore, such general theories are fundamentally unable to predict or control historical processes (as the technical grip on nomologically explained nature is able to do).

Intentional Explanation   A second type of explanation is completely based on the specific human way of life in which intentions determined by meaning determine human action. This is *intentional explanation*. The question of why human beings do certain things and not other things can be answered by examining the intentions behind doing and not doing. We can call such an explanation *Verstehen* (understanding).

It is immediately clear how relevant this type of explanation is for historical thinking. Historical thinking primarily concerns what human beings have done and what their actions have caused, changed or destroyed. We can work with theory-forming knowledge (about the motivational structure of human action) within this explanatory framework. However, it is questionable whether this does justice to the particular temporal structure of historical processes (developments). Entire historiographical works that deal with actions that are in dire need of explanation demonstrably cling to this type of explanation in their way of forming meaning.[154] Still, this type of explanation is not paradigmatic but fallacious for the historical explanation of significant events and processes of the past. Can we, for example, explain a significant process like industrialization in terms of intentions? Who would be the acting subject and what would be the identifiable intention? And finally, does the specific historical character of temporal change in the human world not lie in the fact that change is not always the outcome of deliberate actions and thus cannot be understood within a framework of purposefully defined action?

Narrative Explanation   Finally, the third type that provides insight into what it means to pose a decidedly historical question and to offer a decidedly historical answer. This type is – what else? – the *narrative explanation*. This explains temporal changes through a narrative of the changing process. The logic of this explanation is completely different from the logic of the other two types. It also determines the role and use of the other types of explanation in historical thinking. Nomological and intentional explanations are reliable and necessary when they can be used in a narrative, but they do not determine the logic of it.

The narrativity of historical explanation does not make the rationality of a scientific argument irrelevant. Instead, this rationality develops a specific or special form by narrativity.

c) Is Narrative Explanation Rational?

The starting point of historical thinking is the experience of a difference in time that generates a specific historical question: Why does everything change so much? And then, closely related to this: Why are we the way we are, and why are we so different from what we used to be? As mentioned earlier, historical thinking aims to bridge a challenging temporal divide with an evidence-based concept of the course of time in such a way that the present living conditions in the flow of time between past and future can be understood and human life can be lived in a meaningful way in this passing of time. Historical thinking provides coherence, powerful for orientation, in the temporal differences of the human way of life. When this coherence is achieved through the constructive formation of theory and concepts we can speak of explanatory historical rationality. In such rationality the other types of explanation have exhausted their potential for rationality. More importantly, narration has its own rationality that pertains to its discursive character and high level of complexity through the synthesis of differing forms of communication. It deals with categorical, typological, theoretical and conceptual forms of thinking that occur in the narration of history. Their validity claims are discursively determined. But the rationality of historical thinking is not just limited to this. In other dimensions in the forming of meaning there are discursive practices in which claims of plausibility are raised and determined according to specific criteria for meaning. Indeed, the methodical processes of historical thinking are at the core of scientific rationality. These processes enable categories, typologies, theories and concepts to develop their meaning and their explanatory power.

Table 4.6 Schema for the three types of rational explanation.

Type of Explanation	Explained Through
Nomological	Principles or laws
Intentional	Intentions
Narrative	Narrated course of time

Notes

74. See, e.g., E. Angehrn. 1991. *Geschichtsphilosophie*, Stuttgart: Kohlhammer; H. Nagl-Docekal (ed.). 1996. *Der Sinn des Historischen*, Frankfurt am Main: Fischer Taschenbuch Verlag; J. Rohbeck. 2000. *Technik, Kultur, Geschichte*, Frankfurt am Main: Suhrkamp; J. Rohbeck and H. Nagl-Docekal (eds). 2003. *Geschichtsphilosophie und Kulturkritik*, Darmstadt: Wissenschaftliche Buchgesellschaft; J. Große. 2008. 'Geschichtsphilosophie heute', part I: 123–155; part II: 209–236.

75. In the following I refer to a text that I co-authored with Karl-Joachim Hölkeskamp as an introduction to the volume: *Sinn (in) der Antike*, 1–15, 'Einleitung: Warum es sich lohnt, mit der Sinnfrage die Antike zu interpretieren' ('Introduction: The Question of Meaning in Interpreting Antiquity').

76. This definition was chosen by the study group 'Sinnkonzepte als lebens- und handlungsleitende Orientierungssysteme' ('Concepts of Meaning as Systems of Orientation for Living and Action'). The group was directed by Klaus E. Müller and myself from 1997 to 2002 at the Institute for Advanced Study in the Humanities in Essen.

77. J. Assmann. 1995. *Politische Theologie zwischen Ägypten und Israel*, 2nd ed., Munich: Hanser, 106 f.

78. Above all Reinhart Koselleck: R. Koselleck. 1979. *Vergangene Zukunft*, Frankfurt am Main: Suhrkamp. (*Futures Past*, Cambridge, MA: MIT Press, 1985.)

79. It is less Koselleck's 'veto right of the sources' that has greatly influenced professional historians, and more the authority of the sources that makes plausible present-day actions and interpretations of the world. Such authority does not invalidate the veto right, but rather grants it an interventional role in the area of historical interpretation (Koselleck, *Vergangene Zukunft*, 106 – see explanatory note 45, this volume).

80. For more detail, see also this volume, 206sq.

81. J.G. Herder. 2002. *Ideen zur Philosophie der Geschichte der Menschheit*, edited by W. Pross, Darmstadt: Wissenschaftliche Buchgesellschaft, part I, book 2, 49 ff. For more on the topic area of synthesis of nature and culture at that time, see P.H. Reill. 2005. *Vitalising Nature in the Enlightenment*, Berkeley: University of California Press.

82. I. Kant. 1968. 'Idee zu einer allgemeinen Geschichte in weltbürgerlicher Absicht' ('Idea for a Universal History from a Cosmopolitan Perspective'), in W. Weischedel (ed.), *Werke in zehn Bänden*, vol. 9, Darmstadt: Wissenschaftliche Buchgesellschaft, A 387.

83. For an excellent example of this, see D. Christian. 2004. *Maps of Time*, Berkeley: University of California Press.

84. The same considerations occur in the natural sciences. For a useful summary, see e.g., C. Kueffer. 2013. *Ökologische Neuartigkeit*, in ZiF-Mitteilungen, 21–30.

85. G. Dux. 2000. *Historisch-genetische Theorie der Kultur*, Weilerswist: Velbrück Wissenschaft (*Historico-genetic Theory of Culture*, Bielefeld: Transcript, 2011); W. Welsch. 2011. *Immer nur der Mensch?*, Berlin: Akademie.

86. See also G. Dux. 1997. 'Wie der Sinn in die Welt kam, und was aus ihm wurde', in K.E. Müller and J. Rüsen (eds), *Historische Sinnbildung: Problemstellungen, Zeitkonzepte, Wahrnehmungshorizonte, Darstellungsstrategien*. Reinbek bei Hamburg: Rowohlt Taschenbuch Verlag, 195–217.

87. For more detail, see also J. Rüsen. 2008. 'Der Teil des Ganzen – über historische Kategorien', in idem, *Historische Orientierung*, 2nd ed., Schwalbach/Taunus: Wochenschau, 168–187.

88. H.M. Baumgartner. 1972. *Kontinuität und Geschichte*, Frankfurt am Main: Suhrkamp.

89. See J. Kocka. 1984. 'Zurück zur Erzählung? Plädoyer für historische Argumentation', *Geschichte und Gesellschaft* 10, 395–408; also idem. 1989. *Geschichte und Aufklärung*, Göttingen:

Vandenhoeck & Ruprecht, 8–20; idem. 1986. 'Theory Orientation and the New Quest for Narrative' in *Storia della Storiographia* 10.

90. See also this volume, 203sqq.

91. For more on the subject of memory, see this volume, 170sqq.

92. An older version of this schema appears in Rüsen, *Historische Orientierung*, 187.

93. J. Burckhardt. 1982. *Über das Studium der Geschichte*, edited by Peter Ganz. Munich: C.H. Beck, 226.

94. Koselleck, 'Historik und Hermeneutik', 9–28; also in R. Koselleck. 2000. *Zeitschichten*, Frankfurt am Main: Suhrkamp, 97–118. In Koselleck we also find the category of '*Generativität*' (generativity) as analytical concept in deciphering between man and woman, young and old. Koselleck presented the dichotomies as necessary conditions for the possibility of history, or histories. He did not extrapolate a systematic theory from them. He did not take it a step further. What is critical on an anthropological level for historical thinking is inner temporality, which he only explored in terms of generational relationships. In terms of a transcendental historical theory, his approach did not address a concept of directed time. Without such directionality there would be no narrative form of historical knowledge. There would be nothing to tell.

95. Kant, *Idee zu einer allgemeinen Geschichte in weltbürgerlicher Absicht*, Satz 4, A 392.

96. The 'Universality of the Experience of Suffering' is addressed by J. Müller. 2002. 'Ethische Grundsatzprobleme in der Entwicklungspolitik', in F. Bliss, M. Schönhuth and P. Zucker (eds), *Welche Ethik braucht Entwicklungszusammenarbeit?* Bonn: Politischer Arbeitskreis (PAS); see also idem. 1997. *Entwicklungspolitik als globale Herausforderung*, Stuttgart: Kohlhammer (recommended by Christoph Antweiler).

97. With this I am referring to earlier thinking in the philosophy of history. Kant presented an anthropological basis for this temporal dynamic in historical occurrences: as the '*ungesellige Geselligkeit*' (unsocial sociability) in the lifeways of human beings (*Idee zu einer allgemeinen Geschichte in weltbürgerlicher Absicht*, A 392). Herder also touched upon this in anthropological terms: J.G. Herder. 1883. 'Briefe zur Beförderung der Humanität', no. 122, Abschnitt 5, in idem, *Briefe zur Beförderung der Humanität*, edited by B. Suphan, *Herders sämtliche Werke*, Berlin: Weidmann.

98. Goethe, *Faust* V 3250. If this sounds a little too poetic, then we can turn to the historical anthropology of Karl Marx in his chapter on Feuerbach in '*deutsche Ideologie*' ('German Ideology'). Here Marx points out that the satisfying of desires [after material needs for survival (Rüsen)] leads to new needs; and this production of new needs is the first historical act: 'die Aktion der Befriedigung und das schon erworbene Instrument der Befriedigung zu neuen Bedürfnissen führt – und diese Erzeugung neuer Bedürfnisse ist die erste geschichtliche Tat'. K. Marx. and F. Engels. 1966. 'Feuerbach (Kritische Ausgabe)', in *Deutsche Zeitschrift für Philosophie* 14, 1199–1254, quote, 1211. (*The German Ideology*, part I: Feuerbach, available online at: https://www.marxists.org/archive/marx/works/download/Marx_The_German_Id eology.pdf.)

99. Therefore, the anthropological universal (or the 'existential' as building on Heidegger's existential ontology) of 'historicity' is not yet historical. What is missing is the directionality of time.

100. For an overview, see also: J. Rüsen, M. Fehr and T.W. Rieger (eds). 2005. *Thinking Utopia*, New York: Berghahn Books.

101. K.E. Müller. 1984. *Die bessere und die schlechtere Hälfte*, Frankfurt am Main: Campus.

102. As an example, see I. Lenz. 2010. 'Differenzen der Humanität – die Perspektive der Geschlechterforschung', in J. Rüsen (ed.), *Perspektiven der Humanität: Menschsein im Diskurs der Disziplinen*, Bielefeld: Transcript, 373–405.

103. See also J. Rüsen. 2003. 'Die Kultur der Zeit', in J. Rüsen (ed.), *Zeit deuten: Perspektiven, Epochen, Paradigmen*. Bielefeld: Transcript, 23–53.

104. Walter Benjamin intensified this notion of realism into a catastrophic concept for the historical process of time and allowed its meaning to shrink to contingent moments. He discredited the developmental category as part of this fundamental catastrophe of the historical and transplanted its meaning into the hereafter within a 'weak Messianism'. In reality: this meaning is weak, so weak that genuinely historical thinking, which cognitively views all of time in human culture, cannot be captured by it. W. Benjamin. 1991. 'Über den Begriff der Geschichte', in idem, *Gesammelte Schriften*, edited by R. Tiedemann and H. Schweppenhäuser, vol. I.2, Frankfurt am Main: Suhrkamp, 691–704. ('Theses on the Philosophy of History', in idem, *Illuminations*, edited by H. Arendt. New York: Schocken, 1969, 253–264.) Adorno followed the same line of thought. According to his 'negative dialectic', there is no philosophy of history that can reveal the categorical possibility demanded by historical thinking. T.W. Adorno. 1966. *Negative Dialektik*, Frankfurt am Main: Suhrkamp (*Negative Dialectics*, New York: Continuum International, 2007.)

105. H. Rickert. 1896. *Die Grenzen der naturwissenschaftlichen Begriffsbildung*, Heidelberg: Mohr/Siebeck; see also idem. 1924. *Die Probleme der Geschichtsphilosophie*, 3rd ed., Heidelberg: Winter.

106. W. Dilthey. 1989. *Introduction to the Human Sciences*, Princeton, NJ: Princeton University Press.

107. G. Simmel. 1923. *Die Probleme der Geschichtsphilosophie*, 5th ed., Munich: Duncker & Humblot.

108. A.C. Danto. 1974. *Analytische Philosophie der Geschichte*, Frankfurt am Main: Suhrkamp. (*Analytical Philosophy of History*, 2nd ed., Cambridge: Cambridge University Press, 1968.)

109. Ricoeur, *Time and Narrative*.

110. 'Das Licht, welches jene höchsten Wertideen spenden, fällt jeweilig auf einen stets wechselnden endlichen Teil des ungeheuren chaotischen Stromes von Geschehnissen, der sich durch die Zeit dahin wälzt.' Weber, 'Die "Objektivität" sozialwissenschaftlicher und sozialpolitischer Erkenntnis', 213 f. ('The light which emanates from those highest value ideas always falls on an ever changing finite segment of the vast chaotic stream of events, which flows away through time.' Weber, '"Objectivity" in Social Science', 111.)

111. E. Flaig. 1996. 'Verstehen und Vergleichen', in O.-G. Oexle and J. Rüsen (eds), *Historismus in den Kulturwissenschaften*, Cologne: Böhlau, 262–287, quote, 277.

112. Paradigmatic here is Ricoeur, *Time and Narrative*. Although here the specifically historical aspect of a narrative is treated as a special problem and is conceptualized only partially as a theory of historiographical narrative. Ricoeur does not specifically explore the unique cognitive capabilities of historical studies.

113. See this volume, 145sqq.

114. A.L. Schlözer. 1990. *Vorstellung seiner Universalhistorie* (1772/73), edited by H.W. Blanke, Hagen: Margit Rottmann Medienverlag, 14 ff. Kant took up this formulation: *Idee zu einer allgemeinen Geschichte in weltbürgerlicher Absicht*, A 408.

115. For an example, see Weber, *Gesammelte Aufsätze zur Wissenschaftslehre*, 252 ff. (*The Methodology of the Social Sciences*, 111sqq.)

116. Kant, *Idee zu einer allgemeinen Geschichte in weltbürgerlicher Absicht*, A 404.

117. W. von Humboldt. 1960. 'Über die Aufgabe des Geschichtsschreibers', in *Werke*, edited by A. Flitner and K. Giel, vol. 1: *Schriften zur Anthropologie und Geschichte*. Darmstadt: Wissenschaftliche Buchgesellschaft, 596 f. ('On the Historian's Task', in L. von Ranke, *The Theory and Practice of History*. Indianapolis: Bobbs Merrill, 1973, 15.)

118. See also C. Schneider, C. Stillke and B. Leineweber. 1996. *Das Erbe der Napola*, Hamburg: Hamburger Edition. Also Rüsen and Straub, *Dark Traces of the Past*.

119. I developed the outline of such a humanistic view of history in Rüsen, 'Humanism: Anthropology, Axial Times, Modernities'.

120. I take up here the ideas of Klaus Füßmann. 1994. 'Dimensionen der Geschichtsdarstellung', in K. Füßmann, H.T. Grütter and J. Rüsen (eds), *Historische Faszination*, Cologne: Böhlau, 27–44, and specifically 32–35.

121. A striking example: 'Geschichte … wird im Medium narrativer Textstrukturen allererst gewonnen' ('History … is wrought within the medium of textual narrative structures'). From D. Fulda. 2002. 'Strukturanalytische Hermeneutik', in D. Fulda and S.S. Tschopp (eds), *Literatur und Geschichte*, Berlin: de Gruyter, 39–60, quote, 45.

122. F. Nietzsche. 1988. 'Vom Nutzen und Nachteil der Historie für das Leben', in idem, *Sämtliche Werke*, vol. 1, Munich: Deutscher Taschenbuchverlag, 243–334. ('On the Uses and Disadvantages of History for Life' in idem, *Untimely Meditations*, translated by R.J. Hollingdale. Cambridge, 1983.)

123. As, e.g., in P. Nora. 1990. *Zwischen Geschichte und Gedächtnis*, Berlin: Wagenbach. Determined in Flaig, 'Verstehen und Vergleichen', 262–287.

124. This is the case for Kant when he speaks of 'chiliasm' in the philosophy of history. What he means is that the aim or direction of universal developmental processes in human culture is advanced through the philosophical explication of this process, or through the philosophy of history itself (Kant, *Idee zu einer allgemeinen Geschichte in weltbürgerlicher Absicht*, A 403).

125. Droysen, *Historik* I, 251 ff.

126. Ranke regarded this orientation in an inner relationship between historical cognition and political action: it is 'the task of history to present the nature of the state out of earlier events and occurrences and to make it understandable, while it is the task of politics to take this understanding, this knowledge, and develop it and perfect it further' ('die Aufgabe der Historie, das Wesen des Staates aus der Reihe der früheren Begebenheiten darzutun und dasselbe zum Verständnis zu bringen, die der Politik aber, nach erfolgtem Verständnis und gewonnener Erkenntnis es weiter zu entwickeln und zu vollenden'). L. von Ranke. 1877. *Über die Verwandtschaft und den Unterschied der Historie und der Politik*, collected works, vol. 24: Abhandlungen und Versuche, Leipzig: Duncker & Humblot, 288 sq.

127. L. von Ranke. 1971. *Über die Epochen der neueren Geschichte*, edited by T. Schieder and H. Berding, Munich: Oldenbourg, 80.

128. 'Every epoch is immediate to God, and its value has nothing to do with what comes after it, but rather in its own existence, in itself alone. Through this the considerations of history, or even the views of an individual life within history, attain a singular allure in which every epoch must be seen as something valid in itself, appearing to the observer in the most worthy of terms.' ('Jede Epoche ist unmittelbar zu Gott, und ihr Wert beruht gar nicht auf dem, was aus ihr hervorgeht, sondern in ihrer Existenz selbst, in ihrem Eigenen selbst. Dadurch bekommt die Betrachtung der Historie, und zwar des individuellen Lebens in der Historie, einen eigentümlichen Reiz, indem nun jede Epoche als etwas für sich Gültiges angesehen werden muß und der Betrachtung höchst würdig erscheint.') Ranke, *Über die Epochen der neueren Geschichte*, 59 f. (L. von Ranke. 1973. *The Theory and Practice of History*, Indianapolis: Bobbs Merrill, 53.)

129. 'Allein der Mensch, als Person betrachtet, d. i. als Subject einer moralisch-praktischen Vernunft, ist über allen Preis erhaben; denn als ein solcher (*homo noumenon*) ist er nicht blos als Mittel zu anderer ihren, ja selbst seinen eigenen Zwecken, sondern als Zweck an sich selbst zu schätzen, d. i. er besitzt eine Würde (einen absoluten innern Werth), wodurch er allen andern vernünftigen Weltwesen Achtung für ihn abnöthigt, sich mit jedem Anderen dieser Art messen und auf den Fuß der Gleichheit schätzen kann.' I. Kant. 1968. 'Metaphysik der Sitten', in W. Weischedel (ed.), *Werke in zehn Bänden*, vol. 7. Darmstadt: Wissenschaftliche Buchgesellschaft, A 93. ('Man as a person, i.e., as the subject of a morally-practical reason, is exalted above all price. For such a one (*homo noumenon*) he is not to be valued merely as a means to the ends of other people, or even to his own ends, but is to be prized as an end in himself. This is to say, he possesses a dignity (an absolute inner worth) whereby he exacts the

respect of all other rational beings in the world, can measure himself against each member of his species, and can esteem himself on a footing of equality with them.' Available online at: http://praxeology.net/kant7.htm.)

130. Here I am going beyond Ranke (believing, however, to be upholding the notions that Ranke in his own time could only assert in a limited way). For Ranke, the experience of historical thinking was only something to consider in Western countries (which included Ancient Egypt). This is of course from today's perspective (and not only then) untenable. But there is no necessary reason why we should not also consider his 'Idee der Menschheit und der Kultur' ('Idea of Humanity and Culture') on the basis of its historical-philosophical logic as limited as well. It is similar in terms of its normative implications. These must uphold the concepts of a modern humanism within the Kantian category of dignity. Ranke gave a religious form to humanism. If we were to remove the form from the content we would find the humanistic core of historical thinking at the cusp of modernity. (Though we are also seeing the unresolved issue concerning the relationship of humanism and religion. From today's scholarly perspective, Ranke's 'immediate to God' concept can only be dealt with on secular terms as it pertains to meaning and the criterion for meaning. It is unclear whether within the semantic reaches of this secularism the potential of meaning that is available in modern humanism as well as in historicism with its historical ties to religious traditions could be harnessed.)

131. This is found on a linguistic level in the hyphen between historical and political in, for example, the '*historisch-politische Bildung*' (historical-political education) as a part of any teaching of history and political science (not that this relationship is so clear as assumed).

132. See also this volume, 203sqq.

133. See also this volume, 207sqq.

134. J.-F. Lyotard. 1968. *Das postmoderne Wissen*, Vienna: Passagen Verlag, 14 f. (*The Postmodern Condition*, Minneapolis, MN: University of Minnesota Press, 1984.)

135. E. Runia. 2007. 'Burying the Dead, Creating the Past', *History and Theory* 46, 313–325, quote, 317. See also this volume, 216.

136. *Poetics*, 9 b.

137. See also C. Antweiler. 2011. *Mensch und Weltkultur*, Bielefeld: Transcript. (*Inclusive Humanism: Anthropological Basics for a Realistic Cosmopolitanism*, Göttingen: Vandenhoeck & Ruprecht unipress; Taipei: National Taiwan University Press, 2012.)

138. See J. Rüsen. 2010. 'Klassischer Humanismus: eine historische Ortsbestimmung', in J. Rüsen (ed.), *Perspektiven der Humanität*, Bielefeld: Transcript. ('Classical Humanism – A Historical Survey', in J. Rüsen (ed.), *Approaching Humankind*, Göttingen: Vandenhoeck & Ruprecht unipress, 2013.)

139. K. Jaspers. 1963. *Vom Ursprung und Ziel der Geschichte*, Munich: Piper (*The Origin and Goal of History*, New Haven: Yale University Press, 1953); S.N. Eisenstadt (ed.). 1987–1992. *Kulturen der Achsenzeit*, parts I, II and III (*The Origins and Diversity of Axial Age Civilization*); J.P. Arnason, S.N. Eisenstadt and B. Wittrock (eds). 2005. *Axial Civilisations and World History*, Leiden: Brill.

140. A. D'Haenens. 1983. *Oralité, Scribalité, Electronalité*. Louvain-la-Neuve.

141. J. Kocka. 1975. 'Theorien in der Sozial- und Gesellschaftsgeschichte', *Geschichte und Gesellschaft* 1, 9–42, quote, 9. ('Theory and Social History: Recent Developments in West Germany', *Social Research* 47(3), 1980, 426–457, quote, 426. See also Kocka, 'Theory Orientation and the New Quest for Narrative'.)

142. I explored the development and use of theory in historical studies in more detail in Rüsen, *Historische Orientierung*, 82–115.

143. L. von Ranke. 1958. *Die großen Mächte: Politisches Gespräch*, edited by T. Schieder, Göttingen: Vandenhoeck & Ruprecht. ('The Great Powers: Dialogue on Politics', in idem, *The Theory and Practice of History*, Indianapolis: Bobbs Merrill, 1973.)

144. I attempted this in view of the relationship between enlightenment and historicism and in terms of the problems of methodology in intercultural comparisons: J. Rüsen. 1993. *Konfigurationen des Historismus*, Frankfurt am Main: Suhrkamp, 29–94.; J. Rüsen. 2002. *Geschichte im Kulturprozess*, Cologne: Böhlau, 231–266.

145. This has been made clear in the wealth of empirical material on the 'charismatic leader' found in W. Nippel (ed.). 2000. *Virtuosen der Macht*, Munich: C.H. Beck.

146. H.-U. Wehler. 1987. *Deutsche Gesellschaftsgeschichte*, vol. 1: *Vom Feudalismus des Alten Reiches bis zur Defensiven Modernisierung der Reformära 1700–1815*, Munich: C.H. Beck 6–31.

147. M. Weber. 1968. 'Die drei Typen der legitimen Herrschaft', in idem, *Gesammelte Aufsätze zur Wissenschaftslehre*, 3rd ed., edited by J. Winckelmann. Tübingen: Mohr, 475–488. ('The Three Types of Legitimate Rule', *Berkeley Publications in Society and Institutions* 4(1), 1958, 1–11.)

148. Weber, '"Objectivity" in Social Science', 90.

149. See also this volume, 170sqq.

150. See this volume, 84.

151. See this volume, 86sqq.

152. For more detail see Rüsen, *Grundzüge* II, 22–47. From among the wealth of literature on the subject I will point out here C. Lorenz. 1997. *Konstruktion der Vergangenheit*, Cologne: Böhlau.

153. I am simply summarizing the logical structure of narrative types. These are described in more detail in the relevant chapter found in Rüsen, *Grundzüge* II, 22–47.

154. A noteworthy example is Daniel Goldhagen's historical interpretation of the Holocaust in D. Goldhagen. 1996. *Hitlers willige Vollstrecker*, Berlin: Siedler. (*Hitler's Willing Executioners*, New York: Alfred A. Knopf, 1996.) See also my analysis in J. Rüsen. 2001. *Zerbrechende Zeit*, Cologne: Böhlau, 263–278.

CHAPTER 5

Methodology

The Rules of the Historical Method

1. The Methodological Character of Historical Knowledge

Categories, types, theories and concepts are only valuable when they can be used methodically in historical scholarship. Categories fundamentally determine the particular character of historical methods used in dealing with historical experience, while types, theories and concepts concretize this dealing down into details.

The categorical level is developed through the formal philosophy of history. As noted earlier, the way that historical thinking as process handles empirical evidence of the past is analysed on this level. This primarily means to distinguish it from the methodical processes involved in the rigid and – especially – the experimental and mathematical sciences, while at the same time adhering to the methodical character of historical knowledge. In this respect, there is a clear distinction between types of methodologies. There is a tradition behind this: historical *Verstehen* (understanding) is different from *Erklären* (explaining) in the natural sciences (according to Droysen and Dilthey); idiographic thinking is different from nomothetic thinking (according to Windelband); and individualizing processes from generalizing processes (Rickert and Weber). In more recent times, and to this day, the debate concerning the narrative character of historical thinking has dominated any discussion regarding the particularity of historical knowledge. Even though this has led to a very convincing clarification of the inherent logic of historical thinking, the methodical aspects of historical thinking have increasingly been neglected. We are now faced with the radical question of whether historical thinking could be considered scientific (or scholarly) in the first place.

In order to answer this question properly, we first must concede how misleading it would be to measure historical scholarship against the standards of the highly developed natural or hard sciences, such as physics or biology. Such a comparison consistently and necessarily leads to negative results (for logical reasons). Instead, we need to examine the differences between the established disciplines or institutions that produce 'scientific' knowledge as a way of finding commonalities between them. By doing so, the varying forms of academic study may appear as different expressions of the same spirit of science (*Geist der Wissenschaft*).

This spirit (the German *Geist,* an intellectual spirit or mind) manifests itself in certain features of knowledge and cognition. The most relevant ones are listed below.

The Determining Factors of Scientific Knowledge   For lay people, the specialized language or terminology of many academic disciplines can appear strange or downright alienating. It concerns the use of cognitive constructs, which are based on processes of abstraction. These processes can, but do not necessarily, lead to explicit theories. They must, however, determine how to deal with information. Abstraction means removing the immediacy of perception in order to better understand given material. When we compare historiographical texts with the statements made in other scientific or academic fields, such as the field of mathematics, we immediately notice a relatively low degree of specialized terminology. Historiography cannot avoid borrowing extensively from the language that dominates the historical culture of a particular time outside of academic discourse. This is related to the fact that the formation of historical meaning fundamentally connects scholarly knowledge to the reality of daily life. If academic historical thinking were to linguistically break away from the practice of daily life completely, then it would lose an essential element of meaningful knowledge within its own practical application. On the other hand, the scholarly credibility of historical studies is directly related to the degree to which it is capable of distancing itself from the common world from which it draws its research questions. The purpose of this distance is to relieve the pressure of our historical need for orientation and to allow these questions to be answered (or to contribute to an answer) objectively. Scholarship also addresses questions that do not arise out of daily life but rather occur in the interest of cognition itself for academic purposes.

The second essential characteristic that the field of historical scholarship shares with all empirical scientific fields is its fundamental reference to evidence, characterized by two features: (a) on a specifically scholarly level, historical experience becomes expanded and intensified through research. This evidence-based research goes far beyond that which is usually the case outside of the professional handling of the human past. Therefore, (b) the past, which impacts the cultural orientations of the present, must become objectified and turned into methodically gathered facts. (Whether or how this facticity of empirical knowledge can then be transformed back into the living experience of historical memory is another question altogether. This question goes beyond the methodology of research and into the fundamental problems of historiographical representation.)

A third essential characteristic of specifically scholarly thinking is its procedural character as *argumentation*. The validity claims raised in scholarly thinking must be justifiable. Such justification or substantiation happens through argumentation in discursive practices. Such practices can easily be discerned through the use of terminology and can be (critically) analysed with respect to the cognitive features they have in common: they are held together by logical coherence and a rational and formal consistency.

Scholarship as Research   All three characteristics converge into a fourth: methodically regulated research as a cognitive process. We could simply say: scholarship is method. Method subjects thinking to rules that allow academic study to consistently produce new knowledge. Methodical research enables academic study to make advances in knowledge. This methodical character provides scholarly knowledge with one more feature: its intersubjective justifiability. This pertains to historical knowledge as well, although it is uniquely related to the subjectivity of those who make use of this knowledge (who want to know). Regardless of who is meant here, we are not speaking of something that all human beings have in common as subjects, but rather what distinguishes human beings in their concrete ways of life and temporal dynamic. Historical knowledge can form distinct identities. This has often led to the idea that this knowledge is only true for those who turn to it or use it.[155] Some claim that historical knowledge is characterized by bias and a dependency on perspective, which severely limits, if not damages, all its scientific claims.[156] *But historical objectivity is something different: it is a certain way of realizing this particular and especially distinctive subjectivity, and taking it seriously rather than ignoring it altogether.* This reference to the subject is particular because it is fundamentally comprehensible and can be dealt with on a discursive, argumentative level (or at least it appears to be justifiable). Moreover, those who address this knowledge of the subject can deal with it argumentatively.

These features (the concepts, the reference to evidence, the argumentative character and the methodical research) give historical knowledge that is

produced through scholarly historical research a specifically scholarly character. Historical studies is therefore scientific, or better yet, academic study.
We should not rob it of this quality when we emphasize its particularity
compared to other fields of study.

2. The Unity of the Historical Method

Historical methods are basically the rules that determine historical thinking as a research process. Regulated research allows historical knowledge to
be substantiated, which determines its scholarly character. The existence of
these rules is not up for discussion. What is not immediately clear is that these
rules are related in a systematic context that we can call 'historical method'.

What determines this systematic unity? The word 'method' originally
meant 'way'. If we draw on this meaning, then the uniformity of method
refers to the way or the path along which we must think in order to attain
substantiated knowledge. Such a path can look like this: it starts with a historical question and ends with an answer to this question. The first step in
historical thinking begins with deriving questions from the given temporal
orientations of daily life in the present and the available historical knowledge, that can be answered by experience. At the end we find the answer to
the question. This 'end' would be the historical representation. But does this
representation belong to the research process? Certainly, historical thinking concludes with a representation, with the presentation of the research
findings. On the other hand, the representation is not primarily cognitive in
form. It is not as methodically regulated as research. It presents the research
and incorporates it. It predisposes the research according to the represent-
ability of its results, but it is not a part of research. Rather, it is a way to
deal with research results. As such, despite their shared context and dependency on one another, it makes sense to make a methodological distinction
between research and representation.

In its specifically scholarly form (as research process), historical thinking
constitutes a cognitive procedure that begins with a question. It directs this
question toward empirical findings in which the past is made present, and
extracts information from these findings about the what, where, how and
why of the past. Historical thinking then combines this information into a
contextual ordering of occurrences that clarifies the individual occurrences
in their chronological sequence. This procedure has an open ending. It cul-
minates only in connection to the research in the narrative representation of
this temporal context.

Historical method regulates this cognitive process, and makes individual (and artificially isolated) cognitive processes (or steps in thinking)

comprehensible, which means they can be justified and criticized. The historical method can be seen as a unity of three forms of thinking or cognitive strategies: *heuristics, criticism* and *interpretation.*

This is the traditional concept of methodology in historical studies as developed systematically by Droysen[157] and later by Bernheim,[158] and canonized by others.

The following considerations are indebted to this canonical form of the historical method. They focus on the sequence of steps in thinking and their own internal regulation. I will deal with 'method' in purely monological and not communicative terms. I consciously leave out the fact that the individual steps in thinking in the research and interpretation of historical experience are related to other processes of forming historical meaning that follow other strategies within a communicative context. This may appear as a shortcoming but it is really a benefit, because without such an artificial isolating of cognitive procedures, we would not be able to decipher the methodical regulation of historical thinking that defines the disciplinary character of historical scholarship. Of course the methodically regulated procedures of historical cognition are formulated in communicative terms in the research process. But since we want to characterize research as a (relatively) closed methodical operation of acquiring knowledge, these communicative processes that determine and influence the research process are not relevant for the method.

Preliminary Considerations on Methodical Principles in Historical Thinking In the following I am only concerned with describing the methodical principles of historical thinking that determine its research process. This description has to remain abstract as principles in general can only be imagined as abstract. I am leaving out the wide range of established research practices in order to consider the few dominant perspectives of methodical regulation that underlie them. The downside is that this also leaves out the various schools of thought in historical research in all their variety. Classical historicism, the Annales School, historical sociology, historical anthropology and other directions in research all follow different procedures and clash over varying methodical concepts. But they all accept the methodical process itself, the enquiring character of historical thinking, regardless of direction or school. They take for granted this common character; otherwise, historians from these different directions would not be able to argue with each other. Their arguments are based on varying paradigmatic manifestations of the methodical principles, but not on the concept that principles in general should regulate research.

These different manifestations characterize historical scholarship at exactly the point where the field, through all its conflicting paradigms, reveals its disciplinary professionalism. The field defines its professionalism through internal differences. Some examples are the differences between subject areas, such as between political and economic history, or the regional differences marked by geographical classifications, such as the difference between European and Chinese history, or the temporal differences between ancient and modern history. These distinctions lead to corresponding and methodological differences that suit the circumstances of a given area of specialized study. A methodology of historical scholarship that wants to approach real research practices must embrace these differences in a systematic way and explicate their dynamic character. Finally, they change depending on the interests and questions that prompt an analysis of circumstances of the past.

This kind of methodology is not meant here. It belongs to the tasks of specialized historians for specific subject areas in historical studies and – let us not forget to add – in the self-reflection of other scientific fields that also deal with historical phenomena.[159] As noted earlier, the aim here is to clarify the common features of the variety of research strategies or, in other words, to see the woods despite the trees. With this methodology, we can properly analyse the various different research strategies in the field. Methodology can then provide perspectives that can be used to order, compare and even criticize these strategies.

3. Heuristics

The method[160] known as the *heuristic* approach can be divided into two parts: the enquiring search for historical questions and finding the right evidence for a possible response.

a) The Historical Question

Research begins with a question. The questions that prompt research into historical sources determine the results of the research. Does methodology determine research questions? Are there perspectives that we should follow if we want to be certain that historical questions will lead to productive research? Such perspectives can indeed be identified, both in the negative and positive sense. In the negative sense, historical enquiry should be innovative. It should not be restricted to the usual questions or standardized routines in research. It should be open to explore what is unheard of, unknown, unasked and mysteriously assumed to be self-evident – in short, open to everything that lies beyond the realm of already researched historical experience.

The Three Rules of Heuristics   This heuristic rule of disorder can easily lead to pure arbitrariness in historical enquiry. A fool can pose more questions than one hundred wise men (or women) can answer. We can avoid such foolishness when we subject historical questions to two positive methodological rules: the innovative value of any historical question is not measured by how much existing historical knowledge it overrides. What is important is which empirical dimensions and contents of the past it reveals, and what these dimensions and contents mean in terms of meeting the need for orientation that sets the historical thinking of the historian in motion. Asking such productive questions is of course impossible without a regard for existing historical knowledge. Innovation does not mean ignoring existing bodies of knowledge, but rather developing a reflective attitude of 'not yet knowing'. We need to become familiar with the status quo of thematically relevant research and the fundamental theoretical concepts and methodological processes that underlie this research.

To the negative rule, which opens the doors to the inaccessible realm of intuitions, we can add two positive ones: the first extracts the power of these intuitions from our need for orientation and experiences of contingency of the present. This translates as asking historical questions in such a way that your research leads to results that correspond to the unsatisfied needs for orientation in the present. (Gaps in research alone do not prompt particularly innovative research.) The other positive rule directs the unfettered intuitions toward empirical evidence from the human past. This then translates as asking your historical questions, which are prompted by the need for orientation in the present, in such a way that these questions can be answered through research. This means that the historical questions must make use of sources from the past. A historical question must lead to a search for material in which the past is present.

What Does 'Empiricism' Mean?   The word 'material' refers to a specific form of the presence of the past: its empirical reality found in its so-called remains, or sources. It would be horribly delusional for historians to see this as the only way in which the past is present. The past is a formidable part of the present from within the context of historical thinking as a result of developments or occurrences that happened in the past. This is also the case for all forms of memory and remembering. But this presence of the past is precisely not the empirical evidence that we direct historical questions to. Empirical evidence is the reification of the past. To put it more drastically, the past that lives within the conditions of the present must be methodologically killed to become visible as the past. Only then are we able to perceive the temporal difference between past and present and recognize the particularity of the past. In the heuristic sense, the past becomes the 'object', the objective facts behind empirical evidence of human lives from the past. The past only becomes a subject for research in this objectified form. The historical question in heuristics has to create this objectification (to suffer the dust of the archive), in order to formulate substantiated answers.

Controlling the Question   The substantiation of knowledge is a critical factor in historical research. This is well known in the tradition of metahistory, in that teaching methodology often began with a classification of all possible types of material in which the past is empirically evident in the present. But it is problematic to start methodological research with collecting and examining source material.[161] What I call a source plainly and simply depends on what I want to know. And what I want to know depends on what questions I ask. A question becomes an explicit research question through methodology. Its plausibility can be measured against two things: first, the need for orientation in the present and second, the current state of knowledge. Historical questions should not stay one step behind the current state of knowledge. They must surpass it, not in any random direction, but toward contemporary understanding and substantiated claims. Is this a methodological rule? If 'rule' means that the historian is responsible for fulfilling any given need for orientation, then this would be heuristically counterproductive. It contradicts the commitment to separate the historical question from the pressure of conformity that has crept into research routines and submits historical research to the demands of politically motivated interests that can disturb scholarly correctness. On the other hand, the effectiveness of an explicit research question is not random, especially not when it is open for discussion. This discussion hinges on coherent perspectives that consider the relationship between the research question in hand and the state of knowledge within a given field as well as the historical culture of a given time and real-life context.

The plausibility of a historical research question depends on its capacity for generating discourse. Here, methodology ensures that the posed questions both explicitly refer to the contemporary scholarly historical discourse and (critically) take into account past works and the need for new knowledge. This guarantees that the standards guiding discourse and the capacity for discourse do not fall below the questions and problems of the professional community. They may, though, be surpassed. In that case, the relationship between academic discourse and historical culture must be considered, as this relationship determines the discursive possibilities and limitations of historical consciousness. Historical questions that aim to transcend these limits and expand these possibilities, and can make this aim plausible through a critical assessment of earlier academic achievements, distinguish themselves by a high degree of heuristic productivity.

Certain research questions can arise from interdisciplinary constellations. The problems and insights from other academic fields that deal with human beings and their world can both stimulate and greatly influence the heuristics of historical studies. The field of cultural anthropology in particular has recently influenced historical scholarship.[162] Before that, the social sciences, sociology and economics inspired new historical perspectives.

In addressing empirical evidence of the past, historical questions and problems prove their heuristic value by methodologically assuming the form of substantiated assumptions (hypotheses). In this form, the surplus of possible questions in heuristics is systematically bound by a body of knowledge with the purpose of expanding and advancing it. Knowledge is expanded when the questions leave prior knowledge and its underlying cognitive strategies untouched. Knowledge is advanced when heuristic questions address and change the strategies that organize the bodies of knowledge in historical contexts of meaning. Not only does this direct our view towards new facts, but these facts also appear in a new light: our view changes.

b) Finding: The Empirical Answer

Heuristics is concerned with the second step of 'finding' (the Greek word '*heureka*' means 'I have found') historical facts. To find something, you must look for it. (Of course we can also come across something, but nevertheless we must be on our way to something.) Therefore, rules or norms that concern the productivity of the historical question and the plausibility of the historical problem are necessary for heuristics. At the very beginning of research, methodology helps us clarify what we want to find out. What should be known remains vague, when it is not referring to a methodological clarification of what can be known. Heuristics becomes the methodology of finding sources that contain information that is necessary and sufficient to produce a response to the historical question and a solution to the historical problem.

With this operative step in research, heuristics leads us from the lofty (or shall we say, intellectual) sphere of potentially innovative questions and substantiated assumptions towards the earthly domain of a widely disparate and divided world of documentation with clearly divided academic disciplines that are indispensable auxiliary sciences (e.g. archival science) for historical research. The readiness of this growing potential of technical assistance in finding relevant source materials could only be disliked by historians who consider empirical answers bad for the high art of historical enquiry. Academic professionalism, however, is demonstrated in that historical questions are asked within the realm of possible and meaningful answers. Good historical questions lead to the discovery of the information contained in relics of the past that still exist and can tell us what happened and where, when, how and why. These relics must be systematically collected, examined and prepared for the purposes of research. This entails heuristic operations that transform the productivity of historical enquiry into the plausibility of empirically substantiated answers.

c) Tradition and Remains

It is essential for historical research to discern what is historically relevant from the wealth of material remains from the human past. How do we select information from sources that will disclose the specific historical quality of the human past?

Heuristics qualifies sources by making a distinction between tradition and remains. Sources are qualified as remains when they are a random or unintentional expression of the past and are not made to carry a specific meaning into future memory (like the refuse of our consumption habits). On the other hand, sources have a quality of tradition when their contents have produced certain qualities of meaning (like memorials or historical reports). *Remains* only carry externally the meaning that marks the process of time through the historical interpretation of history. *Traditions* carry meaning within themselves. Remains are the imprints of a past life while traditions are the traces of the past that carry on into the present, mentally rather than chronologically. Remains from the past that do not contain traditional elements provide evidence from the past but not meaning in or of itself. Remains with traditional elements only provide meaning for our temporal orientation in the present.

Possibilities and Limitations of Preset Meaning   Historical research builds on fundamental criteria for meaning that help to interpret the experience of the past and turn it into history (histories). Research must determine the empirical plausibility of evidence that then defines meaning over the course of time and provides it with the persuasive power of processed experience. The heuristic distinction between tradition and relic concerns the possibilities and limitations of such empirical knowledge as well as the corroboration of historical contexts of meaning. The ratio of tradition to remains in the sources depends on the direction of the historical question. If we want to deduce potential meaning from experience of the past for the purposes of existential orientation in the present, then we are effectively reassessing the past for tradition. If, however, we want a more critical distance from the historical patterns in cultural orientation or if we want to find new possibilities to determine a meaning of time in daily life, then the remains of the historical experience that have not yet established themselves as preset meaning are important. Source materials bear witness to facts whose meaning must still be interpreted, whereas the alternative suggests that the sources present meaning as fact.

The distinction between tradition and remains is relative. Research depends on the concept that all traditional sources are, in a way, also remains, since they are factually present and permit empirical examination. Conversely, all remains bore witness to the subjects who left them behind or who at least left traces on them. Without reference to the meaning behind the actions of the human subjects, these relics have no historical quality.

Historical research deals with the heuristic tension between meaning and fact, between relevance and experience when examining source material. The sources do not decide which history is a meaningful response to a historical question. The criterion that determines meaning in the historical question precedes the information of the sources. This criterion determines the quality of the historical assertions that a source can deliver. Heuristics addresses the assumed meaning of the historical question to the sources of the human past in such a way that the answer to this question contains the highest quality of information available from the source in the form of empirically substantiated historical knowledge.

4. Criticism

The first step in forming empirical knowledge is source criticism. This is the research procedure in which reliable and verifiable information is attained from the relics of the past to establish the what, when, where, how and (in certain cases) why. After the appropriate source material (with its complex tradition-remains relation) for responding to the historical question has been collected through heuristic efforts, the source criticism starts with an analysis in which the facts of the past are presented by examining their empirical evidence in the present. Source criticism can be divided into three methodical processes, as follows.

(1) *External source criticism* examines the source itself as a given fact. It clarifies the question of whether the material in hand is in fact a real source or, for example, a forgery. The traditional label of 'critical authenticity' says it all. However, we should remember that even falsified sources are in fact sources, not in the sense of what they pretend to be but in the sense of what they lie about (the actual intentions of its maker, the strategies behind the forgery and the deception, the time-specific views on plausibility, etc.).

(2) *Internal source criticism* examines the quality of the information provided by the source after the fact of the source material has been determined. This occurs according to two perspectives: temporal proximity and objective possibility. Both perspectives help to determine a measure of probability. Temporal proximity has a particular significance in the framework of a research strategy concerning the documentation and sequence of events. Since it is well known that memory becomes less reliable as time passes, documentation tends to be more plausible when it is created sooner after

the event. In creating critical editions of reports and certificates, historical scholarship has turned the reconstruction of original texts from their later variations into a highly developed technology.

(3) The criterion of *objective possibility* checks whether the sources' claims are consistent with verified historical knowledge and all other relevant empirical knowledge in the present. It is common knowledge that sources can be shaped by a completely different understanding of reality than the reality of the historian who works with them. In case of any doubt, the historian's concept of reality rather than the claims of the source is decisive for determining the plausibility of what a source reports as fact.

What is Reality?   The question of whether the present understanding of reality itself must be historicized is a historico-ontological problem of the first order. When we answer this question with an unconditional yes and when we see historicization as way to relativize validity claims, then source criticism as a methodical operation is invalid. This radically reverses the step from myth to history. In terms of a post-colonial ideological criticism, this epistemological basis of source criticism is now seen as culture-specific.[163] This critique argues that a perverted form of Western dominance in the modernizing process influenced all forms of historical thinking. This argument relativizes and dismisses evidence-based controls over historical information or understanding. There can no longer be a scholarly historical discourse across cultures (but only an intercultural power struggle). The intention of this critique then turns at the same time against itself. What experience can we rely on to deal with cultural differences if we no longer have a basis of transculturally valid historical knowledge that allows us to engage in discourse and to disprove illegitimate claims to power? When we dissolve the objectivity of historical knowledge into an endless flow of references, then we no longer have identifiable events in the past and no way of checking the validity of historical assertions. The past becomes simply a matter of perspective.[164]

On the other hand, regarding culturally specific ways of defining sources, it is important to find and analyse *cross-cultural trends* on a theoretical level. They could be made prerequisites for a productive and critical intercultural communication.[165] They can also be used to deal with the variety of historical perspectives. As long as something of the past still appears in these perspectives we can compare the perspectives and examine them critically against each other.

Highly Aggregated Facts   Along with the operations of external and internal source criticism acknowledged and demonstrated by the traditional methods of historical research,[166] there is a third operation that is characteristic of modern historical research: the *constitution of highly aggregated facts*. This concerns the reconstruction of facts that are not documented in the sources as such because they were not facts at the time when the sources were produced. Rather, these facts can only be reconstructed from separate bits of source information. These facts are of a higher order that can be identified through analytical research (mostly through quantifiable methods), such as birth rates, growth rate of a gross national product, agricultural cycles, mental factors (like attitudes) in a political culture, and so on.

Auxiliary Sciences   The field of historical studies has produced a rich arsenal of methodical procedures and technical resources to assist with source criticism. The scope and sophistication of this arsenal represents the complexity involved in deciphering sources according to the distinction of tradition and relic in responding to historical questions. These aids are called 'auxiliary sciences' or 'auxiliaries' (specifically, a group of specialized disciplines within historical scholarship). They deal with chronology, which helps solve dating problems; palaeography, which helps to decipher ancient writing systems; diplomatics, which analyses documents; geneology, which clarifies ancestral lineages and origins; and heraldry, sigillography and numismatics, which analyse emblems, seals and coins. We can also add historical geography, which provides information about sources concerning spatial data. Modern research methods of quantification promote statistics to the highest ranks of auxiliary sciences: it enables source criticism to survey quantifiable data. There are also a great many other academic fields whose bodies of knowledge and research strategies can be used for source criticism. Basically, all other fields of scientific study (e.g., biology, physics and astronomy to determine chronological dates or genetics to clarify the ancestry of different human groups) can function as auxiliary sciences of historical scholarship when they provide procedural methods that help historians identify facts from historical material.[167]

As far as I know, there is no systematically applied and reasonably complete methodology for source criticism that corresponds with the current research practices of historians. This has to do with the fact that, in contrast to nineteenth-century source work, which was easier to canonize, modern historical scholarship has developed completely different research strategies for processing information that is difficult to organize systematically. They refer to varying types of sources, from the rubbish piles of pre-historic peoples to interviews with contemporaries, from the pollen analysis of archaeological remains to the self-portrayals of people personally involved in events, from contemporary historical developments and aerial photographs of old settlements to opinion polls and information from the internet. In theory, all these processes and proceedings can be seen as the investigation and establishment of facts that are necessary to answer a historical question.

The Question of Objectivity   With these processes and proceedings, source criticism guarantees the objectivity of historical assertions that are based on factual data in histories. This objectivity is fundamental and essential for historical scholarship's claim of scientificity as well as for the cultural prestige that comes with such claims. And yet, this claim of objectivity is limited in two respects. The first respect concerns the certainty of historical knowledge about the factuality of the past. Especially when it comes to the distant past, source criticism does not always provide pure facts, that is, exact information about what really happened, where it really happened, how it happened or why. At best, source criticism can provide a certain degree of certainty as to what we know or can know in light of empirical facts and according to a certain form of verification.

The second respect concerns the degree of objectivity that can be achieved through source criticism. Source criticism determines verifiable facts to a particular degree of certainty from the flood of information that historical enquiry acquires from sources. However, this factuality is abstract, as it does not extend to specifically historical connections between individual facts. The actual historical interpretive work that is based on the preliminary source criticism deals with these connections.

The Historical Character of Facts   The facts identified by source criticism do not in themselves have a specifically historical character. They become historical only after they are placed in a meaningful temporal relationship with other facts. They gain their historicity in two ways: through their position in a chronological relationship to other facts or through their position within the framework of a notion of the course of time that encompasses both the present and the future. We could call one objective and the other subjective. The crucial point is that only together do they form the specifically historical in factual occurrences of the past. In this respect, analytical and hermeneutic ways of thinking are inextricably linked in the historical cognitive process.[168] Within this objective and chronological context we also find the procedure of explaining what comes later with what came before. This explanatory character of the temporal context of historical facts connects both dimensions, the objective and the subjective, or if we prefer, natural time and cultural time.[169] Determining this context is no longer the job of source criticism but the work of interpretation.

5. Interpretation

Interpretation is the operation in historical research that *joins together the facts of the past identified by source criticism into intersubjectively verifiable defined movements of time* that have an *explanatory function* and can be presented as *histories.* The interpretation makes the facts historical. The historical contexts in which the facts are placed cannot be derived from the sources themselves. The sources cannot know what came after them. They cannot bear witness to the course of time that is the subject of historical enquiry. This context can only be perceived *post festum*, and not documented *in actu*. However, the context is not simply imposed on the facts; rather, individual facts have already created the context in some way, since they are already part of an encompassing temporal occurrence. The interpretation addresses this occurrence. It cannot simply extract it from the facts, as these facts are linked to many other facts. It is impossible (and not desirable) to gain an all-encompassing insight into all links and associations. The interpretation filters out those relationships or connections that are important for the answer to a particular historical question.

The decision about what is important and what is not depends on the meaning we attribute to an event from the past for the sake of orientation in the present. The way we attribute this meaning is anything but arbitrary or purely functional (turning the event into what we would like to have happened). The results of processes from the past are already a part of the real-life circumstances of the present. Only when we recognize the effect of the past on the present are we able to properly substantiate the historical interpretations of that past.

The pre-modern self-understanding of historical scholarship saw connecting events of the past as the work of historiography, or the process of writing history. The idea of methods was then seen as a question to be dealt with according to this process. Method was a form of representation. It was judged on its comprehensibility and (moral) application.[170]

The Structure of Historical Cognition With the professionalization of historical knowledge, the research operation of interpretation emerges between source criticism (which has developed methodologically since the early modern period with the techniques of the auxiliaries) and the historiographic formation of historical knowledge. As mentioned earlier, interpretation involves empirically determining temporal connections from the information of sources that enable us to answer the historical question. In each historical question there is the notion (in the form of an assumption) of a course of time that encompasses individual facts, the idea of a possible history. Research transforms this idea of a possible history into a real history. Source criticism delivers the building blocks for this reality. The interpretation then builds the historical reality with these blocks (to stick with the metaphor) according to a set construction plan. Such a construction plan is a notion of an overarching course of time in which the individual facts can be inserted. The operative modus for carrying out this interpretation is narrative. Again sticking with the metaphor, the narrative is the mortar that holds the structure together. It is important to remember that interpretation is not the empirical ratification of the constructively developed idea of a possible history. Generally, interpretation involves significant modifications that lead to a result that was not assumed or prescribed before the sources were analysed.

Historical knowledge that is gained through interpretive research and concerns the temporal connections of facts identified through source criticism has to be told in the form of histories. If this is the case, then the question of what exactly the research behind an interpretation is arises. What makes historical interpretation verifiable? Factuality alone does not make facts into history because source criticism and its methodical identification of facts do not present the specifically historical connections between these facts.

Method and Theory in Interpretation   The process of interpretation is methodical when the working concept of an overarching temporal relationship refers to the information extracted from the source material in a verifiable way. This only happens if this concept explicitly presents a particular cognitive construct in handling the individual facts. As such the concept attains a theoretical and explainable status. This means that the concept of a course of time combines the separate moments of time within each individual fact into a general construct, which is concretized in the facts. In this intellectual process, the facts do not lose their factuality; rather, they become *historical facts* at this point. They gain their historical and unique temporal quality. They take on the meaning that they have in the narrative context of a history.

Narrative Use of Theory   The method of historical interpretation can be described as a process in which notions of the course of time are explicated as general and comprehensive elements of knowledge, compared with the facts extracted from source criticism.[171] At the same time, these concepts of time refer to the facts in a way that they merge together into an empirically rich temporal movement. Interpretation is a complex research process in which theories about historical connections are formed and facts derived from sources are historicized. The interpretive notions of time do not absorb facts or rob them of their individual particularity to turn them into an abstract principle. Instead, they bring out a specific quality of time, the particular historical quality, from within the facts. Historical theories have a special function in the interpretive process. Theories help determine the qualities of facts from the past that make them typical of or specific to a particular time.

The methodological form of using theory in interpretation and turning facts from the past into history has not yet been sufficiently explicated.

The comprehensive concepts of the course of time, with which historians create empirically plausible historical correlations or relationships out of facts, are narrative constructs, or *plots*. Their use in research and interpretation can be called *narrative use of theory*. Until now we have not seen the work with theory or the building blocks that form it in historical research attain the status of a standardized and methodical process. Instead, historians use implicit concepts of comprehensive courses of time in their work. As long as this is the case, the problem of the methodical rules of interpretation will remain unresolved. This does not mean that the relevant perspectives for historical interpretation cannot be critically examined for their inner consistency, for their scope and intensity as regards experience or their capability in bringing facts into plausible, explainable and historical contexts and correlations.

These considerations on historical methods are 'monological'. They concern the logic of the process in which a coherent temporal narrative is drawn from a chronological order of information. The relevant concepts of the course of time are explicated as theoretically drawn narrative constructs. Of course, the use of such constructs stands in a communicative relationship with an argumentation, in which it is related to other similar constructs. To borrow a term from literature studies, interpretation is always 'intertextual'; in other words, it refers to other interpretations and thereby attains its particular historical meaning and functional capacity in historical culture.

6. From Interpretation to Representation

Historical interpretation leads to a form of knowledge in which the factuality of past events can be narrated and presented as a history. Interpretation and representation cannot be clearly or sequentially separated from each other (like the traditional methodology of Bernheim and others claimed). Still, they are two different processes. Interpretation is a genuinely *cognitive process* and therefore methodically regulated, while representation does not only work from a cognitive perspective. Therefore, metahistory requires an analysis that does not primarily deal with research methods but rather with the literary (*poetic, aesthetic or rhetoric*) *analysis* of texts.[172]

The overarching connection between both operations is the *plot*, or the concept of time that uses interpretation in the methodical process of explaining a course of events and that is represented as a narrated history. The cognitive dimension of this organization of historical narrative has hardly been addressed in recent discussions about theory of history. However, we cannot dispute the fact that every historical interpretation of past happenings takes place in an interpretive framework that can be understood and

Table 5.1 Schematic representation of methodical operations in historical research.

Methods	Operations	Regulative Concepts, Criteria
Heuristic I	Development of a question that reveals an area of historical knowledge	Innovation, body of knowledge
Heuristic II	Finding, identifying and developing the documentation of events of the past that is relevant to the question	New revelations from known sources; identifying new sources
Heuristic III	Distinguishing tradition from remains as qualities of evidence from the past	Analytical separation of meaning and facts
Critique	Attaining verifiable information about events of the past from documentation in the present	Establishing facts with the help of auxiliary sciences
	– External source criticism: examining authenticity; uncovering forgeries	Proof of origin, temporal quality of language, (temporal) proximity, objective possibility,[173] compatibility with body of knowledge
	– Internal source criticism: examining the reliability of information from sources	
Interpretation	Combining critically attained facts into courses of time that can be narrated and have explanatory value	Theoretical evaluation of concepts of the course of time Reflective perspectives on meaning and significance

critically analysed as a cognitive entity (and is treated as such in discussions between historians). The historiographic form of this analytical framework does not necessarily emerge from its cognitive structure or its interpretive function. This framework can, for example, be made explicit and reflexively explicated, but it can also remain hidden as an implication of the narrative. It is worth asking and investigating whether and how historical knowledge acquired through research should exhibit traces of the methical process it developed from or not.

Notes

155. This is the case, for example, in Droysen, whose *Historik* I cite as paradigmatic here. As to the problems associated with this understanding of objectivity, Wilfried Nippel is very clear on this: W. Nippel. 2012. 'Das forschende Verstehen, die Objektivität des Historikers

und die Funktion der Archive', in S. Rebenich and H.-U. Wiemer (eds), *Johann Gustav Droysen*, Frankfurt am Main: Campus, 337–377). Also see (at a very different level of judgement): K. Ries (ed.). 2010. *Johann Gustav Droysen*, Stuttgart: Franz Steiner.

156. The classical text for this is C.A. Beard. 1935. 'That Noble Dream', *The American Historical Review* 41(1), 74–87. Peter Novick took up the same mode of argument, attempting to add plausibility to it through a grandly conceived empirical study: P. Novick. 1988. *That Noble Dream*, New York and Cambridge: Cambridge University Press. The question remains of whether the results of this study also belong to the 'dream' or whether they have any validity.

157. Droysen: *Historik*, 65–283, 399–406. In the original version, Droysen assumes that representation (*Apodeixis*) belongs to research, while later he treats representation as its own theme (*Topik*) in metahistory.

158. E. Bernheim. 1908. *Lehrbuch der Historischen Methode und der Geschichtsphilosophie*, Leipzig.

159. As for example in art history: K. Badt. 1971. *Eine Wissenschaftslehre der Kunstgeschichte*, Cologne: Dumont; N. Schneider. 1986. 'Kunst und Gesellschaft', in H. Belting et al. (eds), *Kunstgeschichte: Eine Einführung*, Berlin: Reimer, 244–263. Or in Archaeology: M.K.H. Eggert. 2006. *Archäologie: Grundzüge einer Historischen Kulturwissenschaft*, Tübingen: Francke.

160. The following wording goes back to the section '*Regulative der Forschung*' (regulating research) in the text on '*Historische Methode*', which I wrote with Friedrich Jaeger (in Rüsen, *Historische Orientierung*, 116–129). For a much more detailed presentation of the methodical operations in historical research, see *Grundzüge* II, 87–147.

161. As for example in M. Howell and W. Prevenier. 2004. *Werkstatt des Historikers*, Cologne: Böhlau.

162. To this end, the essay by Hans Medick has become a classic: H. Medick. 1984. '"Missionare im Ruderboot"? Ethnologische Erkenntnisweisen als Herausforderung an die Sozialgeschichte', *Geschichte und Gesellschaft* 10, 295–319.

163. See, e.g., Seth, 'Reason or Reasoning? Clio or Siva?', 85–101.

164. As for example in Goertz, *Unsichere Geschichte*; also idem, 'Was können wir von der Vergangenheit wissen? Paul Valéry und die Konstruktivität der Geschichte heute', 692–706; cf. also idem. 2007. 'Geschichte: Erfahrung und Wissenschaft', in idem, *Geschichte: Ein Grundkurs*, 3rd ed., Reinbek: Rowohlt, 19–47.

165. See J. Rüsen. 2003. 'Was ist Geschichte? Versuch einer Synthese', in idem, *Kann Gestern besser werden?*, Berlin: Kadmos, 134 ff. ('History: Overview', in N.J. Smelser and P.B. Baltes (eds), *International Encyclopedia of the Social & Behavioral Sciences*. Amsterdam: Elsevier, 2001.)

166. E.g., A. Feder. 1921. *Lehrbuch der historischen* Methodik, 2nd ed., Regensburg: Kösel & Pustet; W. Bauer. 1927. *Einführung in das Studium der* Geschichte, 2nd ed., Tübingen: Mohr.

167. For the latter see L.L. Cavalli-Sforza. 2000. *Genes, Peoples, and Languages*, New York: North Point Press.

168. The consequences deriving from this inner relationship of methods in historical research cannot be explored here any further. See my ideas on '*substantielle Operationen*' (substantial operations) in historical research (*Grundzüge* II, 117 ff.). Here a more exact analysis of the unity existing between hermeneutics and analytics is lacking. The determinant behind this unity is the philosophy of history in the systematic relationship of its three dimensions (see this volume, 77sqq.).

169. See also this volume, 16sqq.

170. For example, Jean Bodin's *Methodus ad facilem historiarum cognitionem* from 1566. J. Bodin. 1966. *Method for the Easy Comprehension of History*, New York: Octagon Books.

171. Theory of science speaks of 'covering laws'. With their help, information derived from research attains an explanatory character.

172. The difference between interpretation and representation, and the singularity of the latter, is keenly analysed by F. Ankersmit. 2012. *Meaning, Truth, and Reference in Historical Representation*, Ithaca, NY: Cornell University Press.

173. This means examining the question of whether what has been reported could even have taken place according to our contemporary state of knowledge.

CHAPTER 6

Topics

How We Write History

-----

1. The Waywardness of Writing

Writing history is a peculiar process in the formation of historical meaning. This is not only clear in the varying ways that metahistory deals with it as subject matter, but also in the work of historians on a daily basis. The results of research must be obtained before they can be written down. This does not mean that all the information must be collected before it can be turned into a text. The opposite is true. The process of gathering information is only completed and considered finished by the author after he or she has formulated the writing to follow. This act of formulation is part of a process of cognition that differs from the methodical development of historical knowledge from the evidence of the past. Through the act of writing something happens to the research results that goes beyond what happens during interpretation.

Writing and Thinking   Writing does not appear to be different from thinking. It is the continuation of thinking through other (than purely cognitive) means. Conversely, we cannot say that research merely delivers the raw materials for the formation of historical knowledge and that they only take shape in representation. Ultimately, one of the most important roles of interpretation is explaining the temporal course of events in the human world. And explanation itself is a (logical) form. But this does not cover the full extent of the distinct way of thinking that makes the human past

-----

Notes for this section begin on page 165.

recognizable in the present. Thinking extends into the formulation and representation and finds closure only in this process. At the same time, the act of formulating history is influenced by considerations and mental practices that are not purely cognitive. This means that the historical meaning of the past is determined by elements and dimensions of meaningfulness that lie within and beyond the framework of conceptual and explanatory thinking.

It is worth taking a closer look at this duality of cognitive and non-cognitive elements and factors. Leopold von Ranke formulated this precisely in the following: 'History is distinguished from all other sciences in that it is also an art. History is a science in collecting, finding, penetrating; it is an art because it recreates and portrays that which it has found and recognized. Other sciences are satisfied simply with recording what has been found; history requires the ability to recreate.'[174] Collecting, finding and penetrating are the three methodical operations of historical research: heuristics, criticism and interpretation. However, this does not sufficiently describe the specifically historical character of the past as history.

'The ability to recreate' means the capacity of the human mind to bring the past into the present, a capacity that cannot only be achieved through thinking. To do this we need art. Ranke did not bother to contrast art with science. He simply considered it to be a given and not worthy of further analysis. The expertise of historians depends on the scientificity of their work: 'Art rests on itself; its existence proves its validity; science, on the other hand, must be totally worked out to its very concept and must be clear to its core.'[175] This attitude is typical for a metahistory that primarily deals with the scientificity of historical thinking. This scientificity has to overcome a tradition of reflecting on history and historical thinking in which rhetoric is the dominant argumentative form. The field of modern historical scholarship has made a distinct anti-rhetorical turn. Again, Ranke phrased this markedly in his classic work on source criticism in early modern historiography. He explains: 'Naked truth without all the ornament and fuss; basic research over the particulars; the rest for God; no inventive fiction, none whatsoever, no fantasy or pipe dream.'[176]

This realistic turn to a research-based analysis of historical evidence has never completely lost sight of the particularity of historical writing. But the push towards historical method meant that the focus on this particularity became blurry. In more recent developments in metahistory, it is the other way around. Non-cognitive procedures in the formation of historical meaning, which are a conspicuous part of historical writing, have become the focus, while the cognitive side of historical thinking has faded away.

The critical question of a theory of writing history would then be how we can do justice to both: to the *cognitive achievements* that historical thinking gains when it is based on research, and *the aesthetic form and rhetorical effect* with which historical thinking brings the past into the present.

Literary Narration   We need to consider the relevant phenomena that give historical writing its particular place in the theory of historical scholarship. This is where *the practice of narrating histories* and its structures come in. We must distinguish the particularity of historiography and differentiate it from many other narrative practices. These differentiations must of course be made in respect of the literary art of narration. Literature influences the culturally dominant criteria for 'good' narration – if not sets them. These criteria are always already a part of historiography as formal principles against which historiography is judged. Essentially we use the principles of literary scholarship to analyse and understand historiography as a specific way of narrating history. Literary narrative as an artistic performance – or fiction – is often silently assumed to be 'essentially the only "proper" form of narrative'.[177] Historiography is always at risk of being perceived merely as a special case and not an independent modus of narrative. We need to give historiographical narrative its proper due as an act that originates from the functional need for historical orientation in the daily lives of human beings, and give it its traditional place in the narrative culture.

The Limits of Fiction   Therefore, we should not make the fictional difference between literature and reality the benchmark for judging historiographical narrative. Rather, we should identify the integration of fictional imagination into the relationship between historical thinking and experience. Narrative as a mental process that enables us to deal with contingency should not be understood as basically and primarily fictional. On the contrary, an abundance of everyday narrative serves to mediate and articulate our experiences. The imaginative production of fictional worlds through narrative is just as much a special case as the historiographical production of a past world in our present consciousness. The differences and similarities of both of these cases must be understood in terms of their anthropological basis.

This basis, as noted earlier, is the mental process of dealing with contingency.[178] By integrating contingent events into a narrative history we connect them to other events in such a way that they make sense and can be integrated into an interpreted horizon of experience in the present world. The events lose their extraordinary character with the human capacity for bringing them into an interpretive scope or plan. At the same time, they maintain their unique character as events and their distinctive temporal significance in the order of the world. Narrative subjects the peculiarity of events to an idea of ordered time. This idea gives meaning to all that occurs in the lives of human beings. The power of events that threaten to overwhelm us is tamed into a life-serving functional purpose. This is the cultural achievement, the power, of narrative.

2. Imagination, Fiction, Experience

Narrative changes the experience of singular events in the daily lives of human beings into a temporally ordered context of events. This can happen in many different ways. Everyday narrative integrates everyday events into an internal context of meaning. This involves the communicative inter- pretation and mediation of experiences. Obviously, the character of things may be altered to help deal with life's challenges. We cannot maintain the 'purity' of events when we narratively represent and mediate them, because we integrate them with other events. Ideas about how we think things should or could have been play a part in this. Nevertheless, this narration of events is 'empirical'. Their meaning is based on the fact that the narra- tor and the listener share the belief that what they tell each other actually happened.

The narrative interpretation of events draws on imaginative actualiza- tion. The representation produced by narrative does not simply reproduce the events but gives them the quality of meaning. This meaning is not simply assigned to them in a constructivist or retroactive manner. It develops out of a complex and dynamic context of meaning already present, and of meaning yet to come. In the pre-given context of meaningful daily life, the nar- rated events are not meaningless but rather are always already imbued with meaning. This does not mean that they do not then attain their 'true' his- torical meaning through narrative. They become 'true' in the sense that they become significant for practical life, that is, integrated and incorporated within the horizon of meaning in daily life. Narrative changes the event into a carrier of meaning in the entire context of events of daily life, as it is projected and incorporated into the narrative itself.[179]

The 'added' meaning that the narrated event gains through the act of narration goes beyond its factuality. This meaning is introduced through a context of events in which it makes sense to the narrator and the listener. This act of insertion that comes with representing an event or a thing is what we call imagination. It has the 'power' (imaginative power) to transcend the facts of a narrative. In the process of transcendence through narrative the meaning of an event becomes concise, accessible and communicable. Imagination does not just add meaning; it also leaves out what is experi- enced as meaningless and what might hinder, destroy or damage potential meanings. Finally, the narrative presentation of experience serves to repress experience. In the most radical instance, there is no narration but a powerful silence. Experience is excluded from the narrative context of our lives and gives it over to the power of unconscious destruction of meaning.

Fiction   Through the imaginative power of narration, factual events gain a meaningfulness that they did not (yet) have. In order to (artificially) distinguish between the acquired meaning of the narrative and the factuality of the events, we employ the *concept of fiction*. This can lead to a great misunderstanding and an obscuration of the issue – *fiction* as the opposite of fact; this only makes epistemological sense if we systematically exclude any elements that have to do with meaning from factual events. This would mean that all sense and meaning in narrative is fictional. However, such an understanding of fiction omits those elements of meaning that were in fact real during the events. In metahistory this radical separation of fact and fiction is often called 'positivist', which is based on the premise that the pure factuality of events in the human world basically has no meaning or sense. Both are only assigned later through the cultural formation of meaning (in this case: through narrative). But this kind of positivism is completely unrealistic. Events are not in themselves meaningless, but they appear meaningless if we consider them only as pure facts (which we never do in daily life). Factuality as the strict opposite of fiction is an abstract construct that does not address the phenomenology of the event, its lively reality. As such, this factuality is a fiction that depends on an abstraction of the essential elements of an event.

Fiction and Imagination   We should therefore only use the word fiction to describe those features of a narrative that are gained through narration. The features that accumulate through the participation or involvement of the narrator (and indirectly, the listener) are 'fictive'. This accumulation of features brings the narrative into the horizon of meaning that basically localizes the narrative, or better, that the narrative in effect creates. Imagination is not a reproduction, but rather a translation, a transformation, in which the event is processed through interpretation, loses its empirical quality and gains its meaning.

Narrative is never simply a reproduction of events – strictly speaking, it cannot be – since the event can never be narrated in its entirety. It always involves some sort of fictionalization. The imagination uses fictionalization to fit the event into the horizon of meaning that narrative initiates or actualizes. Since narrative is a communicative act that relies on experience, it transcends the experience to connect it to other experiences in an interpretive context. With and in this context we achieve the orientation necessary for human beings to live their daily lives.

The concept of fiction can only acquire specific meaning when it articulates this transcendence over all experience: everything that is imagined but has not happened yet serves to interpret the event or situation in question. Art turns transcendence into its own modus operandi. It imagines a world that is possible rather than experienced. It reveals qualities in the narrated events that do not exist in reality but that still have particular meaning for people.

When you turn such a narrative into the paradigm of all narration and discuss writing history in this context – which many literary narrative theories tend to do[180] – you make a category mistake. This independence of imaginative transcendence removes the reference to experience that is constitutive of historical thinking. In order for us to understand historiographical narrative, we must use the original, fundamental and trimmed-down concept of narrative. Its aim is the interpretive mediation of events as they happened in the horizon of human life and the way in which these events are (and must be) interpreted.

Historical Narration   Historical narration is not concerned with events that happen (or have happened) in an unbroken temporal continuity with the present, but rather with events that carry the special feature of a meaningful past. The past contains a potential for meaning in its temporal distance from the present that we must deal with in its own way in order to form meaning (through historical narration).

Such narration – like all narration – is achieved through the human power of imagination. With this power, the narrated event becomes vivid in the communicative context of narrative. It draws on the imagination's ability to form meaning. A further factor comes into play here. Since the fact that it happened in the past is closely connected to the meaning of the event, the narration brings the past of the event into the present. Historical narration, therefore, distinguishes itself by making the past reappear. This is what Ranke meant when he wrote about the 'power of recreation'.

3. Orders of Historiographical Representation: The Range of Possibilities

There are many different kinds of historical representations. This is all the more true when we consider historical change and the intercultural expressions of historical representation. The analytical concepts discussed thus far (except for the aspects of argumentative discursive concepts) apply to the writing of history in general. They do not address the complexity involved here. They demarcate the field of historiography in terms of cultural orientation but do not help us to discern the complexity or diversity in the field. This complexity poses a particular problem for a theory of historical studies: how can we clarify this complexity as well as emphasize the particular way in which we distinguish the scholarly character of historical studies and the writing of history?

We can use the following strategies for this.

Historization (1) We can proceed historically and characterize the development of historiography from its beginnings to the present in terms of its origins. We could start such an origin story with the aforementioned features[181] of (modern) historiography (especially the genetic forming of meaning and its scholarly component). To establish the scholarly quality of historical representation, we need to emphasize the dominant perspectives on validity. However, in applying an organizational concept, there is a danger of measuring the history writing of the past against the standards of the present. This robs historical representation of its own uniqueness as a cultural phenomenon of its own time and leads to a loss of historical insight. Nevertheless, the insight into the inner rationality of historical narrative over the course of time and in diverse cultures is a cognitive gain. It serves as an inner historicization of the methodical rationality of historical scholarship. Historians today attempt to maintain present standards for scholarly historiography while at the same time considering the relative nature of cognition depending on the specifics of time and place. They do this without undermining the validity claim of the developed methodical standards (which happens when an emphasis on the 'Western character' of modern history writing is used to relativize its validity).

In the historical perspective, the changes in writing history over time could be seen and described as a gain and a loss. The writing of history gains rationality in a complex way that does not fit into a straightforward concept of progress. At the same time, we cannot reject that the (self-)assertion of modern historical thinking in the field of historical culture contains an underlying notion of development. We can see this in a plausible way: if we take up the concepts of a material philosophy of history that we discussed earlier,[182] we see a reference to a fundamentally anthropological fact: for better or worse, all human beings must refer to their experience of the past and demand validity claims to create an orientation in their daily lives. Scholarship can identify in itself the same anthropological tendency, thus ascribing to itself a universalistic element of historical orientation. With such an argument we could contest the popular dismissal of methodical standards in the humanities as an ideological agent of Western dominance over non-Western cultures. (This disdain for methodical standards implies a universalism, due to which the West is characterized as particular and therefore as ideological.)

Philosophy of History (2) We can also use three forms of philosophy of history (material, formal and functional) as an analytical framework for historiography.[183]

(2a) Writing history can be organized according to *historical concepts*: in this case, we make a fundamental distinction between universal history and particular histories and then make further subdivisions. *Universal history* can be divided into world history, global history or universal histories of specific elements of human life, such as culture, work, authority, gender and so on. *Particular histories* can be differentiated according to a vast range of separate subjects, like tribes, ethnic groups, kingdoms, religions, nations, territories, regions, local structures and so on.

(2b) Historiography can also be organized according to the historical-philosophical notion of the *cognitive form*. This can lead to many different forms of representation: analytical, chronological, tabular, catechetical, narrative, essayistic, documental (e.g., source editions) and so on. Here we must also mention non-narrative, that is, descriptive forms (such as, for example, Jacob Burckhardt's work 'Die Kultur der Renaissance in Italien') in order to clarify that the narrative character of historical thinking is more than just a form of representation. This list also includes specifically scholarly forms of representation: scholarly articles, reviews, research reports, source publications, theoretical and methodological texts, monographs on specific topics, comprehensive presentations, edited volumes or anthologies, essays and so on.

The scholarly character of these works is not just determined by their external form but also represented in the narrative mode. The distinction between a closed and an open narrative form or an authorial and personal narrative style is of fundamental importance here.[184] This analysis of historical representation could prove especially fruitful for intercultural analysis. Depending on the cultural context, varying representative forms are valued differently. For example, with Confucius' compiling of the 'Spring and Autumn Annals', Chinese historical thinking establishes a paradigm of historical representation that differs from the pronounced narrative style of classical historiographical representations from antiquity on a culturally typological level.[185] There are of course annals in the Western tradition as well, but they do not have the same level of authority in creating temporal orientation as is the case within the framework of Confucianism. Cultural comparisons that draw upon historiographical theory are unfortunately still in the early (promising) stages of development.

(2c) In the context of practical philosophy of history or pragmatics of historical thinking, the diversity in the writing of history can be organized according to its *life-serving purpose*. This concerns the proximity to or distance from practical interests, how interests are realized in cognitive forms, achieving orientation through distancing, integrating viewpoints in a representation as an alternative to the pretense of writing the one, true history, and more. The *distinction between claims of scientificity and ideological function* is of particular interest for metahistory. Criteria of rationality must be balanced against criteria of relevance. Academic historiography, with its supposed lack of practical relevance, must prove its practical significance (while appearing open to criticism). In terms of practical relevance or irrelevance, we can imagine a spectrum that emphasizes not the contrasts but rather the varying forms and degrees behind the inner relationship between the practical and the academic – and how they are mediated. With this spectrum we can develop analytically illuminating distinctions between *types of historiographies*. Their variety can be seen as a functional differentiation in historical culture.[186]

Scientificity   (3) We can also systematically organize historiography around formal scholarly principles. With reference to the scholarly qualities of the field, we can discover and elaborate on some very striking external features. Surprisingly, this rarely happens in theoretical research of modern historiography. The footnote, for example, has never found the same recognition as an integral element of academic narrative as it has (and continues to have) in the training of professional historians.[187] Instead, narratology has insisted on dispersing the academic form of historical narrative in its analytical framework.[188] The entire inner context in which academic historiography and its established discursive forms of research (such as source criticism) appear is consistently dismissed, even though historiographic works cannot be understood without this context. The literary concept of intertextuality is not sufficient. Clearly, historiography always refers to other historiographies, but at the same time it refers to archival work, excavations and documentations that may be formed through narrative representation but that are not written as narrative.

We have already referred to *scholarly narrative forms*. On a theoretical level these forms can be characterized and analysed as inner discursiveness of historical narrative. In other words, we must look for the 'inner footnote' in the *ductus* of historical representation. This shifts the focus to the *language of the historian*. With respect to academic presentations we must focus on the conceptual terminology of the historian and distinguish it from metaphor (which historians of course always and necessarily employ). Avoiding the use of conceptual language for the sake of clear and easily understandable metaphors appears to increase the vividness and conviction of the historical representation, but at the same time it does not appeal to the thoughtfulness, the reflectiveness or the critical capacities of the audience.

The aesthetics of reception has shown that a possible and hoped-for reception (partly) determines the way in which a text is written. In this respect, the scholarly quality of historical writing lies in the meaningfulness of a narratively constructed past in a form that is not necessarily easy to grasp but that allows the reader to participate in the creation of meaning.

This does not necessarily mean that the receptive capacity of historiographical texts is reduced. The opposite is true. If, for example, historiography were based more on a multi-perspective process, then the allure of the text would increase. The reader must position him or herself among the divergent perspectives presented. (Is there an equivalent of the multitude of perspectives that Günter Grass offers in his novel *Crabwalk* in the historiography of contemporary history?[189]) This complexity is not only compatible with all the standards of academic rationality. Rather, these standards are required to explicate the generational mark of historical interpretations and thereby reveal the historical place and time of a given historiography. Multiperspectivism does not belong to the virtues of academic historiography, although it has proven to be an indispensable formal principle of historical representation in history education (that is, when we want to actualize historical experience in the learning process).

4. Typology of Historical Narrative I: Droysen, Nietzsche, White

Typology is the most important classification scheme for the field of historiography. It condenses the diverse forms of historiographical presentations into a few fundamental forms, bundling the characteristic features in such a way that they cover the unity and diversity of the entire field of historiography. A typology depends on the points of view that the types are based on: they have to synthesize particular elements into a fundamental form that can clearly delineate areas of historiographical representation. Together, the areas must cover all possible forms of historical representation. The principles of forming historical meaning that underlie all of its various (substantial, formal and functional) aspects are critical for the definition of these areas. These formal principles are relevant for historical narrative. They are conceived of as principles, as something fundamental and constitutive, as something that defines the entire spectrum of phenomena and makes them transparent and understandable.

In the following I will single out three typologies that have had a special impact on thinking about the writing of history. Johann Gustav Droysen, Friedrich Nietzsche and Hayden White have all analysed historical writing on a typological level in different ways. (We could even speak of three types of historiographical typologies.) I will characterize each one briefly and then offer one of my own.

a) Johann Gustav Droysen

Droysen differentiates between *investigative, narrative, didactic* and *discursive* representations of history.[190] The first and last are bound to the enquiring character of historical thinking. The first describes the cognitive process from heuristics to interpretation and forms historiography as a research report. The last is dedicated to one specific research problem and presents historiography as part of a professional discussion. The *narrative* representation brings the results of research together into a historical process. It expands the research by synthesizing its results and allows acquired historical knowledge to enter into a representational form that follows the course of time. The third, *didactic* representation encompasses the full extent of historical details and individual developments and presents a comprehensive concept for the course of time. It offers a comprehensive history in which all the separate parts have their meaning and significance. The material philosophy of history transforms historical representation into a *great narrative*.

The Role of Research and Unified Meaning   This typology connects the research aspect of historical thinking with the broadest conceptual framework of historical interpretation so that the various historical representations, from detailed accounts to general histories, become anchored in this framework. The particular importance of the relationship between research and writing history on the one hand, and on the other meaning generated by a general concept for the movement of time for historiography is evident. Droysen's typology is firmly rooted in modern historical thinking, with its cognitive validity claims and its theoretical figuration in the form of a comprehensive conception of the temporality of all human ways of life. This temporality is recognized as the basic characteristic of the cultural nature of human beings in all its diverse manifestations and changes over time.

It is worth nothing that this typology is based on the idea that the temporal process in the human world is fundamentally meaningful. Historical meaning does not unfold into a typology of fundamentally different forms, concepts or ideas. Droysen's typology merely reveals various strategies of representation in the field between methodical processes of establishing historical knowledge and the comprehensive concepts of time that make this knowledge specifically historical.

b) Friedrich Nietzsche

Nietzsche's typology[191] is based on a fundamental critique of the academic presentation of historical thinking. This criticism refers to the life-serving purpose or function (*Lebensdienlichkeit*), which must be recognized on a fundamental level in historical thinking. Nietzsche does not perceive this purpose or function as being found within historical studies, and confronts it with possible life-serving forms (or types) of historical representation. The *monumental* form inspires human beings with a great paradigmatic organization of the temporal human world. The *antiquarian* directs human interest in the past towards its many relics to challenge the interpretive powers of human beings as they appropriate the past in concrete detail. It reveals the unique possibilities that human beings have in forming the world and comprehending human culture. Finally, the *critical* form or type resists the preset order of the human world and makes room for new formations. The present gains future perspectives when we distance ourselves from the prescriptive elements from the past.

Limits   This typology is purely functionalistic and determined by the fact that modern historical thinking has no place in it: neither its logic of a fundamental temporalization of the human world nor its practical importance for the articulation of historical identity (in Nietzsche's time, this identity was mainly national) are dealt with or recognized as legitimate phenomena.[192] It is a typology in the sense that it suggests important historically and culturally significant distinctions, though at the same time disregarding an entire realm of historical thinking and its particular relevance in the context of modernity.

c) Hayden White

White's typology[193] is entirely based on the literary and linguistic character of historical writing. He develops a highly complex analytical framework for historiographical texts and thereby contributes enormously to the understanding of the writing of history as a core phenomenon in historical culture and theory. These poetics outline a refined poetic analysis of historical representation. It explains the meaning of historiographical texts and the diverse forms of connecting temporal happenings as narrative units (histories), and systematically presents the linguistic tools of narrative synthesis that underlie these connections. Historiographical narratives are constituted by their *explicative* character.

   White's thesis is based on the idea that histories are understood through their narrative character. Their explanatory mode is typologically revealed as a narrative mode. The explanatory power of historiography lies in the way it organizes its narrative according to literary patterns (*emplotment*). Furthermore, historiography explains through *formal argumentation* as well as through *ideological implication*. All three explanatory modes can be revealed on the typological level: the *literary* narrative style in the form of romance, tragedy, comedy and satire; *formal* argumentation as formist (emphasizing the particularities of events), as mechanist (working with causal principles), organicist (working with the notion of historic wholes) and contextualist (explaining events through their contexts). The *ideological* direction of explicative narrative is typologically revealed as anarchistic, radical, conservative or liberal.

On the functional level of narrative syntheses, rhetorical *tropes* determine the comprehensive meaning of historical narratives. As locutions, they linguistically prefigure the specifically historical character of the presented information and constitute the realm of historical interpretation. White considers four of such tropes to be critical for the various historiographic concepts of meaning: *metaphor, metonymy, synecdoche* and *irony*.

The Poetics of Historiography   These criteria of meaning are linguistic forms, or figures of speech, that give factual information its meaning: the *metaphorical* form refers one happening to another; the *metonymic* form refers a part to a whole; the *synecdochic* form refers an element of an event to the event as a whole; and the *ironic* form reflects on the assumed meaning.

White developed his typology as an analytical tool for the (Western) historiography of the nineteenth century, and as such made no claim for its universal validity. However, the typology comes very close to it: the narrative forms are not limited to a specific period of time, and neither are the formal argumentation or the ideological implications. Only the typological unfolding of these three modes of narrative explanation is limited to the nineteenth century in the Western world. However, these modes could be expanded to include other areas of experience. Tropes as figures of speech are universal.

Due to its analytic diversity and systematic complexity, White's poetics of historiography actually offers a methodical tool for examining historiographical forms. It can be used to describe specific manifestations of historiography in precise terms. It does, however, have one major flaw: the tropes do lend the events a meaning that goes beyond a purely factual level. But beyond that, they say nothing about how this linguistic reference deals with the specifically temporal context of past events, which is what historical thinking is about. The tropes are not specifically historical. This does not mean that they are not significant for the literary formation of historical representation. They just do not determine or characterize what distinguishes historiography from literary narratives. The reference to evidence and experience that is constitutive of historical thinking cannot be discerned through tropes in the linguistic formation of meaning. The specifically historical disappears in these poetics of historiography.

5. Typology of Historical Narrative II: Classifying the Formation of Historical Meaning into Four Types

In the following, I will develop a typology that is different from the previous ones.[194] It primarily differs from the Droysen typology in the sense that it does not focus on the research aspect of historiography. Moreover, it aims to characterize historical thinking itself rather than just modern historical thinking in its forms of representation. It circumvents the specifics emphasized by Droysen. It does, however, claim to develop the decisive criteria of representation that were part of the forms defined by Droysen.

Similar to Nietzsche's typology, my approach will also advance a functional distinction that claims to cover the entire range of historical thinking. However, I will not ignore its specifically modern feature but typologically present it in its particularity. These two typologies only have one type in common: the critical narrative. Nietzsche is also not primarily concerned with the forms of representation but with the fundamental and determining criteria for meaning that characterize the cognitive and the aesthetic-rhetorical dimension.

In contrast to Hayden White, I do not concentrate on the literary form of historical writing. I focus on systematically identifying those aspects that determine the interpretation of the human past as something specifically historical. I will develop these aspects as narrative types that can be found as formative principles in every historical representation. As mentioned earlier, these four types together cover the entire spectrum of historical representation of the past. Their diversity and their systematic interrelationship should define this spectrum. At the same time, and most importantly, they should help us to investigate all the possibilities for keeping the past alive or bringing it to life in the cultural orientations of the present. They systematically organize these possibilities. They form a typology that lies somewhere above general and fundamental historical meaning and below a conceptuality that must be developed to characterize concrete forms of representation (which Droysen did to some extent).

I work with *ideal types*, single logical components of meaning in history. They are deliberately abstracted from concrete phenomena and developed as 'pure' narrative structures of meaning. As logical components of the formation of historical meaning they are effective and verifiable in the concrete forms of historical culture. However, they seldom or never appear clearly or distinctly in concrete phenomena. The practical applicability of this typology lies in helping us to recognize and discern specific structures of meaning and their guiding principles for historiographic forms, and even for historical thinking in general. Its analytical value lies in its clear logical difference and in the scope of possibilities in its complex system of relationships.

Four Types of Historical Narrative   There are four possible ways to actualize the human past in the structural meaning of narrative for the sake of cultural orientation. They are *traditional*, *exemplary*, *genetic* and *critical* types of narrative.

A *traditional* narrative represents history in such a way that its primary meaning (that grants meaning and practical orientation) is presented as staying the same over time. Historical meaning here attains the form of an inner-temporal eternity: that which perseveres in the world appears in the shifting winds of time as perpetual meaning, an enduring concept in the ordering of human life. This inner meaningfulness of the human world is historically tied to the origins of life and universal order. These origins are not just the beginnings. They are the first and the last of all things throughout time. As sources of meaning in the daily lives of human beings, they underlie the distinction between then and now, between today and tomorrow. They combine these dimensions in a continuous and consistent concept of meaning.

Historical representations that follow this logic serve to confirm and reinforce this continuity. The dominant notion of the course of time in *traditional narrative* is that of continuity through the ages. These traditional histories are mediated through a produced and continuously reproduced agreement about the validity of universal origins. They can form identities by prompting us to accept the predefined world orders. They form human subjectivity in a mimetic way. These histories are relatively lacking in evidence since they refer to information that is relevant for the human community and disregard all other possible ways of forming the human way of life. All the changes that might occur in the temporal happenings of the human world are fixed in the permanence of one normative and paradigmatic event (in the pre-historic time, if you will).[195]

The Exemplary Formation of Meaning   In contrast, the second type, or the *exemplary* formation of meaning, opens up the horizon of experience in historical thinking and turns all its accumulated experience and evidence into a pillar for orientation in the present. Our view of history becomes open to everything that happened in the human past. Historical thinking approaches these events as a plethora of events or situations that, despite their spatial and temporal diversity, present concrete cases that demonstrate the *general rules of action with timeless validity*. Here, time is not immobilized in an inner-temporal fashion of eternity through historical meaning but instead has a timeless quality. History functions as a teacher of life (*historia vitae magistra*).[196] The contingent nature of time in actual historical events gains its meaning because these events reveal principles that drive action that spans across all differences in time. In the framework of this exemplary form of narrative, historical thinking unfolds its power of judgement: history teaches us to generate general principles regarding the human organization of life from separate, isolated or individual events or things. We can apply these principles to concrete cases of actual events occurring around us in real time.[197] In the words of Jacob Burckhardt, we can say that history does not make us smart for another time, but wise forever.[198] History facilitates our agency. As a form of communication, it occurs as a form of societal discourse in which the power of human judgement can develop and be tested. Historical identity is defined as *Regelkompetenz* – the competence to understand or work within rules or regularities. In the perspective of timelessly valid rules of engagement, the events of the past span across space and time into diverse processes and activities. In a metaphorical sense, we could say that *exemplary narrative spatializes time as meaning* in the case of a historical event that leaves the narrowness of a predefined universal order and grounds human action in general rules through reflexive insights.

As with the traditional narrative, the exemplary version immobilizes time, but it does so on a higher level of *timeless and accepted insights*.

The Genetic Formation of Meaning   The logic behind the *genetic narrative* is based on the idea that *change creates or makes meaning*. The events of the past in their temporal movement no longer appear within the confines of fixed practical principles of human ways of life. Rather they establish a dynamic process of transformation that takes the edge off change in the human world and shakes off the eternal value of accepted norms. Instead, change itself becomes the proper human way of life. The past appears as change that relates our own way of life to previous ones in such a way that change can be seen as an opportunity. The relevant notion of the course of time here is one of *development*, in which the change occurring in human lives is understood as a dynamic process by which they gain continuity. Genetic historical narratives are based on the idea that differences in time that orientate human action towards future situations have not been predefined by the past. The relationship between experience of the past and our expectations for the future is asymmetrical.

Within the framework of such a dynamic formation of historical meaning, human identity has the opportunity to individualize. To temporalize means to change in a meaningful way. It strips human subjectivity of the foundation of an identity anchored in normative precepts. Change burdens us with the responsibility of forming our own identities (making us neurotic) but also allows us to be creative in dealing with ourselves in a process of self-education (*Bildung*). Formally, self-education is temporalized subjectivity. This form is filled with the contents of historical experience in the sense that it concerns development as the formation of meaning from historical happenings or situations. The classic case of this kind of individualization on the level of collective identity that is tied to the historical concept of a temporalized humanity is the modern concept of the nation.

In summary, we can say that *time is temporalized as meaning*.

Critical Formation of Meaning   The fourth type of historical narrative is the *critical narrative*. It has a special status. It only asserts itself as a negation of the

Table 6.1 Schema: the four types of forming of historical meaning.

Types of Forming Meaning	Reference to the Past	Concept for the Passing of Time	Form of Communication	Self-education (*Bildung*) as Identity	Time as Meaning
Traditional	Origins of universal order and ways of life	Continuity through change	Consensus	Adopting predefined universal orders ('imitation')	Time is immortalized as meaning
Exemplary	Events and situations that demonstrate general rules of action	Timeless validity of rules of action that encompass temporally different ways of life	Normative argumentation	Competence in the rules of action and behaviour ('intelligence')	Time is spatialized as meaning
Genetic	Changes introduced into one's own way of life by others	Developments in which ways of life change in order to remain dynamic	Discursive references between differing points of view and perspectives	Individualization ('*Bildung*')	Time is temporalized as meaning
Critical	Events that challenge the dominant historical orientation	Disruptions, discontinuity, contradictions	Consciously held position and dissociation from other positions	Rejection of prescribed ways of life (self-will)	Time is assessable as meaning

other three narratives. Critical narrative destroys and deconstructs culturally predetermined *traditional, exemplary* and *genetic* interpretive patterns. It
focuses on events that challenge established historical orientations. Its relevant notion of the passing of time is one of *disruption, discontinuity* and
contradiction. A critical narrative of history is about deviating points of view,
differentiation, rebuttals and the transformative power of 'no'. In the historical pragmatism of forming identity, critical narrative develops self-will.
The structure of meaning of a history is characterized through (negative)
interpretation or assessment of the past.

What Does this Typology Achieve?   This typology is anthropologically fundamental and universal. In theory, all types can be found in all time periods
and all cultural contexts. The possibilities for forming meaning through historical thinking that logically follow from these four types are found at all
levels, from daily life to the lofty realm of highly intricate historical culture.
In view of the empirical findings addressed here, it is obvious that the types
hardly ever appear as pure, separate entities but always together in varying
constellations.

   These constellations can be outlined and empirically tested as perspectives of broad historical change. On a purely logical level, the *traditional* narrative shapes the conditions for the other types of narrative. The *exemplary*
transcends the realm of experience established by the *traditional* type, while
the *genetic* brings time into the timeless dimension of meaning as articulated
in the *exemplary* type. *Critical narrative* is manifest in the execution of changing from one type to another (when it does not remain within the horizon of
meaning in one of the other three and only offers alternatives, for example,
making one tradition replaceable by another). In a very schematic form, this
typology can be constructed as an outline for a universal history of the formation of historical meaning.[199] Due to its abstract nature, we can trace this
schematic concept across all cultures. The narratives in this schema do not
simply replace each other. Instead, the forms overlap and inform one another
in many ways.

6. Typology of Historical Narrative III: Meaning and Rationality

Within the framework of a metahistory, a typology of historical narrative
must also address the *specifically scholarly character of historical cognition*.[200] This
is done by identifying and emphasizing the scholarly principles in the narrative types. The scholarly character of historical narrative does not develop a
type of its own but rather lies in a specific combination of types. Scientific

rationality is rooted in the living world and requires a particular development that leads to its own particular articulation of the types.

Whether separately or combined in a wide variety of constellations, the narrative types become specifically scientific when they take on research-based *argumentative features* in historical representation. Historiography is then determined by *terminology, research dynamics* and *intersubjective verifiability*. These scientific attributes give the types a certain contour or shape.

History as academic discipline is a phenomenon of modernity. Modern historical thinking is determined by the *genetic* formation of meaning. However, not all genetic narrative forms are modern or specifically scientific. Moreover, the other types do not disappear within a historiography dominated by genetic thinking. Rather, they combine with the genetic form in such a way that the particular character of the genetic form allows the others to take on a modern form.

The critical narrative type is also closely related to science. All historical thinking that wants to be academic must adhere to the rule that all its claims about events of the past must be empirically verifiable. A narrative about historical events must make fundamentally clear if it is reliably substantiated, what can still be doubted and what the possible alternatives are. This can disrupt the narrative ductus, but its coherence cannot take precedence over the certainty of historical knowledge. Criticism then determines form.

As essential as critical thinking is to science, the *critical narrative type* is hardly scientific. Its negation of predefined historical orientations is normatively determined. The narrated historical events serve to make these norms empirically plausible by invalidating the norms negated by them with contradictory historical evidence. Scholarly thinking would even be critical of the normative standards that are brought into this. It rejects the one-sided selection of historical evidence by referring to relativizing experiences. Scholarly thinking has to take into account even evidence which contradicts the intended negation. In preserving an inner cohesiveness, events or occurrences from the past are judged by whether their normative relevance or meaning might refute or destabilize historical orientations, making them basically relative in the full context. Critical historical representations are notorious for their bias. They challenge the methodical principle of historical thinking that the representation of past occurrences must incorporate its different meanings for different people. It is of course impossible to reach strict neutrality. The perspectivist structure of historical representations influences the interpretation of the past as effected by the varying mindsets of those involved. If only one of many perspectives is considered in a historical representation, it is an example of bias that needs critical assessment.

Tradition and Science   Traditional narrative in its scholarly form is critically assessed according to the empirical plausibility of the information behind the tradition. This dissolves the mythical character of the emphasized origins sustained throughout the course of historical change. Within this concept of time we recognize the importance of maintaining a clear continuity in the prescribed lifeways in change over time. But the traditional narrative cannot avoid placing temporal changes in the context of a continuity that is set by tradition. Due to its functional role of providing orientation, it is not enough for this kind of narrative simply to motivate its addressees into a mimetic behaviour of the ways of life that are described. On a functional level, this would take away the critical and reflexive approach to the past that is also constitutive of scholarly thinking as historiography.

The argumentative character of a specifically scientific or academic narrative does not take away *the eternal quality of traditionally conceived historical meaning*, but *alters its temporal character*. Scholarly historical thinking is modern historical thinking, which is determined by the genetic narrative type. Inner-temporal continuity takes on an anthropological dimension. Historiography cannot exclude temporal change from traditional concepts of order in human life, but must reveal change as part of these concepts. Only then can the resistance to change inherent in traditional concepts be made plausible. The dynamic of genesis must be understood as part of the traditional order. This is possible due to the fact that historical events occur in an anthropological context, revealing normative factors of being human which endure through all temporal change.

Exemplary Thinking and Scholarship   The *exemplary* historical narrative is defined by the role that judgement plays in providing a detached reflection that is critical for scientific thinking. A change in form occurs due to the specific nature of science. This happens when we derive a general regularity in human behaviour out of the plethora of historical events from the past. Modern scholarly historical thinking is committed to the following hermeneutic rule: we do not do justice to the human past if we do not interpret events and ways if life in the context of the self-understanding of suffering and acting human beings. This does not dismiss the trans-temporal validity of an exemplary understanding of history when viewing human behaviour – something that would make all of history appear relative – but empowers the temporal component. In exemplary representation, the general behavioural structures of human beings are systematically related to their contexts. The commonality of mediated structures and normative mindsets is recognized for being abstract, and can be concretized through references to time that go beyond specific happenings (concepts of development).

Genetic historical thinking provides a scientific quality to historical representations through the narrative framework, or plot structure. This does not mean that all genetically organized representations are specifically scientific. This is only the case when their form makes argumentative use of human understanding in the presentation of the events of the past and their significance for the present.

Scholarship and Multiformity Since all types are systematically related to each other, together they mediate effective modifications in the forming of meaning through the rationality of scholarly thinking and provide a highly complex fabric of possible strategies of historical narrative. Scientificity certainly does not mean an impoverishment of historiography. On the contrary, it increases its inner complexity. In historical theory, this complexity does not lie so much in the claim of regulating historical representations but in the impulse to deal with this complexity. This occurs in literary forms, which are not dictated by historical theory. A metahistory that presents itself as a normative poetics of historiography would violate the principle of argumentative openness. The multiformity of historiography must be substantiated and not limited to normative precepts. The exact literary form and method used to realize the inner rationality of the formation of historical meaning cannot be dictated, only suggested. Literature contains a multitude of examples of how narrative is open to argumentative reasoning. But it does not contain the reasoning structure that scholarly history has developed. Here lies a chance for professional historiography to take such literary forms and transform them into historical narratives and rhetorically and aesthetically validate its understanding rather than lose it.

Notes

174. Ranke, *The Theory and Practice of History*, 33 (idem, *Vorlesungseinleitungen*, 72 f.).

175. Ranke, *The Theory and Practice of History*, 34 (idem, *Vorlesungseinleitungen*, 73).

176. L. von Ranke. 1874. *Zur Kritik neuerer Geschichtsschreiber*, 2nd ed., *Sämtliche Werke*, vol. 34, Leipzig: Duncker & Humblot 24.

177. S. Jaeger. 2002. 'Erzähltheorie und Geschichtswissenschaft', in V. Nünning and A. Nünning (eds), *Erzähltheorie transgenerisch, intermedial, interdisziplinär*, Trier: WVT (Wissenschaftlicher Verlag Trier), 237–263, quote, 250, relating to ideas from Fludernik (M. Fludernik. 1996. *Towards a 'Natural' Narratology*, London: Routledge; see also M. Fludernik. 2001. 'New Wine in Old Bottles? Voice, Focalization and New Writing', *New Literary History* 32, 619–638). For the logic behind fictional historical narrative see the exceptionally nuanced discussion in Ansgar Nünning. 1995. *Von historischer Fiktion zu historiographischer Metafiktion*. Vol. 1: *Theorie, Typologie und Poetik des historischen Romans*; vol. 2: *Erscheinungsformen und Entwicklungstendenzen des historischen Romans in England seit 1850*, Trier: WVT (Wissenschaftlicher Verlag Trier).

178. See also this volume, 14sqq.

179. Just how significant narrated events can be is best illustrated through how traumatic events or occurrences can be kept from being narrated in the present, effectively falling silent. This is similar in the case of experiences concerning the overpowering of meaning.

180. Cf. the edited volume by D. Fulda and S.S. Tschopp (eds). 2002. *Literatur und Geschichte*, Berlin: de Gruyter.

181. See this volume, 97sqq.

182. See this volume, 80sqq.

183. See this volume, 77sqq.

184. See also F.K. Stanzel. 1979. *Theorie des Erzählens*, Göttingen: Vandenhoeck & Ruprecht; E. Lämmert. 1955. *Bauformen des Erzählens*, Stuttgart: Metzler.

185. See also the exceptional studies of Fritz-Heiner Mutschler. 1997. 'Vergleichende Beobachtungen zur griechisch-römischen und altchinesischen Geschichtsschreibung', *Saeculum* 48, 213–253; also idem. 2007. 'Sima Qian and His Western Colleagues: On Possible Categories of Description', *History and Theory* 46, 194–200.

186. See also this volume, 177sqq.

187. See (at times with humour) P. Rieß, S. Fisch and P. Strohschneider. 1995. *Prolegomena zu einer Theorie der Fußnote*, Münster: Lit; A. Grafton. 1998. *Die tragischen Ursprünge der deutschen Fußnote (The footnote)*, Munich: Deutscher Taschenbuchverlag.

188. The fact that footnotes can be used as a literary tool in fictional narratives does not reduce their importance in checking fictional exuberance through the referencing of experience in historiography. One is able to distinguish between authentic source referencing in footnotes and their fictional use.

189. G. Grass. 2002. *Im Krebsgang: Eine Novelle*, 3rd ed., Göttingen: Steidl. (*Crabwalk*, Orlando; Austin; New York; San Diego; Toronto; London: Harcourt, 2002.)

190. Droysen, *Historik*, 217–283.

191. Nietzsche, 'Vom Nutzen und Nachteil der Historie für das Leben', 243–334, esp. 258–270. ('On the Uses and Disadvantages of History for Life', 83–100.)

192. Nietzsche's fundamentally anti-modernist attitude kept him from perceiving the political function of historiography in his own time, and more precisely its all too relevant importance in the forming of national identity. This attitude also kept him from reflecting on the political importance of his own concept of life-serving purpose in history as one that is purely aesthetic. Aesthetics functions as political substitute: something that until today has remained a highly problematic element in historical culture.

193. White, *Metahistory*, introduction.

194. I have presented this typology on many occasions, but in most detail (though since then in a more developed form) in J. Rüsen. 2012. 'Die vier Typen des historischen Erzählens', in idem, *Zeit und Sinn: Strategien historischen Denkens*, 2nd ed., Frankfurt am Main: Humanities Online, 148–217.

195. Klaus E. Müller described this concept of meaning as 'being without time', introducing then a universally historical paradigm in the traditional forming of meaning. K.E. Müller. 2003. 'Sein ohne Zeit', in J. Rüsen (ed.), *Zeit deuten: Perspektiven, Epochen, Paradigmen*. Bielefeld: Transcript, 82–110.

196. Cicero, *De oratore* II, 36.

197. This way of thinking defines the concept of history in the quote from Shakespeare; see this volume, 14sq. For a more recent example: 'History shows that political factors can be important when trying to determine if a sovereign borrower – normally the State – is capable or willing to meet its obligations.' Interview with Moritz Krämer, responsible for evaluating states at Standard & Poor, '"Wir sind apolitisch". Ein Analyst erklärt sich: Warum die Rating-Agentur Standard & Poor's an Italiens Reformfähigkeit zweifelt' ('We Are Apolitical'. An

Analyst Explains Why the Rating Agency Standard & Poor Doubt the Reform Capabilities of Italy), in *Die Zeit* 22.9.2011, no. 39, 4.

198. J. Burckhardt. 1949. *Weltgeschichtliche Betrachtungen: Historisch-kritische Gesamtausgabe,* compiled and edited by R. Stadelmann. Pfullingen: Neske, 31. Alternative edition: *Gesamtausgabe,* vol. 7: *Weltgeschichtliche Betrachtungen,* edited by A. Oeri and E. Dürr. Stuttgart: Deutsche Verlagsanstalt, 1929, 7. (*Force and Freedom: Reflections on History,* New York: Pantheon Books, 1943, 86.)

199. Rüsen, 'Die vier Typen des historischen Erzählens', 200 ff.

200. For more detail see Rüsen, 'Die vier Typen des historischen Erzählens', 219–230.

CHAPTER 7

The Basis of Historical Culture

1. Historical Culture as Societal Practice

The theme of 'historical culture' brings metahistory back to its origins: historical thinking in the daily lives of human beings. We began here in order to reveal how historical thinking develops from our needs for orientation, and also to characterize its particularity. We then turned to the possible ways to fulfil these needs, and discussed the specific way in which academic study approaches the human past. We now return to the sphere of practical human living to consider the function of the cognitively acquired and narratively presented historical knowledge. By looking at the practical side of applied historical knowledge we can better discern and describe the role that history plays as a scholarly discipline.

Historical culture is the *product of our historical consciousness and its power to form meaning*. It contains the cultural practice of the orientation of human action and suffering in time. Historical culture localizes human beings in the temporal changes under which they suffer and in which they must act and that are in turn (partly) determined and enforced by human action and suffering. The orientation achieved by historical culture is our way of interpreting our experience with the human past so that we can understand the present as well as develop strategies for the future.

This definition of historical culture (once again) expands the reflective metahistory perspective beyond the disciplinary confines of historical studies. If we were to dismiss this expanding reach, then historical culture would primarily be the business of a specialized group of people, namely professional historians. Without challenging their pre-eminent role, we must always consider the societal context in which history takes place. It is within this context that historical thinking is professionalized in the first place. And it is here where, however mediated, historical thinking impacts us on a practical level. We therefore need to discern and (through examples) describe historical thinking within the depth and scope of the cultural orientation of human life.

Who owns history? Some have quite rightly asked this question.[201] Considering the fundamental meaning of human time consciousness and historical consciousness for all people and their ways of life, there is only one answer: everyone. In other words, 'every man his own historian'.[202] This universal belonging poses a significant problem in historical theory, because in reality there are many different allegiances, modes of belonging and identities. It is manifest in the diversity of and the contradiction and tension between a multitude of perspectives on the past. In this diversity, historical scholarship must find its place and purpose. We can only determine this place and purpose if we consider the limitations as well as the achievements of scholarship.

Who Owns History?   It is easy to say that if history belongs to everyone, then historical thinking is democratic. We can take it away from the privileged, specially appointed few (who are often close to those in power) and make it the subject of public (and of course private) discourse. But in this wide scope historical thinking begins to blur into different expressions and becomes an instrument for pursuing different interests. Democratic intentions can lead to a kind of anarchy that, at best, could be called confusing. We cannot assume that all the ways in which human beings deal with history are equal. However, they all claim to be valid, so their legitimacy can be debated with arguments and counterarguments. This is where the field of historical scholarship comes into play again, because it has developed the most elaborate form of justification for working with the past. As a special societal institution it offers a powerful and rational response to questions of perspective and legitimacy. It does this through conceptually mediated experience, critically examining experience, argumentation and advancing knowledge through research. These activities place it above any interest-motivated opinion, maintaining a fundamental level of critical distance. But because of this, historical scholarship also risks being too far removed from its own rootedness in the practical lives of historians. Historians might see their own perspectives as the most valid ones and dismiss all others as irrelevant. But they do not always succumb to this danger.

In the following I want to determine the cultural function of historical scholarship within the framework of a general discussion about the capacities of historical consciousness in the human ways of life. To do this we must first focus on the meaning and cultural significance of *memory* and its expression in historical consciousness.

2. Historical Consciousness and Memory

Cultural orientation in the daily lives of human beings through interpretation of the past is a creative human activity. It constantly relates to prior interpretations that are entrenched in the circumstances of our lives. This continuation of the past in the present in the need to come to terms with the past is obvious. It is especially obvious when we consider the fundamental capacity of human consciousness to deal with time. This human awareness of time is a complex interaction between memory and expectation.[203] The temporal span of our lives stretches between our experience of the past and our expectations for the future. Memory constitutes one direction of the timeline between past and future. It is intrinsically tied to the other direction that points to the future, but is more often than not treated as a separate phenomenon in the memory discourse of the humanities.

We can argue over whether historical culture is a phenomenon of memory or not. Depending on how far we stretch the reach of memory, it can extend across all of historical culture or only encompass the past in the consciousness of a single human being. But even in the narrower understanding of personal and individual memory, the past cannot be contained within the lifespan of a single human being. What we remember always includes events that we did not personally experience. These become effective conditioning factors behind our own experiences or a past that has been relayed to us by others and has grown into our concept of time. The category of memory is fundamentally significant for the understanding of human historical consciousness. It shows that the particular activities of human historical consciousness form the groundwork from which the past emerges, brought to life through interpretation.

Memory[204] has received a great deal of attention in the last thirty years. In reflecting on the meaning of history in the lives of human beings, this discourse is clearly different from the common understanding of history from the previous century. Until recently, history was primarily assumed to be the result of professional historical thinking. This involved conceptualizing what happened in the human past through specific procedures of the human mind. History appeared as something distant and fundamentally different from the present and the active processes in human culture.

Memory, on the other hand, was seen as an active part of culture. This shifted the focus to phenomena that until recently did not belong to the subject matter of historical thinking. This concerned phenomena in which the past has become an integral part of contemporary culture. The past no longer appeared as something that could only be conceptualized in the present through the procedures of professional historical thinking. It was identified as already manifest in the present. Historical knowledge and its professional articulation were strictly distinguished from things that already contained their own historical relevance, making them culturally significant. As 'places of memory' they were assigned a place in real life. And making the past tangible in the present, these phenomena were described as something very special.[205] A living and influential quality was given to the past that would have been lost or overlooked if it had been made into the material for academic research and historiography.

Memory Versus History   Memory and history could thus be pitted against each other. The allure of memory lay in the prior liveliness of the past in the cultural processes that shape our practical orientation in daily life. In contrast, the relevance of history for the presence lost plausibility. While memory made or kept the past alive in the present, history made the past distant through temporal difference. It gave the past a quality of otherness, of different from the present. Historical culture, though, has acquired a new profile as memory culture. It is seen and defined as an outcome of the past coming alive in the present on the practical level of cultural orientation. Scholarship itself (which has made memory culture a topic of discussion) has not been assigned a 'place of memory'. At best, it functions as a tour guide in its own territory. Implicitly, this means it has the status of an alienated and alienating consciousness. The enthusiasm with which academic study has engaged with 'places of memory' reveals that historical scholarship was searching for ways to reinvigorate its cultural attractiveness. It happily turned to the cultural institutions that contained abundant sources of living memory.

This explains the new importance of memory for understanding the capacities of human historical consciousness and the forms and effects of historical culture. This is best illustrated by focusing on the (ideal-typical) differences between memory and academic historical understanding. We find the following contrasts.

Memory appears as original and history as derived and construed. Memory is subjective, and history is the reflection of research results of historical studies through intersubjective validity that is often (and mistakenly) called 'objective'. Memory is emotionally powerful and lively; history on the other hand is '*von des Gedankens Blässe angekränkelt*' ('*sicklied o'er with the pale cast of thought'*). Memories can therefore be a greater motivation for action than history. Memory is spontaneous, impulsive and untethered. In contrast, history is tethered, at least in view of the methodological procedures of historical knowledge. We could even say that history appears to be subject to the forces of rational thinking and discursive argument. Memory follows aesthetic and rhetorical criteria when it is articulated and communicated on an intersubjective level. In contrast, historical thinking is bound by perspectives of empirical and explanatory validity. Memory is coherent on a formal (imaginative) level, without having to adhere to the dictate of accuracy. For history, this accuracy is imperative. Memory distinguishes itself through a play of forces in the human mind, guided by desire, with the contents of experience, while history must follow the constraints of argumentative rationality, particularly a strict control over experience.

Relationships　An insight into these capabilities and capacities of memory gives thinking about history a new perspective on the mental powers in and with which the past becomes part of the living world of human beings and even belongs to the vital powers of culture itself. The assumed contrast between memory and history is effective on a discursive level but not so convincing on the level of historical theory. (This would also have become clear had the memory discourse realized the older discussion on the topic of historical consciousness.[206]) 'History' uses the same criteria of meaning that preserve the past in memory and give it meaning. On a purely logical level, a sharp division between memory and history cannot be sustained. This does not mean that the two are joined together and cannot be distinguished. The discourse on historical consciousness has made clear that the phenomenon of 'history' is characterized primarily through cognitive processes that do not necessarily have anything to do with memory. The non-cognitive forces of

Table 7.1 Schema showing the ideal-typological contrast of memory versus history.

Memory	History
Original	Derived, fabricated
Subjective	Objective
Strong on emotion	Strong on rationality
Motivates action	Motivationally weak
Spontaneous, impulsive, untethered	Controlled by reason
Criteria of aesthetic and rhetorical acceptability	Criteria of empirical and explanatory validity
Formally coherent	Accurate
Guided by desire, play of the imagination	Constrained by argumentative rationality

memory are absent from this discourse. In contrast, the memory discourse has hardly touched on the future-oriented aspect of historical consciousness or the cognitive elements of a rational critique. However, it is important to note that memory and history use the same sources of cultural formation of meaning in asserting the past as a powerful element in cultural orientation.

But what does it mean to say that memory is the source of the cultural effect of historical thinking? Fundamentally, the issue is the introduction of the past into the horizon of meaning in the present. This easy-to-grasp plausibility is evident in *personal* memory. However, as argued by Maurice Halbwachs,[207] every personal memory exists in social contexts that contain references to the past. The past is manifest in the present in these references. This is especially true when it comes to the strong convictions we hold regarding inclusion and exclusion in the normative structuring of our own lives. Every memory has a social dimension and every personal memory is influenced by a social memory.

With *social* memory and the effects of collective memory, the temporal scope of memory expands considerably. The lifespan of the individual human being is sustainably transcended. Memory reaches into the depths of the distant past in order to assure a promising future.

The Human Dimension   We should add, at least tentatively, a third dimension (along with the personal and the social), to define memory as a source of historical meaning: the human dimension. Every individual represents humanity in general in a socially mediated form and every memory contains perspectives that can be seen as anthropologically fundamental and universal.[208] What that means specifically cannot easily be simplified to a common denominator. Elements that form humanity and characteristics of being human that have their own cultural manifestations all belong to the forms of social memory that remain alive. For example, stories about the origins of humanity belong to the old traditional master narratives articulated by social remembering. The following point can be seen as a *topos* of a socially manifested historical orientation concerning humanity: we ascribe to ourselves and our own group a unique status in humanity, such as a higher degree of civilization or a particular relationship with the divine world, and thereby devalue others. By doing so we distinguish ourselves from other communities, which are then portrayed as barbarian and as stereotypes in the everyday anthropology of normal life.[209]

The Significance of the Unconscious   Particular dimensions of memory develop and we need to keep them theoretically separate when we want to distinguish degrees of consciousness. The power of the past over the present in the realms of the unconscious has been known since before the relevant work in psychoanalysis.[210] The human dimension of the unconscious is especially interesting here. Sigmund Freud approached this dimension with the help of anthropology and religious criticism.[211] Above all, with his analytical psychology of the collective unconscious, C.G. Jung was able to uncover an inner human dimension in the unconscious formation of meaning that reveals its own historical dynamic.[212] Historical theory has largely ignored these unconscious levels in the formation of historical meaning, although there is no doubt about the power of unconscious drives in human behaviour.

Three Stages of Memory Memory is not only articulated in these three intimately entwined dimensions. It also asserts itself in various forms of its communicative force, its defining power in historical culture. We can distinguish three stages in the manifestation of memory in historical culture: a *communicative*, a *social* and a *cultural* stage.[213]

With this distinction we can identify and analyse the developmental processes in which culturally and historically relevant forms of memory are formed. In terms of ideal-typical steps, the first step of such a developmental process is an open communication about various and complex forms and contents of memory and remembering (*communicative memory*). It then further develops to a second step, in which certain forms and contents get a higher social relevance. This *social* memory represents those elements of present past that communities refer to in order to be seen as a community and to dissociate from others. Social memory can now develop further into *cultural memory*, which forms a framework for integrating different social memories and excluding other memories.[214] The three steps can be seen as increasing sustainability or resistance to change. With this ideal-typical distinction of different inner concepts of time in the functions of remembering, historical culture gains its own temporal signature or configuration.

Two Modes of Remembering Another fundamental distinction is important for the mental practice and operation of memory. Remembering can be *spontaneous and responsive*, or the opposite: it can be *purposeful and constructive*. In the first case, the past pushes into the present, challenging the mental powers of human consciousness to cope, interpret and work through it. In this mode of remembering, the past enters into the present, challenges and imposes. It 'invades'. In this case, meaning is received, or maybe better: it is experienced or perceived. The potential for meaning in human consciousness can be called upon in various ways. In extreme cases, it is an overpowering of meaning, as in religious or aesthetic experiences, or a destruction of meaning due to a traumatic experience.[215]

The other mode represents the opposite: this is when what has remained present in the memory of the past is dealt with in a purposeful way. Meaning is formed intentionally. This is where histories are told and interpretations negotiated; here the great narratives are formed. Traditions are adapted to new living conditions; powerful normative standards of memory can be changed, rejected or replaced with others. From communicative remembering comes memory that is social and cultural. This is where all mental practices occur that bring the remembered past back to life. Above all, this is where the sting of malady or affliction is pulled from the past. Perpetrators can become victims; defeats can become victories. Guilt or responsibility can be dismissed and placed onto others, and so on. This is also where things are repressed, which carries over into the unconscious dimension of memory with a force that is hardly possible to control.

The spontaneous or 'invasive' memory pops up on a contingent level. It can suddenly descend upon us, often triggered by a sensory experience. It is essentially *receptive*. In contrast, intentional and constructive memory is *productive* and a result of its conscious formation. Spontaneous memory is articulated in literature as a reflection of lost innocence (at least when it employs the metaphor of childhood), of a lost origin or as a promise of an '*anderen Zustand*' (Musil's 'other condition'). In Kleist's essay on the marionette theatre,[216] he impressively describes the past as a present longing. This kind of memory provokes. We cling to it in the hope that it will bring happiness, and keep the memory alive. As productive intuition it demands elaboration, becoming an unexhausted source of meaning. As a source of terror, a traumatic destruction of meaning, it wants to be rejected, transformed or reversed. It provokes for the sake of relief from the conditions of life and the relief from expectations. In any case, it releases an impulse, producing mental activity. It evokes the *productive or constructive* mode of memory. We need to bring that promised happiness of the past into the present world in order to (reflexively) regain that lost innocence (the 'third stage' in Kleist's 'On the Marionette Theatre'). The overpowering of meaning is tempered by an attempt to channel or integrate it. The (traumatic) experience of the destruction of meaning is transfigured into the search for undamaged sources capable of producing potential meaning. With great mental effort, the depletion of meaning is transformed into gaining meaning.

In summary, we can compare and contrast the modes as follows: the *receptive* mode draws from the power of the unconscious; the *productive* mode counters it with the power of reason. The one is unprethinkable (preconscious) and the other is reflexive. Both types of memory are of course closely connected; you cannot imagine one without the other. Together they become what we could call the formation of cultural memory. They are both the impact and result of an activity.

Memory and history are not the same thing. But we cannot think of history without memory. On the other hand, memory without history is cut

off from the expansiveness within memory from which history develops. A
theory of historical culture needs to explicate the potential of memory since
it charges historical consciousness with the vitality of a past made present. At
the same time, however, the conscious processes that go beyond the reference to experience and turn memory into history should not be left out.
Only in this step can history to be culturally localized as science.

Historical consciousness as a mental place of historical culture is based
on memory, but is 'more historical' in terms of its complex reference to
time and especially its cognitive capacities and procedures. It is tied to the
productive character of memory. It expands these capacities through a systematic collection of historical experience and through a systematic application of thought-out interpretive patterns. In the developmental steps towards
a memory culture, historical consciousness acquires essential features for
establishing social and cultural remembrance. A master narrative is a good
example of the powers or achievements of historical culture. The collective
memory of a nation is not even conceivable without the achievements of a
national historiography (especially in the nineteenth century).

Historical Consciousness and Science   In view of the particular characteristics of
historical consciousness in the activities that constitute historical scholarship,
the cognitive elements of memory culture play a critical role. How does
this work? We can identify five processes and their respective features: (1)
their systematic development and improvement through research methods
and the discursive strategies of history writing lead to the manifestation of
the distinct cultural form of an academic discipline. This form or shape is
the result of a comprehensive and fundamental process of rationalization. In
this process, memory expands and intensifies into its own cognitive process.
(2) This process takes the past out of the living memory of the present and
transfers it to the ensemble of temporally distant events. It is objectified and
turned into a source of information that can methodically be made accessible. (3) In this objectified form, the past becomes the content of a cognitive
process. This process creates a lasting form of attaining knowledge through
research. (4) The separate bodies of knowledge develop independently of
their orientation purposes and become ends in themselves in the professionalism of history and the production of historical knowledge. (5) With this
new formation of historical knowledge comes a new formation of meaning.
Meaning is detached from the content itself and becomes part of a reflective
and interpretive process. The dynamic of the production of knowledge corresponds to a dynamic of changing interpretive perspectives and processes.

In this disciplinary form of a rationalized handling of the human past, historical consciousness loses its mental embedding in the timeframe of current
action and suffering. It avoids being used for practical purposes but certainly

does not lose its place in real life. It might have lost the often-invoked use-fulness it claimed and reflected upon in its historical development, but it has gained cognitive substance, and with that, cultural prestige. Claims for historical education are substantiated with reference to its usefulness in a framework of a purely instrumental and utilitarian way of thinking. Uselessness can make sense when there is an established culture in which knowledge for its own sake is considered valuable. In theory of memory, this removal of purpose in rational historical thinking is characterized by Aleida Assmann as '*Speichergedächtnis*' (stored memory).[217] Scholarly produced historical knowledge becomes an inventory that can supply elements of knowledge to serve cultural purposes. The self-serving purpose of cognition was originally the defining characteristic of one of the most important cognitive achievements of the human mind: metaphysics. With regard to memory culture, metaphysics has lost some of its shimmer. But if we ask what the meaning is of the knowledge that the memory discourse has revealed and still reveals, things look very different (that is, if we do not want to be subject to a performative self-contradiction in following a criterion based on liveliness).

3. Five Dimensions of Historical Culture

Like any other culture, historical culture as source and functional field of historical thinking is determined by a complex array of factors. Thinking, knowing, recognizing, judging, feeling, hoping, fearing and believing are some of these factors. How can we locate historical studies in this intricately woven fabric of historical culture? How can we clarify how historical scholarship influences and is influenced by this context? To do this we must consider the cognitive elements of the formation of historical meaning in relation to other distinct elements. Otherwise we cannot appreciate the

Table 7.2: Schema: historical consciousness and science.

Processes operating within historical consciousness	Results
The cognitive elements are systematically expanded and developed	History as discipline
The past becomes an object of research	Methodological handling of sources
Knowledge becomes a research process	Lasting form of acquiring knowledge
Areas of knowledge become independent	Knowledge as an end in itself
Meaning of knowledge is the result of reflection	Construction of perspectives

particularity and the cultural quality of historical scholarship. In view of the diverse character and transformative capacity of historical thinking, and especially with regard to the current challenge posed by different cultural traditions, it is important to address and explicate the mental factors that are essential for historical culture on an anthropological level.

Five Factors   Allowing for some generalization, we can distinguish five fundamental determining factors: (1) thinking, (2) feeling, (3) wanting, (4) judging and (5) believing. We can then distinguish five corresponding dimensions of historical culture, which can be analysed separately and in relation to each other. They include the (1) cognitive, (2) aesthetic, (3) political, (4) moral and (5) religious dimensions. This classification is ideal-typical and is based on exaggerated abstraction and sharp logical contrasts. It excludes other dimensions that by all rights could also be seen as primary and distinct and that also allow (to varying degrees) for generalization. An example of this is the ideological (although this could be considered a specific manifestation of the cognitive dimension) as well as the psychological dimension. The latter is particularly interesting because it deals with a dimension that historical theory has not yet researched extensively: the collective unconscious.[218]

The following analysis of the five dimensions and their formation and criteria for meaning is influenced by the current problems of historical culture in modern societies. The first three dimensions – the *cognitive*, *aesthetic* and *political* – are the most important for locating the institution of historical scholarship in historical culture. Today the particular nature and capacity of historical studies are only conceivable in the secular culture of a civil society. This gives the *religious* dimension a special status. Its historical significance and immense influence (in the pros and contras about the secular character of modern academic study) are undeniable. Also, the distinction between secular and religious is not so unambiguous as it would at first appear (e.g., as in Confucianism). As such, we cannot deny the religious dimension when we attempt to discern the setting and function of historical studies in the historical culture of a particular time. The same goes for the *moral* dimension. The notion of professionalism in historical scholarship includes a rejection of a moral evaluation of the past, even though these moral judgements play a big role in historical culture. At any level, the concept of being 'value-free' in historical scholarship does not mean that normative factors have no influence.

Five Dimensions   In the following we will be considering each of the five dimensions named above separately, and examining the criteria for meaning and their manifestation in the framework of cultural orientation in the daily lives of human beings. We will also discuss their systematic relationship to each other. We must pay particular attention to whether, or how, the different criteria for meaning in the cognitive, aesthetic, political, moral and religious dimensions converge in the differentiated unity of a specific cultural act.[219]

(1) The *cognitive* dimension of historical culture takes shape in the knowledge and cognition of the human past. Its defining criterion is *truth*, or the degree to which the statements made about the human past can be substantiated with empirical, theoretical and normative content. We cannot imagine historical culture without such cognitive claims of truth, not even when it has not yet produced a form of (modern) scientificity.

(2) The *aesthetic* dimension of historical culture concerns the perception of representations of the past (in various media). Traditionally, its defining criterion is '*beauty*'. This refers to a capacity of these representations to effectively address the mind and spirit of its audience so that the audience absorbs these representations and incorporates them in the framework of orientation in daily life. The quality of form depends on its coherence. Regarding the narrative character of all historical knowledge we can also speak of a *narrative coherence* in the form of representing historical knowledge or historical cognition. In its modern development, in the context of aesthetics existing within its own independent realm, the formative principle gains a special significance: it oscillates between the senses and rationality, in that it relates the compulsory elements of both areas (the pressures driving our physical or sensual nature and the empirical pressures of the mind and the normative demands of our rational or intellectual nature) to each other, so that their interplay can develop a free human subjectivity. We could also employ the Freudian distinction between the super-ego, ego and id.[220] In the Freudian context, the aesthetic dimension can be described as that place where the interplay between the super-ego and id occurs and constitutes (or at least should constitute) the ego. The aesthetic dimension opens up a chance for humanization through historical thinking that the other dimensions do not share.

(3) The *political* dimension of historical culture has to do with the role that historical thinking plays in the power struggles in which human beings have to relate to each other and themselves. According to Max Weber, power is the probability of obedience as a response to a command.[221] The ability to command and having to obey are two elementary forms of human life. They are mutually exclusive, but at the same time are necessarily mutually dependent. One is inconceivable without the other, and yet they demand very different attitudes. While the ability to command causes pleasure, having to obey is characterized by an innate resistance. Historical thinking is a cultural form in which this fractured social relationship is presented and understood as bearable in view of the past. Human coexistence relies on the condition

that those who command can expect that their commands will be obeyed. At the same time, those who obey must have reasons to obey. The legitimacy of relations of power and authority in which human beings must live determines the meaning of the political relationships and all ensuing struggles for power. The legitimacy makes them bearable and merges the subjectivity of those commanding and those obeying into a shared humanity. (Legitimacy humanizes power and authority.[222])

Historical thinking plays an essential role in this process of legitimation. It organizes the experience of the past, which is always an experience of (often inhumane) power and authority. It happens in such a way that legitimacy, and the need for legitimacy, represents the innate meaning of political action from the past, making the events of the past plausible and even obvious in the present. The legitimizing efforts that power relations must expend in order to persist are formidable. Without the temporal dimension of continuity, authority is vulnerable. Here lies one of the most important means of livelihood for the professional historian. This also pertains to historical scholarship as a provider of historical knowledge. (Without the need for historical legitimacy of modern states there would not be organized history education in schools.) There is also a firm political interest on the part of the authorities to know the activities of the historian.[223] In authoritarian power relations, historians are permanently suspected of endangering the legitimacy of power since they can present knowledge of inhumanity or alternative, more humane power relations in a particular political setting. On the other hand, in political systems in which exercising power and authority is dependent on an agreement among free subjects (citizens), historical thinking legitimizes human freedom. This is one of the most important political reasons why historical thinking in its scholarly form is necessary.

(4) In the *moral* dimension of historical culture we determine the value of past events according to the measure of social and moral norms of the present. The *defining criterion of meaning is the difference between good and evil.* Every actualization of the past by way of historical culture gains its meaning through interpretation according to this distinction. This holds true for historical thinking in general: its narrative shape is not at all conceivable without normative elements. These elements are inscribed into our knowledge of the past by way of perspective, through the standpoint taken by the subject of historical thinking in practical life. This standpoint is always determined by a reference to norms and value systems in the context of historical thinking.

In fact, there is a specifically historical ethic in the historical culture of the present. It depends on the criterion of meaning of historical responsibility.[224] With this criterion, the morality of historical thinking extends beyond an external consideration of historical events to an internal connection with these events. The moral of history is external when the values of the present are used to judge the events of the past. The judging subject of the present has an external relationship to the human beings of the past, their actions, their omissions, abuses and sufferings (as a judge relates to the defendant in a fair trial). This relationship can turn into an internal one. In that case, the person in the present feels responsible for what happened in the past.

Historical Responsibility   Historical responsibility is a widespread issue in today's world. However, the question of how we can be responsible for something that we did not do (or failed to do) ourselves cannot easily be answered. Thinking about responsibility brings us into an internal relationship with the events of the past. It extends the subjectivity of historical thinking into the subjectivity of the actors of the past (and their victims). Such an internal relationship determines the relationships across generations, between grandparents, parents, children and grandchildren. In such relationships, our own generation flows into the next and influences the formation of the next generation's mental dispositions. This trivial psychoanalytical point requires a decidedly historical-theoretical analysis. Such intergenerational relationships, or intergenerational subjectivity, knows no temporal limits (while psychoanalysis sets these limits every three generations). It concerns the temporal dimension of historical identity that extends beyond the lifespan of the individual subject and his or her social affiliations. The further our identity stretches back into the past, the more the future perspectives in our intended actions in the present and their underlying interpretations of the world open up.

Human beings in the present can then refer to the events of the past as if they themselves were actors in these events. It is this moral responsibility for the past that brings about an increased interest in the political handling of historical interpretations. For some time, identifying with the victim and not the perpetrator has been a way of dealing with morally reprehensible events of the past. While once people tended to identify with the victor, victimization has become a more powerful trend in the recent history of historical culture. We thereby equate our own historical identity with moral innocence, which strengthens this identity by drawing a clear line between ourselves and the descendants of the perpetrators.

(5) The *religious* dimension of historical culture develops from the depths of human subjectivity, in which it draws on a fundamental meaning of life. This meaning is religious when it is experienced, known, believed and lived as transcendent, as exceeding the mortality of the human subject and all its negative experiences, especially suffering and death.[225] The defining criterion here is human redemption, or deliverance from our own mortality. It becomes a dimension of historical thinking when this redemption, this

input of transcendence into the inner-worldly realm of creating and warranting meaning is understood as an actual event in life. Then, the historical figure of a saviour can become very important. But it is also possible that the temporal events of the human world are projected on a transparency of transcendent meaning from which it gains redeeming depth of meaning in its entirety. This can happen in various ways: history can be formed into an encompassing realm of meaning that is manifested in the occurrences of the world (eschatologically at its end or as *kairos* at varying times). Or this total meaning occurs as apocalyptic, as beyond worldly events, as negation of its lack of meaning. Historical meaning is always imbued with transcendence and thereby gains a spiritual quality. With this quality, the human mind transcends or circumvents inner-worldly or mundane meaning in order to be filled with complete and absolute meaning.

Dimensions Intertwined   The inner coherence of the five dimensions and their respective criteria for meaning are characterized by a tense relationship of contrasts and dependency. Tendencies to instrumentalize and efforts to find a balance define the inner dynamic of a complex network of relationships.

The various criteria for meaning are not fundamentally mutually exclusive. In some constellations they are even dependent on each other. But in practice, historical culture always comes down to asymmetric and hierarchical relationships. Historical cognition tends to view aesthetics as simply a means to articulate certain truth claims and reduce narrative coherence to successful argumentation.[226] In extreme cases, this attitude can (on the metatheoretical level) abandon historiography for the sake of a publication of sources. For example, Paul Fridolin Kehr (1860–1944) saw a critical publication of sources (*Quellenedition*) and not a historical presentation as the conclusion of the research process.[227] But even then, historical knowledge does not lose its narrative structure, much less its function of determining significance.

In respect to the political dimension, cognition is dominant when historical knowledge is used for political orientation, or even worse, when

Table 7.3 Schema: five dimensions of historical culture.

Dimension	Anthropological Basis	Defining Criterion for Meaning
Cognitive	Thinking	Truth
Aesthetic	Feeling	'Beauty'
Political	Wanting	Legitimacy
Moral	Judging	Good and evil
Religious	Believing	Redemption

political orientation is masked as cognitive form and becomes an ideology. The value-free ideal can blur the *moral* dimension. This does not mean that it loses its effect, but rather that it comes to bear in a way that is unnoticed. The *religious* dimension could be considered obsolete due to the secular character of modern thinking. This, however, would obscure a limit of historical knowledge. Some demands for meaning in the cultural framework of orientation in daily life cannot be fulfilled in a secular way but also cannot simply be left out of the cultural processes that form meaning.

The *aesthetic* dimension can engulf the *cognitive* one and fictionalize events of the past (e.g., the films of Hans-Jürgen Syberberg).[228] Historical knowledge then becomes a quarry from which pieces of history are mined to enhance 'images' of the past. Their coherency feigns a validity that cannot be obtained empirically or theoretically. The *political* dimension can dominate the *aesthetic* dimension in such a way that the latter becomes a tool for propaganda purposes. It can then bend the *cognitive* dimension to its will and easily turn the legitimacy of power into a perspective of interpretation.

The *moral* can incorporate the *cognitive* dimension to create ideology to defend political power claims and dissolve religious redemption into a hopeless inner-worldliness. The *religious* dimension can remove the boundary between belief and knowledge, limit knowledge for the sake of faith or burden it with an impossible redemptive function. It can dehumanize authority by theocratic means and downgrade morality to a coercion of salvation.

The Role of Scholarship　Of course, all of this affects historical scholarship. In cognitive self-disregard, it can present implicit political tendencies of historical interpretation as cognitively necessary without much ado and provide them with validity claims. Divergent tendencies and their perspectives are then qualified as objectively false (and one's own tendencies as established fact). Historical scholarship can misjudge the aesthetic significance of historical representation and regard copious footnoting as proof of greater rationality in historiography. We must remember that historiography itself has its own discursiveness because of the way it is formed (e.g., because of the multitude of perspectives and their dynamic relationship). This impacts on how receptive the audience of historiography is (not only in the area of literary consumption but also in the area of *Bildung* and education). Historical scholarship can conceal its moral implications and use its intersubjective validity claims to avoid having to reflect on meaning. Finally, historical scholarship can invoke its secular character and ignore the unique meaning of religion and thus unwittingly mistake cognitively suspect replacements for religion as conducive to knowledge (as in certain varieties of Marxism or the reception of Walter Benjamin).

Balance   How do we avoid these distortions, restrictions, exclusions and falsifications? The relationship between the five dimensions and their criteria for meaning must be defined on a theoretical and practical level in such a way that they validate each other. This kind of coherence opens up many possibilities for the development of historical culture and enables historical culture to more convincingly negotiate its specific function in the cultural orientation in the daily lives of human beings.

What does such coherence look like? To find out, we first need to clarify what constitutes the internal unity of the dimensions as a coherent construction of meaning. How do we make time liveable? The unifying element of the dimensions lies where human subjectivity looks for orientation in time through the mind's activity. External time (natural time and the constraints of events) must be transformed into internal time as a synthesis of interpreted experience and intentional expectation. With this the human (personal and social) self acquires its own time; the human self becomes a figuration of time. This time provides the criterion for meaning in which the dimensions of historical culture converge and through which they are constituted.

Integration through the Meaning of Time   Traditionally this criterion would be conceived of and lived as something religious. For a long time, religion was the authority on integration. The concept of the divine has merged cognitive truth ('I am the way and the truth and the life'[229]), formal coherence ('God is beautiful'[230]) and the legitimacy of power ('all authority in heaven and on earth has been given to me'[231]). Divine time gave history meaning. In the modern period it became necessary to transcend and relativize the religious criteria for meaning for the sake of secular circumstances. It is worth noting that these criteria have not been eliminated but rather have remained a force to be reckoned with. They have remained potent in different ways – in the implicit form of assumptions,[232] or in the explicit form of secular (pseudo-)religiosity (as in certain forms of nationalism, Marxism and racist ideologies).[233] The dissociation from religion has established a secular metaorder that 'civilizes' the religious and ties its validity to standards of humanity that comprise the spectrum of beliefs.[234] This secularization is a necessary prerequisite for the establishment of history as academic study.

The Human Being as Source of Meaning   Currently, under the auspices of cultural difference and intercultural communication, it stands to reason that we should derive the integral meaning of history out of the humanness of human beings. This basis is not actively created by human endeavour – this would be anthropocentric self-empowerment, a mode of authority with external legitimacy. This basis is already there in the naturally predetermined self, in that which we already are as human beings. We must form meaning from this basis. The defining criterion for meaning in modern culture is based on this self-reference. (Since this always means a transcendence of our natural predispositions, we can say that transcendence is a fundamental part of the relationship that we have with ourselves. As such, secular meaning and religious meaning are not mutually exclusive.) It is the capacity of the self to form meaning from the cultural quality of being human that unites the different dimensions of historical culture and asserts itself as time of the human self.

Of course, this cultural meaning occurs in various and shifting forms. When we consider this pluralism as a manifestation of one and the same cultural capacity of human beings, made apparent from its anthropological basis, then we have found the sought-after basic principle that is the fundamental and comprehensive basis of historical culture. Immanuel Kant described it thus: each and every human being is not just a means to the ends of others, but is a purpose in itself. This being a purpose in itself represents human dignity.[235] This dignity must be granted to all human beings on the most fundamental level – regardless of their way of life.[236] It gives human life meaning. (It was the task of the philosophy of history to reveal this quality of meaning in the lives of human beings from within its specific historical dimension.) The concept of dignity synthesizes the different dimensions of historical culture into one single, comprehensively human dimension.

The different dimensions of historical culture must be interconnected in such a way that the humaneness of human beings is fully appreciated. How does this happen? The different criteria for meaning must be recognized (1) in relative autonomy and (2) in mutual recognition and integration in the interpretive achievement of historical consciousness. They must thereby (3) develop and assert their orientating function in social reality. (4) In this productive context, the criteria for meaning at the same time check their own reach and (5) criticize any instrumentalizing overreach in other areas. These five qualifications arrange the five dimensions into a complex and coherent entity.

The New Media   The new forms of media in the world today represent a special problem in the framework of a theory of historical culture and a particular challenge for historical scholarship as a cognitively distinct formation of historical meaning. Currently, human beings are experiencing and realizing a cultural transformation that can only be compared to the shift from an oral to a written culture. This change transforms the dominance of the written word (that of course carries the work of historical scholarship and defines its logic) into one of the new media. Writing, of course, does not disappear, but its capacity as bearer of meaning and as symbolizing form develops in a new way: it is constantly understood in terms of and as dependent on the new forms of articulation and new practices of imaginative meaning. New rules for cognition and aesthetics come with that. Historical culture is now shaped by an overarching simultaneity of everything that is historically different in the new media. It is characterized by an overwhelming immediacy of sensorial viewing, an excessive amount of information that bombards us without cognitive ordering or temporally differentiated meaning. In the long term, this may well have an enormous impact on what we consider history and how historical understanding is asserted as cultural orientation.

Metahistory, due to its strong ties to the written word, has reacted slowly to the new situation. The significance of figurative sources for historical knowledge has been recognized and implemented in methodological processes. But the question of an inner rationality of the imaginative actualization of the past as a chance for an academic use of the new forms of media is rarely raised. However we may answer this question, the point remains that the scholarly principle of knowledge-based and conceptually realized argumentation has yet to prove its sustainability in the current structural transformation of cultural communication.

4. Orientation and Criticism: The Purpose of Historical Studies

The field of historical studies has a specific function in historical culture: critique. 'Criticism' means to examine the plausibility of all knowledge about the human past that is used for the purpose of orientation. This is done so that the knowledge prevails in the struggle between opposing interests and can be successfully used as argumentation.

All ways of orientation in historical culture incorporate knowledge about the past. These ways may have developed differently. But orientation in the daily lives of human beings in the temporal changes of their circumstances and conditions must always contain cognitive elements. The present cannot be understood without knowledge about how things used to be and how things came to be. Historical scholarship generates practical orientation of time from the cognitive dimension. It is and remains rooted in the living world, however distant broad areas of research and research practices might seem. Of course, not all the fruits of historical research are involved in the practices of cultural orientation in time. Research is limited to providing knowledge that can (also) have practical value. However, the scholars do not decide its practical value; the practical needs of life in society do.

The Life-serving Purpose of Knowledge Scholarship serves life by providing this practical value with its claims of validity. To put this more ambitiously: its practical and cultural purpose is its ability to deliver useful knowledge for the purposes of orientation that holds up against critical examination its empirical data, theoretical consistency, explanatory power and its normative implications and their intentions. At the same time, it must refute claims about the past that either do not stand up to empirical examination or whose explanatory embedment within broad temporal contexts linked with other facts or events do not meet the standards of historical explanation.[237] This purpose creates a tense relationship between historical scholarship and politics.[238] It confronts power with truth. This confrontation does not represent an external relationship between cognition and authority. The relationship is inherent in the entanglement of both dimensions to daily human life, where historical thinking plays its particular part. It is therefore clear that, due to its underlying critical form, this life-serving purpose of historical cognition represents a constant threat for historical studies to become corrupted or subjected to repressive measures.

Historical scholarship validates historical culture due to the particularity of its thinking rather than its production of useful knowledge. Its critical function comes into play when it is about more than just individual facts; it pertains to the processes and forms of cultural orientation, to historical thinking itself. On this level, it is not just about testing the validity of claims about what, when, where, how and why things happened in the past. This critical function concerns something more fundamental that goes to the very heart of the cultural character of historical orientation.

Scholarship as Critique of Ideology This critical function is one of the most important practical functions of academic thinking in historical culture: its fundamentally critical relation to all forms of ideology. By ideology I mean a world view that provides orientation on a cognitive basis. It can appear in interpretations that obscure rather than clarify real-life situations. By obscuring reality, it serves to protect the interests of those who stand to gain from it. In this sense, ideology is a false consciousness of the reality of human life in societal relationships. Historical scholarship counters ideology and its attempts to obscure reality by offering a knowledge-based critical analysis. Historical knowledge can introduce facts and interpretations of the real conditions of daily life that are obscured by ideology with the intention of creating an appearance of reality for its own purposes. (Of course this ideological obscuring can also occur in the name of academic study. Marxism called historical studies 'bourgeois', though this is simply an example of false labelling.)

Another aspect of ideology does not have the element of false consciousness. Instead, it presents the formal structure of a comprehensive interpretation of the world, often fortified with claims of scientificity. This encompasses the entire framework of practical life. It produces cognitively constituted world views. These views promise a reliable orientation in the experiences of life. As a rule, such world views are 'closed' and organized according to easily comprehensible criteria of meaning. Today, these ideologies readily claim to be 'holistic' and ignore or cover up the heterogeneity and internal contradictions of the temporal constitution of human lives. They take the defiance of 'otherness' out of historical experience and shut out any view of the contingency of temporal change in our lives. Ideologies are resistant to experience, are incapable of learning and do not accept alternative modes of thinking or interpretive perspectives. Their most critical deficit is their limitation of the possibilities for discursive flexibility and change in the spectrum of meaning of historical thinking. Ideologies codify history and let us believe that there is such a thing as a reliable orientation that we can only have if we accept rigid dogmatism and lack of knowledge.

Ideologies shackle the dynamic of cultural orientations to a fixed concept of meaning. Historical scholarship, on the other hand, can offer historical culture a discursive dynamic in which experiences are dealt with and do not necessarily have to be rejected. It asserts the wealth of historical experiences of otherness and opens up possibilities for human action and suffering to accept alternative possibilities in articulating chances in human life (even if only by reflecting the denial or refusal of these chances).

The Practical Reason of Scholarship   This life-serving critique is based on *principles of practical reason*. They determine historical thinking in its cognitive and poetic-rhetorical form. They are perspectives of a humanity that enables the interpretation of historical experience and advances the search for orientation. They assert the methodically tamed and discursively stimulated subjectivity of the historian. This approach is what puts (or should put) the historian a step ahead of his or her contemporaries.

The Humanism of Scholarship   The practical reason that defines scholarship can be applied to the empirical, theoretical, normative and narrative criteria for meaning of historical thinking. It makes the cognitive achievements of scholarly historical thinking necessary and powerful in historical culture. If we take 'humanism' to mean a way of thinking that is systematically committed to this practical reason,[239] then we can see the role of historical scholarship in the cultural life of a given time as a form of institutionalized humanism. Its critical function in historical culture can be pinpointed as such: it always and fundamentally serves to criticize the inhumanity of human beings. It operates wherever there is a struggle for balance between contradictory principles and strengths in the framework of cultural orientation.

As mentioned earlier, Immanuel Kant gave us a modern standard of humanity: every human being always and fundamentally is more than just the means to the ends of others. Rather, the human being has a purpose in and of him or herself and must be seen as such. In this quality of self-serving purpose lies the dignity of human beings.[240]

Finally, the rationality of historical thinking in its scholarly form is based on the anthropological foundation of this dignity.[241] Human beings have the capacity to employ reason without the instruction of others (to use Kantian terms) and to communicate with other human beings at the same time. They, too, use their reasoning capabilities when they interpret historical experience in the temporal framework of daily life.

Historical culture is always moved by power struggles. Historical scholarship introduces practical reasoning from historical knowledge into these struggles. It confronts the struggle for control over the interpretation of history with a perspective that legitimizes thinking that is based on self-purpose and therefore supports the dignity of human beings. This can occur in different ways. However, it is and remains a decisive fact that historical knowledge used for orientation always carries a trace of humanity in it: this includes its failure in the face of inhumanity but also its success in the promise of a more humane future.

5. The Role of Value Freedom

So far, the considerations on the role of historical scholarship in the historical culture of its time seem to contradict an essential concept of historical scholarship: value-freedom. For a long time, this concept has defined the self-understanding of historical scholarship. Scholarly historical thinking is characterized by a value-freedom with which it distinguishes itself from the normatively determined historical culture. If historical thinking is based on normative standards derived from its social and political context, then this has serious relativistic consequences. Its validity claims become limited to the audience that subscribes to or wants to subscribe to these standards. This, however, is incompatible with the scientific character of historical scholarship. If we let go of the postulate of value-freedom, then we hand historical thinking over to a cultural relativism that is incompatible with the criteria of a scientific methodical rationality.

This argument poses an epistemological dilemma for the theory of history: Can it adhere to this rationality while at the same time emphasize its practical reason? Can historical knowledge that is imbued with this rationality be or become effective in the historical culture of its time? This seems to concern a fundamental contradiction in the logic of historical thinking.

But this is only a seeming contradiction. The practical function in normative cultural orientations on the one hand and the 'value-freedom' in the methodical rationality of historical research on the other do not necessarily contradict each other. They work together and depend on each other in the complex process of historical cognition.

Scholarship and Lifeworld   In order to make this plausible we must refer back to the disciplinary matrix. It shows the systematic interrelationship between the different criteria for the formation of meaning and defines the particularity of historical thinking. It is able to offer a solution: two dimensions correlate here. On the one hand, there is the life world from which questions arise that are relevant for historical thinking. On the other hand, there is academia, which distinguishes itself from this life world and its mental activities of cultural orientation as an independent cognitive activity. Because of this, it is not exclusively determined by the needs of this orientation.

Normative perspectives unquestionably influence historical thinking in the dimension of the life world. Without norms, we cannot imagine the semantic discourse of symbolization. This is where the meaning of the past as history is ultimately decided. In the scholarly production of historical knowledge, these perspectives transform into another way of thinking: the experience of the past methodically develops according to universal perspectives of validity. Normative standards are included in questions and perspectives. Evidence provides answers and concrete content. As a repertoire of information, it must be drawn upon to produce reliable historical knowledge. The normativity of the heuristic approach, factuality and an explanatory use of historical experience do not contradict each other. Rather, they complement the unity of the historical thought process.

We must not forget that the scientific character of historical thinking itself has a normative quality. Its experience-based, conceptual, explanatory and discursive form of argumentation represents an insurmountable normative basis of scientific thinking. It is this basis that can only be or become practically effective when the historical knowledge produced by historical scholarship is used in the cultural framework of orientation of a way of life.

Notes

201. E. Foner. 2002. *Who Owns History? Rethinking the Past in a Changing World*, New York: Hill and Wang.

202. C.L. Becker. 1935. 'Every Man His Own Historian', in idem, *Every Man His Own Historian: Essays on History and Politics*, New York: F.S. Croft & Co, 233–255.

203. See Rüsen, 'Die Kultur der Zeit', 23–53.

204. On a fundamental level see J. Assmann. 1992. *Das kulturelle Gedächtnis*, Munich: C.H. Beck. (*Cultural Memory and Early Civilization*, Cambridge: Cambridge University Press, 2011.); A. Assmann. 1999. *Erinnerungsräume: Formen und Wandlungen des kulturellen*

Gedächtnisses, Munich: C.H. Beck; A Assmann and U. Frevert. 1999. *Geschichtsvergessenheit, Geschichtsversessenheit*, Stuttgart: Deutsche Verlagsanstalt; E. Flaig. 1999. 'Soziale Bedingungen des kulturellen Vergessens', in *Vorträge aus dem Warburg-Haus*, vol. 3. Berlin: Akademie Verlag, 31–100; H. Welzer. 2002. *Das kommunikative Gedächtnis*, Munich: C.H. Beck.

205. Nora, *Zwischen Geschichte und Gedächtnis*.

206. This was therefore not the case because the topic of historical consciousness in the teaching of history has been dealt with in a manner not suited to historians or specialists in the humanities interested in the topic of 'culture'. The relevant literature cannot all be listed here. I mention only the following: K.-E. Jeismann. 1985. *Geschichte als Horizont der Gegenwart*, Paderborn: Schöningh; B. von Borries, H.-J. Pandel and J. Rüsen (eds). 1991. *Geschichtsbewußtsein empirisch*, Pfaffenweiler: Centaurus; B. von Borries and J. Rüsen (eds). 1994. *Geschichtsbewußtsein im interkulturellen Vergleich*, Pfaffenweiler: Centaurus; J. Rüsen (ed.). 2001. *Geschichtsbewußtsein: Psychologische Grundlagen, Entwicklungskonzepte, empirische Befunde*, Cologne: Böhlau; C. Kölbl. 2004. *Geschichtsbewußtsein im Jugendalter*, Bielefeld: Transcript; P. Seixas (ed.). 2004. *Theorising Historical Consciousness*, Toronto: University of Toronto Press.

207. M. Halbwachs. 1985. *Das Gedächtnis und seine sozialen Bedingungen*, Frankfurt am Main: Suhrkamp; idem. 1985. *Das kollektive Gedächtnis*, Frankfurt am Main: Suhrkamp. (*On Collective Memory*, Chicago: University of Chicago Press, 1992.) See also Welzer, *Das kommunikative Gedächtnis*.

208. See Antweiler, *Mensch und Weltkultur*.

209. See this volume, 207sqq.

210. Rüsen and Straub (eds), *Dark Traces of the Past*.

211. S. Freud. 1975. *Der Mann Moses und die monotheistische Religion*, Frankfurt am Main: Fischer Taschenbuch. (*Moses and Monotheism*, London: Hogarth Press, 1939.); S. Freud. 1964. *Totem und Tabu*, Frankfurt am Main: Fischer Bücherei. (*Totem and Taboo*, London: W.W. Norton, 1989.)

212. C.G. Jung. 1990. *Die Beziehungen zwischen dem Ich und dem Unbewußten*, Munich: Deutscher Taschenbuchverlag; see E. Neumann. 1986. *Ursprungsgeschichte des Bewußtseins*, Frankfurt am Main: Fischer Taschenbuchverlag. (*The Origins and History of Consciousness*, Princeton, NJ: Princeton University Press, 1973.)

213. I am following the argument of Aleida Assmann (footnote 204).

214. An example is the topic of the Holocaust in German historical culture. At first it was simply one of many topics. It then attained its own particular profile and growing political relevance, finally becoming an integral part of the historical subject matter forming Germany's identity.

215. See this volume, 216sqq.

216. H. von Kleist. 1961. 'Über das Marionettentheater', in idem, *Sämtliche Werke und Briefe*, edited by H. Sembdner, vol. 2, Munich: Hanser, 338–345. ('On the Marionette Theatre', available online at: http://www.southerncrossreview.org/9/kleist.htm.)

217. Assmann, A. 1999. *Erinnerungsräume: Formen und Wandlungen des kulturellen Gedächtnisses*. Munich: C.H. Beck, pp. 130–139.

218. See M. Erdheim. 1984. *Die gesellschaftliche Produktion von Unbewußtheit*, Frankfurt am Main: Suhrkamp (especially 'Adoleszenz und Kulturentwicklung', 271–367); Rüsen and Straub (eds), *Dark Traces of the Past*.

219. For a more detailed account, see J. Rüsen. 2008. 'Was ist Geschichtskultur?', in idem, *Historische Orientierung: Über die Arbeit des Geschichtsbewusstseins, sich in der Zeit zurechtzufinden*, 2nd ed. Schwalbach/Taunus: Wochenschau, 211–234; Klas-Göran Karlsson has suggested further distinctions. See K.-G. Karlsson. 2003. 'The Holocaust as a Problem of Historical Culture', in K.-G. Karlsson and U. Zander (eds), *Echoes of the Holocaust: Historical Cultures in Contemporary Europe*, Lund: Nordic Academic Press, 9–58; see my added contribution in

J. Rüsen. 2004. 'Interpreting the Holocaust', in K.-G. Karlsson and U. Zander (eds), *Holocaust Heritage*, Malmö: Sekel, 35–62. For the relationship between secular, scientific thought and religion in the reflection of the relationship of historical studies and theology, see Rüsen, 'Faktizität und Fiktionalität', 119–133.

220. S. Freud. 2000. 'Das Ich und das Es', in idem, *Studienausgabe*, vol. 3: *Psychologie des Unbewußten*, Frankfurt am Main: Fischer Taschenbuchverlag, 273–330. (*The Ego and the Id*, Seattle: Pacific Publishing Studio, 2010.)

221. M. Weber. 1964. *Wirtschaft und Gesellschaft*, edited by J. Winckelmann, Cologne: Kiepenheuer & Witsch, 38.

222. Legitimacy can be called humanistic when the criteria for recognizing (and for criticizing) authority are taken from the humanness of human beings and substantiated with the principle of human dignity.

223. 'Historians are dangerous people. They are capable of upsetting everything. They must be directed.' Nikita S. Chruschtschow (cited in N.W. Heer. 1971. *Politics and History in the Soviet Union*, Cambridge, MA: Cambridge University Press, 11).

224. See J. Tillmanns. 2012. *Was heißt historische Verantwortung?*, Bielefeld: Transcript. See also C. Kühberger and C. Sedmak. 2008. *Ethik der Geschichtswissenschaft*, Vienna: Turia + Kant.

225. R. Otto. 2004. *Das Heilige*, 2nd ed., Munich: C.H. Beck. (*The Idea of the Holy*, London and New York: Oxford University Press, 1970.); see also G. Essen. 1996. 'Geschichte als Sinnproblem', *Theologie und Philosophie* 71, 321–333.

226. This is the case, for example, for Ernst Bernheim, with the 'task of representation' being 'research results communicated with as little distortion as possible' (Bernheim, *Lehrbuch der historischen Methode*, 778; from the German).

227. He no longer considered historical writing to be science or academic study, but rather journalism. W. Paravicini. 2008. *Die Wahrheit der Historiker*, Munich: Oldenbourg, 15.

228. Further examples are found in S. Friedländer. 1986. *Kitsch und Tod: Der Wiederschein des Nazismus*, Deutscher Taschenbuchverlag. (*Reflections of Nazism: An Essay on Kitsch and Death*, New York: Harper & Row, 1984.)

229. John 14, 6. Haffmans, P. and G. (eds): 2011. *Das Neue Testament viersprachig*. Berlin, Zürich: Haffmans & Tolkemit, 433.

230. N. Kermani. 2011. *Gott ist schön*, 4th ed., Munich: C.H. Beck.

231. Matthew 28, 18. Haffmans, P. and G. (eds): 2011. *Das Neue Testament viersprachig*. Berlin, Zürich: Haffmans & Tolkemit, 131.

232. See also W. Hardtwig. 1991. 'Geschichtsreligion – Wissenschaft als Arbeit – Objektivität', in *HZ* 252, 1–32; Rüsen, 'Historische Methode und religiöser Sinn', 9–41

233. See also G. Küenzlen. 1997. *Der neue Mensch*, Frankfurt am Main: Suhrkamp.

234. For a more detailed account, see J. Rüsen. 2006. 'Zivilgesellschaft und Religion – Idee eines Verhältnisses', in idem, *Kultur macht Sinn*, Cologne: Böhlau, 227–239.

235. Kant, 'Metaphysik der Sitten', A 93.

236. Herder was more historically concrete in describing this viewpoint as the recognition of cultural diversity.

237. The treatment of slavery in African historical culture and in post-colonial thinking represents a blatant example of this. See also E. Flaig. 2009. *Weltgeschichte der Sklaverei*, Munich: C.H. Beck.

238. See this volume, 179sq.

239. For a more detailed account, see Rüsen, 'Klassischer Humanismus', 273–315. ('Classical Humanism: A Historical Survey', in idem (ed.), *Approaching Humankind*, Vandenhoeck & Ruprecht unipress, 2013, 161–184.)

240. Kant, see footnote 235.

241. See J. Rüsen. 2008. 'Vom Geist der Geisteswissenschaften', in C. Goschler, J. Fohrmann, H. Welzer and M. Zwick (eds), *Arts and Figures*, Göttingen: Wallstein, 25–31.

CHAPTER 8

Practical History

Learning, Understanding, Humanity

1. The Theoretical Foundations of History Didactics

a) The Relevance of Metahistory for History Education

One of the most important practical uses of historical knowledge is the teaching and learning of history.[242] This of course primarily concerns history education in the classroom. Other institutions could also be considered 'places of learning' for historical thinking: historical museums, cultural monuments, memorials and a wide range of possibilities in adult and higher education as well as the modern media.

Teaching and learning history have their own specific field of study: history didactics. It has developed into its own academic field with its own theoretical debates and research methods,[243] which cannot be thought away out of the academic realm. It owes its disciplinary particularity to a functional demand in cultural life: whenever the learning processes of historical thinking are institutionalized, a need for teaching expertise arises. History didactics analyses this expertise on a scholarly and analytical level for the purposes of developing useful strategies and practices. Teaching history on an expert level of course presumes a familiarity with the content and form of historical thinking, but the scholarly approach to historical learning is much more than that. Learning history also occurs in the academic institution of historical scholarship (after all, this is where the professionals are trained). But this type of learning is not the actual subject matter of historical thinking (except for the history of historical learning).

History didactics explores its own field, which is fundamentally different from the field of historical studies. It is *the academic discipline of historical learning*. It generates scholarly (specialist) knowledge that we need to understand the learning processes involved in history and to allow it to operate on an expert level.

What role does metahistory play in history didactics? There is no doubt that it should play a role, because to know what historical learning is, we must know what history is and what determines the particular quality of historical thinking and its modern scholarly character. The focus here is on the educating and training processes that develop the capacity for historical thinking.

The Substantiating Function of Metahistory   Metahistory acquires a fundamental substantiating function in history didactics. This function generally concerns asking and answering the following question: What is history? The answers are derived from relevant comments from professional historians or works of renowned and classic representatives of the field. They refer to either the content of 'history' or the cognitive handling of this content. However, the complex relationship between both dimensions of the historical generally remains unexplored. Nevertheless, it comes down to this: learning is a mental process. We can only understand the particularity of historical learning if we also understand the corresponding processes and forms for dealing with the experience of the past. These processes turn the past into history. What this experience means or entails is a completely different question. It refers to history as a specific and temporal happening in the human world. One cannot be sufficiently explained without the other.

This is exactly where the *foundational* function of metahistory for the teaching of history comes in. It adds another historical dimension to the other two (the *substantial* and the *formal* dimensions): the *functional* dimension, which is necessary to understand learning as cultural practice.[244] All three dimensions converge in the focus on human historical consciousness. *Hence, historical consciousness is the basic category of history didactics.* History didactics conceptualizes historical learning as a process of historical consciousness. It focuses the relevant metahistorical considerations on the theory of learning and the pragmatism of teaching. The *theory of learning* analyses the processes in the formation of historical meaning, while the possibilities to influence or steer these processes are researched in view of the *pragmatism of teaching*.

Any study on the teaching of history should start with an analysis of the mental processes involved in the formation of historical meaning. Metahistory supplies the relevant insights and arguments for this. Obviously, the *cognitive* factors and elements of this formation of meaning play an important role here. However, it is important for the study of history didactics that the learning process is not reduced to its cognitive dimension. (Unfortunately, this happens far too often, not necessarily in the discourse of specialists but more often in public debates on what should be learned in history classes. Success is almost always defined by the amount of historical knowledge that has been learned.) The extraordinary significance of the *aesthetic* dimension in the formation of historical meaning (not only in this era of new media or only among children or teenagers) is too often marginalized, although it would be difficult to overestimate this significance. In contrast, the *political* dimension is always considered, and for clear reasons: governments and societies have always had an interest in preparing future generations for the political culture as a means of strengthening the viewpoints that are essential in maintaining the historical legitimacy of power.

The other two dimensions – the *moral* and the *religious* dimensions – are also relevant for history didactics and require a historical-theoretical analysis to reveal their didactic function.

Morality and Religion as Factors in Historical Learning With respect to the *moral* dimension there are three issues that are especially relevant in history didactics: (a) the role that historical thinking plays in the cultural orientation of our daily lives; (b) the distanced and critical handling of historical thinking with the normative claims that arise from the societal context of teaching and learning history; and finally, (c) the hermeneutics of the normative particularity of the past in contrast to the present and the historicization (and not the relativization) of the norms in the present.

Concerning (a): normative elements are not assigned to historical thinking from the outside but originate in its cognitive processes and practical functions. At the same time, historical scholarship raises validity claims that are based on a distancing from the normative standards that are imposed on it from their – often political – context. These validity claims concern both the inner normativity of historical thinking and its distance to and critical assessment of norms and values that affect our daily lives. Both must be brought into the framework of a specifically didactical argument with reference to the normativity of learning and teaching history. In this context, the study of historical didactics has a propaedeutic function as a scholarly field of study, not only for introducing a specifically scientific rationality but also for realizing the role that reason might play in the practical needs for cultural orientation.

Concerning (b): this is highly connected to the learning opportunities that the factor of 'criticism' presents. This factor anchors historical scholarship in the historical culture of its time (or at least, it could or should do so).

Concerning (c): it is impossible to understand the human past in the past's own terms, through the notions or constructs that were self-evident at another place and time, without distancing oneself from the pressures of current systems of norms and values. Historical writing with its *exemplary* forming of meaning presents a historical mindset that is didactic at its very core. Cicero formulated the famous saying that history is the teacher of life. This line of thought is as powerful as ever, especially in the teaching and learning of history. It teaches us the power of judgement. This point alone makes history and the teaching of history indispensable. Nevertheless, history didactics cannot neglect the importance of not only exemplary but also *genetic* thinking. The capacity to understand human ways of life on their own terms can only be developed if the logic of judgement is transcended through a temporalizing of moral principles and ethical concepts. The super-temporal validity of learned and taught norms must be transformed into a temporalized concept of the development of ethic and moral principles.

With regard to the *religious* dimension, history didactics need a historical-theoretical clarification of the genuinely secular character of modern historical thinking. Essentially, this secular character should not be played out against religious beliefs. Instead the different logical constructs of the religious and secular formations of meaning in dealing with historical experience must be identified.

Experience and Interpretation versus Knowledge   The cognitive achievements of historical consciousness are too often measured against the academic state of knowledge. In doing so we accept reductions and simplifications without questioning their necessity. 'Knowledge' at any level remains the key element of learning. Here lies an important task for metahistory: it furthers the teaching of history by explicating what this knowledge is all about, and what is involved when we are dealing with this knowledge. It is by no means as simple as it seems at first glance. Historical knowledge is the result of a mental synthesis of experience and interpretation. Experience and interpretation must be learned and not confused with the fundamental mental capacities of absorbing and recounting knowledge. Historical learning adds two essential components to knowledge as the synthesis of experience and interpretation: orientation and motivation with regard to what is known. There are, then, four mental processes. If we reduce this complexity to the one-dimensionality of knowledge as facts, we lose sight of what is essential in the teaching of history, namely, learning these four mental skills of historical consciousness.

Historical Learning and Narrative Competence   Along with the analytical precision with which metahistory considers the mental operations involved in historical consciousness, it also offers further insights in the learning and teaching of history. To put it simply, historical didactics is about properly learning how to think historically. In the academic context, this 'proper way' is called competence. Learning history means to obtain or gain competency.[245] And to what end? This is the main question in determining the normative base of the process of historical learning. Metahistory gives us a clue: simply put, historical competence lies in the ability to narrate the histories that we need in order to come to terms with the temporal dimension of life. *Historical competence is narrative competence* in respect to the presentation of the past and its experience. The interpretation of this experience gives us an understanding or appreciation of the present and the ability to assess our future opportunities.[246] Metahistory explicates the specific factors of this competency and its systematic coherence.

Of course, the work of historical didactics should not only analyse the competency that we (should) attain through historical learning. It must also consider the mental processes in the formation of historical meaning as a *movement* or development of learning. Metahistory can also contribute something fundamental to this analysis. First of all, it expands our view on the specific operations of historical consciousness that affect the formation of historical meaning. They include *experience or perception, interpretation, orientation* and *motivation*.

Each of these represents its own dimension of historical competence. Of course, they all are tightly interconnected. But only when we clearly and analytically distinguish them from one another can we assess their particular importance in the formation of historical meaning and in the processes of learning. We need metahistory to clarify these factors; otherwise, we fail to see the process of historical learning as anything but a diffuse process for the purposes of acquiring knowledge and the skills necessary for it. The *orientational function* of this knowledge, for example, is presupposed, but not seen as an inner quality of the learned knowledge. In order to understand this function we need to consider how it operates from within its own processes. The *motivational function* can easily be suspected of moral or belief-forming instruction and thereby dismissed as a learning opportunity. Opportunities with respect to *perception* often remain limited to an analysis of aesthetics in semantic symbolization and historical representation.

However, metahistory is not the same as didactics. It articulates the procedures involved in the formation of historical meaning. But as learning processes, these procedures need to be analysed on the specific level of didactics. In a certain way, historical didactics takes on the task of revisiting the insights from metahistory in the achievements of historical consciousness. This is not about the constitution of historical thinking but rather about how this thinking can be *learned*. It assumes a working knowledge of this constitution. As such, the teaching of history remains dependent on metahistory.

Not only can we identify the four mental operations in the formation of historical meaning (experience, interpretation, orientation, motivation) as learning processes with specific competencies. We can also discern the four types of formation of historical meaning (traditional, exemplary, genetic and critical),[247] as learning methods. The logic of these types, or more precisely, their systematic interrelationship, allows them to be interpreted as having a *developmental logic*. Metahistory can offer history didactics a theoretical foundation for the development of empirical and pragmatic concepts for the learning processes of history.

b) Approaches to a Developmental Theory of Historical Competence

Metahistory deciphers the logical order of the formation of historical meaning. Its analysis deal with all forms of human historical consciousness, including its ontogenetic development. The typology of the formation of historical meaning can contribute something fundamental to the clarification of this development. These types can be *understood as stages of development in historical consciousness*. Traditional, exemplary and genetic thinking represent these stages. Critical thinking plays an important role in transforming one stage into another. From these considerations we need only take a small step further towards creating a developmental theory of historical competencies. Such a theory organizes these stages into the conceptualization (or

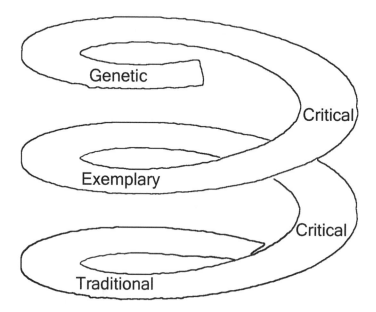

Figure 8.1 Schematic spiral of the levels of competency in historical learning.

hypothesis) of a dynamic transformation. This transformation can be illustrated as a spiral.

The oldest, most original (and mentally most profound) form of historical interpretation of the past is the *traditional formation of meaning*. This does not just apply to a general theory of universal development of historical thinking. It also concerns the mental processes in which historical consciousness unfolds in the life of a human being (ontogenesis). With growing cognitive competencies, we can reach and practise a (logically) higher level of forming historical meaning, an *exemplary formation of meaning*. To reach this level we need the development of the power of human judgement, or the development of cognitive competencies whose origins have been intensely studied in the field of developmental psychology.[248]

Deficits of Developmental Psychology   The developmental psychology of cognitive competencies has devoted little time to human historical consciousness, at least it has not bothered to classify the sequential ordering of competency levels in historical experience, as it has done with temporal and moral consciousness. It has stuck by the concept that moral competence and its corresponding ability to generalize represent the most developed forms of human thinking in dealing with (moral) orientation in practical life. Regarding historical consciousness, this corresponds with the findings that *exemplary* thinking dominates in the learning processes of historical instruction and education when the issue is a general moral competence. Nevertheless, this cognitive level can and must transform into a higher level in which the *genetic formation of meaning* dominates, because only in this interpretive form can we properly deal with specifically modern historical thinking.

The *critical* formation of meaning is not in itself a separate cognitive level but crosses the other three. It has the indispensible function of enabling us to move between levels and problematizing the interpretive power of older or more primal types in favour of new ones. The sequential order of the competence levels and their inner coherence are indeed complex. One level does not simply dissolve into another, but rather receives a different status in the network of mental operations of our historical consciousness. For instance, traditional thinking does not become dysfunctional or simply disappear in the framework of exemplary thinking. It persists (without tradition there is no such thing as historical culture), but it no longer supplies the leading criteria of meaning for dealing with the past. Each type has its own specific orientating function, and they must fulfil this function, though in completely different structures of historical orientation. Different types of thinking are connected in historical culture in completely different ways and in very different constellations. The processes and forms of historical learning and teaching are just as complex. Metahistory gives the teaching of history the theoretical means to clarify this complexity and the opportunity to organize it in a rational way.

To name just one example: human rights and civil rights are a central theme in historical learning. Learning is considered to be a success when these rights are given high importance as an iron bulwark in prevailing historical traditions. But this concept of a fixed (and sustainable) set of norms that regulate the political and social conditions in the present is not valid. The contemporary set of norms calls for a temporal dynamic. Only then can the demands of the ever-changing human ways of life be met. This idea that we need to develop human and civil rights is tied to a historicization that accompanies the insight into their original formation and continuing development. It is easy to see this further development vis-à-vis a rough start and later success. This kind of development already appears in debates in the late eighteenth century. This became clear in view of the problem of how to secure socially active political participation on the basis of human and civil rights.[249]

On an abstract level, this example represents an idea of how the human past must be learned: it involves the *capacity to interpret the past* and to get an *insight into its logical form and development*. In terms of history education, this insight can be further developed into a theory on history learning. However, it should not be limited to the sphere of specialists in teaching or education. Rather, it should be consciously implemented into the processes of learning and reflected upon. This is absolutely possible: relevant phenomena of daily human life and material that has not been prepared for education can be taken up and analysed. At the beginning of history classes in schools, educators could teach fundamental insights into the logic of historical thinking that could be used throughout students' further education.[250]

It is up to history teachers to enhance and further develop these insights, and not only on an abstract level, but also in dealing with the historical material in the curriculum. In this way, historical theory is an indispensable part of history didactics. (Nothing is more practical than a good theory, both for the practice of teaching and for all other forms of historical presentation.[251])

2. Standards of Historical Judgement: Understanding and Morality

Which Values? Every cultural orientation is determined by norms. They indicate the aims of future-oriented action. Through historical interpretation we connect these objectives to the past. This almost necessarily leads to historical knowledge, for the purposes of orientation, being channelled through values that determine present-day ways of life. The past is then judged within the orientating framework of historical culture according to values that do not correspond to its historical particularity. The real normative quality of the past is, in other words, cast out. The norms of the present rather than the past are involved in the practical use of the historical knowledge generated by the work of historians. The fact that other norms applied in the past is another matter. In this sense, the fundamental orienting function of historical knowledge can de-historicize the past. This can completely frustrate the cognitive effort that is needed to pursue genuine historical understanding. After all, this understanding includes the self-conception of actors and victims of the past.

Metahistory finds itself faced with the dilemma of having to defend the particularity of the past against the normative foundations of present-day culture without challenging these foundations. If metahistory were to question these norms, it would undermine the orientation capacity of historical knowledge. Is it possible to integrate these contrasting normative focuses of the formation of historical meaning? Only then is a temporal orientation in practical life without de-historicization of the past possible. How can we solve this problem?

An Aesthetic Devaluation and a Historicizing Revaluation   One common but thoughtless solution is to give the particularity of the past a specifically aesthetic significance for the present. Creating aesthetic coherency can be an unproblematic venture. The normative dilemma is not really dealt with, but avoided aesthetically.[252]

We can also give the past more than just aesthetic significance when we rid past norms of their power by historicizing them, like in the following example. The ritual sacrifice of a fourteen-year-old Inca girl is celebrated as the 'glory of humanity' in the Museo Santuaros Andinos in Arequipa, Peru, which exhibits her well-preserved frozen mummy. (This is literally how it is described in the introductory film that all museum visitors must see.[253]) When I asked the director of the museum about this, she defended this value judgement by saying that we need to judge the past by its own standards. Since this is an example of a pre-Columbian past displayed against the geopolitical backdrop of European colonialism, these hermeneutics of 'historical waywardness' are well received in the current identity politics of Latin America.

But not only in this unique case do we find past and present kept apart in a manner that we could call 'historicistic'. In the framework of modern historical thinking, we cannot argue against the hermeneutic principle of understanding a time on its own terms. But this does not alter the fact that this principle splits the temporal coherence between past and present. If we take this coherence seriously (and only then is historical consciousness possible) it is then necessary to avoid a relativism of values in the name of a strict historicization of the past. In the aesthetic form, this temporal coherence does not matter. This form dissolves the temporal differences in the reality of human ways of life into the beautiful shine of their cultural importance. The course of history is thereby brought to a standstill. It turns historical orientation into nothing more than building a protective shield against the knowledge of what human beings in different normative structures can do to each other.

Is Every Epoch (Only) Immediate to God?   Those who defend this historicizing often do so by referring to Leopold von Ranke's dictum '*jede Epoche ist unmittelbar zu Gott*' ('every epoch is immediate to God'). However, this relativism is not what Ranke had in mind. His explicit insistence on an inherent relationship between 'earlier' and 'later' (and thus essentially the inner connection between past and present) makes it obvious that he was not speaking of an aestheticization of historical experience. According to Ranke, historical thinking connects the two in a *coherent narrative style* ('*Duktus*').[254] What does this mean for the moral divergence between different time periods and the coherence between them? They merge when the moral standards of the past are historicized in light of present standards and when this historicization can be conceptualized in an all-encompassing temporal and developmental context. Within the framework of historical thinking based on philosophy of history through a cultural evolutionary theory based on developmental psychology, this is not just possible, but necessary.[255]

The relativist concept of historicization is based on a questionable philosophical premise. It is based on the notion that historical thinking, with its valid hermeneutic focus on the particularity of the past, can forego (or simply forget) a critical premise of philosophy of history: when we truly think historically we need to bring the particularity of the past into the temporalized horizon of meaning of the present. To forego or forget this means to cast history out of the human world with all its historicity. Here lies a potential danger of the new media. Among the abundance of representations of the past in arbitrary simultaneity, the meaning and particularity of history can be lost in sensory overkill.

3. Politics of Memory and Historical Identity

The practical relevance of historical thinking for the formation of human identity is beyond dispute. Human life is tied to the condition that every human being exhibits to his or her relationship to themselves and to others, a basic level of stability and continuity in the temporality of living. First and foremost, this temporal consistency of the human self comprises the natural continuity of a life between birth and death. But this physical reality is not sufficient to produce identity. It needs a cultural component to vault and 'humanize' it. (This cultural continuity can exceed the physical continuity.) Selfhood is a matter of mental operations, a constant self-reference, an emotional and intellectual interaction with the self. The durability of human subjectivity in the course of time as a condition for our ability to live is commonly called 'identity'. Identity is an essential element of human subjectivity, both in the personal and the social sense.

Identity because of History   As mentioned earlier, historical thinking plays an essential role in the mental processes in which the human subject establishes the certainty of identity over all temporal changes in life. We cannot answer the question of who we are without telling a history of our own life. Personal identity is tied to the more or less conscious awareness that we carry, live and tell our own biography. This identity extends into the future together with our hopes, wishes, anxieties and fears. The same holds true for social identity: we articulate, confirm and of course change and reject an inner belonging to a social formation through historical narratives. This identity is inconceivable without historical consciousness, as it thrives on the emotionally powerful idea of belonging to others that persists through all temporal changes and a difference between our group and others.

   The formation of identity therefore is one of the most important, if not the most important function of historical thinking in the way of life of any given time.[256] There is a surprising discrepancy between this absolute fact and the highly disputed concept of historical identity.

a) What Is Historical Identity?

The concept of identity in question is not based on the purely logical fact that something is what it is and not something else. It is much more about the mental process in which human subjects form their subjectivity, or their self-referentiality,[257] which fundamentally determines their life.[258]

   The human subject always relates to something outside itself (in psychological terms, to an 'object'). This can happen in different ways. One mode of behaviour can be to identify with something outside itself, making this thing its own. This appropriation (the psychological term is 'introjection') gives the self a profile and shapes individual features. The most intensive form of this appropriation is love (or its opposite: hate). Human subjectivity develops through a wealth of identifications in varying degrees of intensity and in high degrees of variability. In other words, the individual, or self, dons a great many identifications as he or she goes out into the world. This trivial fact must serve many theoreticians in rejecting the notion of one single human identity. Human beings have not one, but many, often contradictory identities. However, this notion distorts our view of what the concept of identity is about. What is important is that within the variety, dynamics, changeability and inconsistency of these many identifications and everything that comes with them, we have first and foremost the self. *Identity refers these identifications back to the self-identifying subject.* The self does not lose its many identifications; on the contrary: it develops in and because of these identifications and forms its own individual features. This is true for individuals as well as for social entities. The latter are constructed through conscious belonging as a specific way of identifying subjects with other subjects and separating them from others.

Identity as Work of Consciousness   Identity is the result of mental processes in which the different identifications of the self or subject with something beyond the self are integrated in terms of this self or subject. This is an act of human consciousness (including the unconscious). If it fails, it can cause behavioural disorders in one's relation to the self and to others. It must at least be successful enough to keep us or make us capable of action. Identity is determined by a minimal degree of coherence in the many relations the human subject has to the world. (This also holds true for the post-modern notion of identity as a 'patchwork'; even here the different pieces must be combined to produce a solid whole.)

Since aggressive behaviour is also tied to notions of identity, the concept of identity itself has come under massive criticism. This particularly pertains to essentialist ways of thinking. This way of thinking fundamentally separates us from the 'other' in a relationship that only has an external quality. An essentialist concept defines identity 'objectively', (in terms of kinship or 'blood ties') or quasi-objectively (in terms of ethnic origins or racial ties). For a long time, gender was defined in these terms, too. With regard to this essentialism, the idea that identity defines (or de-fines, as it were, in the sense of separating and isolating) human subjectivity has been fundamentally criticized.[259] The term 'hybridity' was introduced as antonym of essentialism and quickly gained intellectual popularity. This contrast is a clear critique of essentialism. As a cultural entity, human identity (whether personal or social) is susceptible to those changes that fundamentally pertain to the inner temporality and developmental capacity of human ways of life. One can, with good reason, assume that there is a universally historical development from an objective to a subjective determination of human identity, in which the former does not disappear in or become neutralized by the latter.[260] Nevertheless, it does not stand to reason that we pluralize human identity (we do not have just one, but many identities), because it ignores the problem of coherence.[261]

Dynamic Self-reference   Identity is anything but a given. It has many variations, is context-dependent and can change. Traditional concepts of identity often emphasize the essential character of identity, for example in terms of status, tribe, gender, language, a specific place and so on. Identity is seen as something quasi-self-evident. This idea of fixed identity can no longer be sustained in the circumstances of the present. The (post-modern) critique of such a conceptualization of identity justifiably places emphasis on the value of diversity, change and context-dependency in the concepts of identity that determine life. The metaphor of a 'patchwork' identity does this justice. However, this critique often throws the baby out with the bathwater and questions the existence and practical effectiveness of a general and coherent self-referentiality in the human subject. (I can claim with absolute conviction that there is no 'I', but then I must be silent when I am asked who makes this claim.) This self-referencing is fundamental and obvious, for example, in the certainty that it is 'I' who feels pain, who does not like a smell or a taste or who likes a certain colour. Is it possible to fluidify or even dissolve our self-referencing through discourse? That would mean the mental death of those concerned. As mentioned earlier, this does not mean that self-referentiality only appears in rigid forms; rather, it underlies *all* flexible forms as transcendental subjectivity.

The Self in Times of Change: Historical Identity   Historical identity is the epitome of coherently mediated different identifications in a temporal perspective. It integrates events, people and facts from the past in the relation to the self of a personal and social subject. A standard measure for coherence is a concept of time that makes the temporal extent of the human self tangible and real. It is important that the self remains 'the same' in the processes of temporal change (metaphorically speaking: that the human self does not sink, but swims in the current of time).

In this temporal extent, the human self unites its 'now' with the factuality of 'what has been' and this with the desirability of wanting to become and the reality of having to become. What prompts the necessary synthesis of empiricism and normativity in the daily lives of human beings? The answer is: the telling of historical narratives.

Historical identity synthesizes the having been of a subject or a social entity with its future projections. It centres this synthesis in the practical living of the present day, in the subjective establishment of personal and social relationships of subjects with themselves and with other subjects. It also synthesizes experience and expectation, facts and norms in the self-referencing of human beings into a vital notion of the temporal extent of their own existence. In this synthesis, human beings generally move beyond the boundaries of their own temporal life. This is not only the case in social identity; here, the social formation of identity – whether it is a tribe, a religious community, a nation or an entire culture – extends beyond the lifespan of a human being into the past and future. In the great narratives of history that articulate powerful ideas of belonging and not belonging, this temporal direction encompasses significant periods of time. These histories can encompass the time on earth of the human species or, in certain religious identities, even the entire history of the cosmos. Historical narratives of the formation of identity basically produce a temporal expansion of the horizon of our human self. They remove some of the fear of its own mortality. The conceptualization of time in individual identity can also expand beyond the limits of its own lifespan. Examples of this are notions of reincarnation or the idea of resurrection, immortality and so on.

b) The Power Struggle for Identity

The formation of historical identity is a political matter. It is laden with power claims and conflicts and represents a constant state of uncertainty in the cultural life of a human being. Identity does not just happen. It requires serious effort to make the (individual) relationship between a person and a society, as well as the (social) relationship between one society and another real and effective. In our identity all the elements that are predetermined and construed in the circumstances of human life are anchored in the depths of our own subjectivity. As they are 'absorbed' within us, these elements carry a potential for conflict and they carry this potential into the formation of the human self.

As such, the legitimation of political power relations, for example, extends into the depths of the human subject. The constitution of our subjectivity in the tense dynamic between the superego, ego and id is defined by power. The localization of the subject within such a framework of tense oppositions that in effect structure our practical lives also shapes our subjectivity. Every human must relate to this framework and operate within it in the inner core and in the development as a person in all action and suffering. Conversely, the circumstances of life are imprinted in our psychic structure and require us to constantly come to terms with life through the formation of meaning. Historical scholarship is the institutional form of such an imposition. Through its cognitive processes it is both: an instrument of legitimization of power and a criticism of this legitimacy.

c) Potential for Reason in the Formation of Identity

Historical studies is not in the business of creating meaning or identity. Rather, it is an important element in the mental and cultural procedures that form meaning and identity. In its academic form, with its specific focus on methodical research and argumentative substantiation, it introduces possibilities for reason and rational thinking into its processes of orientation. Its contribution to culture lies in application of the forms of knowledge and the argumentative handling of that knowledge that are essential to academic thought. In view of the formation processes of human subjectivity, this application can be conceptualized and carried out as the *humanization* of human beings.

Making Human Beings Human   Undoubtedly, the capacity of human beings to think rationally (that is, to think in an argumentative and substantiating way) in dealing with reality, themselves and others, is a basic quality of being human. Academic study is based on this reason. If reason makes us human, then we can understand academic study as a factor of humanization in historical culture. The rationality of historical thinking belongs to the historical process that it realizes. It structures the temporal processes in our lives its own way, revealing them as a comprehensive developmental process of culture. It also contributes to the practical viability of our lives.

It promotes the fundamental direction of our lives toward the acquiring of meaning. The human self becomes more directed or strengthened by experience and more confident due to the meaning that is determined for its inner temporality. Neither is possible without mental efforts: the strength in experience requires the pain of integrating negative (self-)knowledge as well. The 'dark' sides of historical knowledge in the framework of one's own history must be considered and dealt with. (Without these efforts, an identity is not viable.) Experience leads to normative strength. It feeds off the strength of conviction, which is gained in argumentation and reflection on identity-forming values. However, this necessarily requires a (self-)critical examination of how generally it can be applied. In the application of the relevant criteria of rationality in academic thought, the meaning and meaningfulness of the human self increase for itself and for others.

4. Overcoming Ethnocentrism through Historical Humanism

The Human Being Is Its Own Centre   The aforementioned possibility of reason in historical thinking allows us to approach one of the most significant problems in historical culture: ethnocentrism. It is a way of thinking that is fundamental and universal for the mental procedures of the formation of human identity.[262] What is the nature of this problem? First, we need to establish that every historical identity is 'centric'. This simply concerns the centre of human subjectivity, its identity, the human self as a central quality of being human. This centring in itself is not a problem, but it commonly occurs in a way that has an enormous effect on the potential for conflict in historical culture. This is because the self or the 'I' or 'we' (as determining

factor in historical orientation) fundamentally demands normative self-affirmation. The reference to the self in the relationship of human beings to their
world, to themselves and to other human beings must be in a normative
sense positively charged. This necessarily belongs to the practical viability
of human life. The cartoon character Garfield the cat sums this up with the
quip: 'if I weren't me, I wouldn't like me very much'.[263] The self-referentiality of human subjectivity, which is realized in the cultural processes involved
in the formation of identity, always has a normative side. This determines
our relationship with ourselves as well as with others, from which we must
distinguish ourselves in order to be who we are. Here lie the mental roots
of ethnocentrism.

Asymmetrical Centring 'Ethnocentrism' means that this identity-forming
self-affirmation has a necessary consequence for the relationship to the otherness of others. Identity is always marked by a difference from others, whether
from another person in the case of our personal identity or from other social
formations in the case of social identity. In order to say 'I' or 'we', we necessarily need to assume a 'not I' or a 'not we'; every self assumes the otherness
of others. More precisely, this distinction occurs simultaneously with the
self-reference of human subjectivity.

How does this distinction lead to ethnocentrism? In determining value,
this distinction normatively charges the self while devaluing the otherness
of the other. The classic and universally accepted example from historical
culture of this *asymmetric valuation* is the distinction between civilization and
barbarism. Of course this asymmetry determines the conceptions of identity
developed by the other, as well. This inevitably leads to a tension, a contrast, a conflict (or 'clash') between 'us' and 'them'. And this conflict is the
problem.

This intensifies because of a further process: ethnocentric thinking proj-
ects those features that the subjective, identity-forming self finds problematic
or even unbearable, onto the otherness of the 'other'. It frees itself from
the burden of its own insufficiencies. Through this extra-territorializing of
the dark shadows of our own past, we experience the otherness of others
as a constant challenge or even a threat to our own self, just as we imagine
ourselves to be bright and pure. But we cannot escape our own shadow.
Through this estrangement, the shadow acquires a power over us that
deprives us of any control.

Coercing a Teleological Perspective   Because of this asymmetry, the temporal
direction that is so critical for the formation of identity takes the shape of a
mono-perspective teleology. It directs the horizon of historical meaning toward
the 'centre' of the self. This automatically constitutes a marginalization of the

'other'. These others are pushed to the edges of our own world. In traditional world views, this is where the barbarians lurk, if not the monsters and demons. In ethnocentric historical thinking, both a spatial and a temporal extra-territorializing of the other occurs. Its logical form is a teleology of our own culture.

The Course of Time and the Ordering of our Daily Lives The historical experience of the past is integrated into this notion of the passing of time, resulting in a present perspective of the future. This occurs exactly at the point where all time intersects in the inner self of the subject, where the human being with their social affiliations finds temporal orientation at the intersection of experience and expectation. The goal here is to create order in life, as it appears within the inner self of the subject. This order is conceived as a future constructed from the building blocks of historical experience and functions as the driving force behind daily life. This future orientation feeds off a notion of the past as already containing the origins of our own way of life. In many old master narratives, this origin is located in a mythical time in which past and future are one. But origins play an essential role in secular thought as well: they mark the direction of time, from past to present, often in a normative way. The true way of life is already laid out in the very beginning. This historical promise enters into the normative rules of present living circumstances and charts the perspective of a future in which the promises of the past are fulfilled. We could call this logic of forming historical meaning an *origin-oriented teleology*. It appears in most master narratives, from its mythical forms to the secular forms of the present. Because of this, festive commemorations of origins and beginnings play an important role in the public displays of historical culture in most cultures and societies.

The Self as the Centre of the World In the historical perspective that this logic reveals, the self (alternating between the personal and the social) finds its place in the centre. Here the self finds its temporal place in life, where past and future converge in remembering and expectation. This is where the inner temporality of the human subject is defined. We could say: in this historical dimension of the self, the human subject itself is time. Within this self in the self-referencing of identity, the otherness of the other is also assessed, since the human self can only be formed by way of distinguishing itself from the other. In the ethnocentric mindset, the otherness of the other is devalued and marginalized. (An inversion of ethnocentrism also exists. In that case, a longing for a more valuable life is projected onto the otherness of the other through the image of the noble savage. This 'inverted' ethnocentrism does not alter the conflicting tension between the self and the other. Its asymmetry and marginalization are reproduced in the inversion.) How do we then deal with this basic potential for conflict in human subjectivity?

Taming within the 'Clash of Civilizations'?   One of the most important demands in present-day historical culture is the containment, the taming and possibly overcoming of potential conflict inherent in ethnocentric thinking. Its power cannot be overestimated. This potential for conflict has deeply informed the relationships between cultures as well as the historical thinking of all humanity in its diverse and complex forms. Even today, it still defines wider areas of historical culture. This is especially the case when we consider the external relationships of our own culture, that is, the relationship between one's own affiliations and the affiliations of others. We cannot ignore this potential as simply a natural tension, and leave it at that. Rather, we must see the potential for conflict as a pressing challenge because, in today's process of globalization, there is no clear separation between the inside and the outside in the cultural processes that form historical identity. Globalization creates a closeness that demands new means for distinguishing ourselves from others. If we were to remain in the ethnocentric tradition, then historical orientation would represent a constant danger to peace. Within the framework of this tradition, the reason of historical thinking has a merely instrumental character. It is simply a tool to keep the other out, to distinguish between us and them, and no longer a chance to create understanding.

We cannot remove the distinction between us and them from the world, since, as repeatedly emphasized earlier, it is a constitutive part of human culture. (It is also deeply embedded in our biological evolution.) We can relocate it in the selfhood of the subject and allow it to multiply. We can then speak of hybridity as a new form of human identity. But even then we cannot solve the conflict between us and them. Hybrids are distinguished from one another at an even greater degree of complexity.[264]

Is Relativism a Solution?   What possibilities are there for taking the ethnocentric sting out of historical culture? At first glance, cultural relativism appears to be a plausible solution to the problem. Historical identity is expressed in an unlimited variety of manifestations that are all regarded as equal. One could wonder whether such relativism can really curb the mental power of self-affirmation. It ignores all validity claims presupposing that reason has a role to play in historical cognition. The cognitive price of historical relativism is too high. Moreover, it does not end the conflicts that are embedded in the relationship between the self and other. Historical relativism does not solve these conflicts but makes them unsolvable on the level of argumentative thinking. It is interconnected with the normative postulate of equality, varying historical affiliations and distinctions. But this postulate invalidates relativism, since it must be applied universally. It thus subscribes to a normative dimension of historical identity that has to be unfolded and strengthened against relativism. How is this possible?

Remain Human, Always and Everywhere   First and foremost, we must hold on to the human dimension of historical culture that is implicit in the claims of reason of historical knowledge. Forming an identity through the centring of the self should address the human quality that we all share. This would validate or even ratify the historical-philosophical conception of a cultural evolution of humanity in respect to the pragmatics of identity formation. The category of equality, which is contained within the universalizing quality of the concept of humanity, reduces the ethnocentric sting of devaluing the other to a reduced humanity. Where then do we find the shadows of negative historical experiences if we cannot unload them by differentiating ourselves from others? We cannot avoid integrating these shadows into our own self-image. When we do so, the relationship between the self and the other changes significantly. Negative historical experiences of the self are no longer extra-territorialized in the conceptualization of the otherness of others. Rather, they are – and this is the critical part – transformed into an ambivalence towards one's own historical self-image.[265] Within this ambivalence, the self and the other stand on equal footing. Then, we can see something of ourselves in the other due to our shared human quality: we can recognize our own humanity in the features of the other and catch a glimpse into their own particularity and individuality. If this happens, the asymmetry of the ethnocentric relationship between the self and the other transforms into a balance.

Dealing with Each Other Equally and Critically   Within this balance there is also (or there should be) room for criticism. This does not mean that we somehow make our shadows acceptable. This would open the doors to barbarism in historical culture. Without critical thought, the reason of historical culture is lost. Admittedly, criticism is also only plausible for the other in so far as it is based on standards that span differences. Such standards can only be derived from a desire for recognition that motivates every formation of historical identity. It is the desire of a person to be recognized as having purpose in oneself (to use Kant's formulation of self-purposefulness of all human beings). This self-purpose can be seen as a universal (humanistic) norm in the relationship we have to ourselves and to others (this can also often be counterfactual). This can be substantiated in philosophical terms, as it touches on the cultural attempts to make the 'asocial sociability' of the inner contradictions of our daily lives manageable. These attempts aim to make temporal changes conceivable and comprehensible as directional developments.[266]

With this goal of furthering humanity, the formation of identity in historical culture enters into the temporal change of our present living circumstances that will be interpreted and realized as historical in later times. Self-purpose as determining factor of historical identity has a focus on the future that overcomes the problematic constrictions of an origin-oriented teleology. *An origin-oriented teleology leads to a future-directed reconstruction.*[267] This expands the referential framework of historical identity: it concedes the ethnocentric pressure to conform, in which the developmental process towards our own way of life is seen as a continuous development. Instead we now accept a high degree of contingency, as well as fragmentation and contradictions.

Polycentricism in One World

Within the framework of this kind of historical thinking, the monocentric perspective of ethnocentric thinking breaks down. Our own history moves towards a plurality of different perspectives that refer to each other through discourse in an interplay between critique and recognition. This opens up chances for an intercultural understanding on the deeper level of historical culture and its identity-forming processes. The shared human quality is asserted in two ways: first, one's own way of life appears against the background of a comprehensive, transcultural, temporal form of humanity. At the same time, one's own identity does not lose its particular, individual features, but rather gains something: our individuality expresses itself to the same extent (and becomes recognizable) as the individuality of others as a manifestation of our own humanity, with our capacity to be recognized as well as criticized. These cultural achievements of forming identity can only occur on this particular level: when the movement of history occurs through the explication of one's own humanity, *from an exclusionary to an inclusionary concept of humanity.*

But the Human Being (Also) Remains Inhuman   This all sounds too good to be true. It is true, though, that, when we understand what it is to be human (that is, to have self-purpose), we must also systematically consider what it is to be fundamentally inhuman. This inhumanness occurs daily and systematically in the tense relationship between competing directions of human ways of life. It works as a motor in the temporal movement of human ways of life that can be interpreted as historical. Historical thinking is valid in terms of this inhumanness when it abandons the bias with which it relates the temporal movement to human action. The categorically action-oriented view needs to be fundamentally expanded to include the perception of suffering that causes or is caused by action. The inner humanism in the forming of historical identity is only realistic when human suffering is perceived and understood as an outcome of the same temporal movement with the same categorical importance. This realism takes nothing away from the humanity of human beings in view of their inhumanness. In view of the inhumanness of humanity it reveals a desire for meaning that gives the temporal movement of the human world the character of a development and thereby an implicit reference to the past. This development can and must occur in the processes in historical culture that form identity.

Humanizing Hermeneutics   Such an understanding carries and supports the hermeneutic process of historical cognition. Through the demands for orientation in our lives from within historical culture, the hermeneutics of historical thinking can and must be characterized as humanistic. It cultivates our capacity to not judge human ways of life by comparing them to our own. It makes it possible to interpret historical changes as more than just developments towards the present. It makes ways of life in different places and times understandable according to the perspectives of the human beings in question and systematically incorporates this understanding into all historical interpretations. Humanism grants human beings of the past the freedom of self-determination. It demands an understanding of other, less familiar ways of life. Humanistic hermeneutics enables different ways of life to meaningfully reflect on each other, so that we recognize our own particularity in the reflection of the other.

Humanism therefore means a mutual recognition and acceptance of cultural differences. Obviously, such recognition and acceptance cannot occur without criticism. On the contrary, humanistic hermeneutics assigns all human beings in their different ways of life a fundamental value. This has enormous potential for criticism (also towards our own way of life). Humanism is synonymous with criticism of all ways of life in which human beings must live by rules that they did not establish or accept, and in which they are humiliated, repressed, exploited and de-humanized.

Notes

242. For the following, see J. Rüsen. 2008. *Historisches Lernen*, 2nd ed., Schwalbach/Taunus: Wochenschau.

243. A good example here is W. Hasberg. 2001. *Empirische Forschung in der Geschichtsdidaktik*, 2 vols., Neuried: ars una.

244. See this volume, 100sqq.

245. Also W. Schreiber et al. (eds). 2006. *Historisches Denken*, Neuried: ars una.

246. See also M. Barricelli. 2007. *Schüler erzählen Geschichte*, Schwalbach/Taunus: Wochenschau.

247. See this volume, 157sqq.

248. I refer only generally to the work of Jean Piaget and Lawrence Kohlberg. For this topic area, see Kölbl, *Geschichtsbewußtsein im Jugendalter*. In terms of meaning and theory, developmental psychology can contribute something important on religious attitudes in explaining the ontogenesis of historical consciousness. See J.W. Fowler. 1991. *Stufen des Glaubens*, Gütersloh: Gütersloher Verlagshaus Gerd Mohn; as well as C. Noak. 1994. 'Stufen der Ich-Entwicklung und Geschichtsbewußtsein', in B. von Borries and H.-J. Pandel (eds), *Zur Genese historischer Denkformen*, Pfaffenweiler: Centaurus, 9–46.

249. See K. Fröhlich and J. Rüsen. 1991. 'Menschenrechte im Systemkonflikt', in idem. (eds), *Menschenrechte im Prozeß der Geschichte*, Pfaffenweiler: Centaurus; J. Rüsen. 2008. 'Die Individualisierung des Allgemeinen: Theorieprobleme einer vergleichenden Universalgeschichte der Menschenrechte', in idem, *Historische Orientierung*, 2nd ed., Schwalbach/Taunus: Wochenschau, 188–231.

250. I. Rüsen. 2008. 'Das Gute bleibt – wie schön!', in J. Rüsen, *Historisches Lernen*, 2nd ed. Schwalbach/Taunus: Wochenschau, 144–159.

251. For further considerations, see Rüsen, *Historisches Lernen*, above all 70–114.

252. Typical here according to my experience is the way in which indigenous culture of the Aborigines is presented in Australia. This is similar to what is found in Latin America and the attempts at conceding a normative or proper right to pre-Columbian culture (while reducing or relativizing the European heritage there).

253. In the accompanying information sheet given to the visitor (29.10.2010) the situation is described as follows: 'Juanita [the sacrificed girl] asks us … to treat with respect our rich cultural heritage now and in the future'. The problem of if and how we can respect ritualized human sacrifice does not appear to be a concern for the author of the information sheet. Rather than respecting the ritualized killing of a human being we should be asked to empathize with the victim.

254. It is worth citing this passage in full: 'Every epoch is immediate to God and its worth is not at all based on what derives from it but rests in its own existence, in its own self. In this way the contemplation of history, that is to say of individual life in history, acquires its own particular attraction. … The historian must … secondly, perceive the difference between the individual epochs in order to observe the inner necessity of the sequence. One cannot fail to recognize a certain progress here. But I would not want to say that this progress moves in a straight line, but more like a river which in its own way determines its course.' (Ranke: *The Theory and Practice of History*, 53 sq.) (*Über die Epochen der neueren Geschichte*, 58 f., 60, 62.)

255. For a fundamental treatment see Dux: *historisch-genetische Theorie der Kultur*. Important aspects are also found in G.W. Oesterdiekhoff. 1992. *Traditionales Denken und Modernisierung*, Opladen: Westdeutscher Verlag. He developed his theory on cultural evolution in numerous studies and belongs to the few evolutionary theorists who investigate human cultural evolution closely in line with the traditional concept of progress, as, for example, in G.W. Oesterdiekhoff. 2010. 'Die Humanisierung des Menschen', in J. Rüsen (ed.), *Perspektiven der Humanität*, Bielefeld: Transcript, 221–256. See also S. Pinker. 2011. *The Better Angels of Our Nature*, New York: Viking Adult.

256. Hermann Lübbe drew clear attention to this in his work: H. Lübbe. 2012. *Geschichtsbegriff und Geschichtsinteresse*, 2nd ed. Basel and Stuttgart: Schwabe.

257. Kierkegaard described this self-referentiality in concise terms by saying: the human self is a relation's relating itself to itself in the relation. S. Kierkegaard. 1962. *Die Krankheit zum Tode*, Reinbek: Rowohlt, 13. (*The Sickness unto Death*, Princeton, NJ: Princeton University Press, 1983, 43.)

258. The relevant literature on the topic is vast. I will simply point out the work of Jürgen Straub (e.g., J. Straub. 2004. 'Identität', in F. Jaeger and B. Liebsch (eds), *Handbuch der Kulturwissenschaften. Grundlagen und Schlüsselbegriffe*, vol. 1. Stuttgart: Carl Ernst Poeschel,

277–303). Straub deals with the specific concept of identity in modern psychology, as, for example, it has been developed by Erik Erikson. In this case a specific aspect of the human self is explored that derives on a psychological level from the special conditions developing out of our confrontation with modernity. In this respect, Straub can say that we need to be careful of an anthropologically universalizing conception of identity. But what concept is available to us if we want to speak of the fundamental and universal quality of being human that allows us, even compels us, to behave on a reflexive level as a morally responsible and temporally coherent subject? I am interested in this anthropological universality when I discuss identity in the following. See also A. Assmann and H. Friese (eds). 1998. *Identitäten*, Frankfurt am Main: Suhrkamp.

259. E.g., L. Niethammer. 2000. *Kollektive Identität*, Reinbek: Rowohlt.

260. See B. Giesen (ed.). 1991. *Nationale und kulturelle Identität*, Frankfurt am Main: Suhrkamp; also idem. 1991. *Die Entdinglichung des Sozialen*, Frankfurt am Main: Suhrkamp.

261. See J. Straub. 1998. 'Personale und kollektive Identität', in A. Assmann and H. Friese (eds), *Identitäten: Erinnerung, Geschichte*, Frankfurt am Main: Suhrkamp, 73–104.

262. For the following, see Rüsen, 'How to Overcome Ethnocentrism: Approaches to a Culture of Recognition by History in the 21st Century', *History and Theory* 43, 118–129; also idem. 2004. 'Tradition and Identity: Theoretical Reflections and the European Example', *Taiwan Journal of East Asian Studies* 1(2), 135–158.

263. I found this quote as expressed by the comic character Garfield (01.10.1984). It appeared in the essay on ethnocentrism and how to overcome it as listed above in footnote 262.

264. The hope tied to the metaphor of the hybrid in overcoming the sharp distinction between the self and the 'other' as a way of creating a new form of inclusiveness is lost in the metaphor itself. Hybrids are creatures that are incapable of reproducing themselves. As such, a hybrid identity would lose its temporal dimension, which the human self wants (or needs) in the formative processes of creating identity.

265. We see this, for example, in the treatment of the Holocaust in German historical culture. For more on this, see J. Rüsen. 2005. *History: Narration, Interpretation, Orientation*, New York: Berghahn Books, 189–204, esp. 201 sqq. ('Holocaust-Memory and German Identity').

266. See this volume, 87sqq.

267. See this volume, 72sqq.

Final Reflections

Finding Reason between Meaning and Meaninglessness

One of the main themes of this book is that historical thinking brings together past and future in the temporal orientation of the present way of life and that this is carried by a consistent level of meaning.

Without this consistency in meaning, historical thinking would be meaningless and historical scholarship left lingering in a realm of uncertainty without knowing what it is for. Historical thinking is based on a fundamental reliance on meaning that is anchored in the depth of human subjectivity. One of the most important tasks of metahistory is to explicate this reliance on meaning, substantiate (or question) it and show how it drives historical scholarship. In doing so, it is confronted with the difficulty of having to face and contend with the undeniable experiences of meaninglessness that an unbiased look at the beginning of the twenty-first century inevitably reveals. Such experiences alter the contours of the basic historical question on human identity. In the words of Eelco Runia, 'Who are we that this could have happened?'[268] How do we respond to this question?

1. Meaning and Meaninglessness

Let us first pause at the fundamental elements of historical meaning: it has many dimensions covering a wide operating range.[269]

(a) The first and simplest is the *comprehensibility* of historical representation. Historical texts are meaningful if they can be understood. This dimension is in fact so elementary and narrow that we can easily overlook it. But it already involves the meaning of historical knowledge produced by historical scholarship.

(b) Historical meaning gains a more far-reaching dimension when the comprehensibility of a text is seen within the context in which it is developed and in which it operates (for instance, the formation of personal or social identity). Meaning takes on *practical and normative significance*. A text is not only meaningful in the sense that it can be understood, but also in the sense that its comprehensibility contributes to the orientation of those comprehending it. But what makes texts understandable and (practically) meaningful?

(c) Specifically historical texts acquire a more comprehensive relevance when their meaning illuminates the temporal coherence between past and future. Meaning now refers to real-life temporal processes that are empirically (pre-)given. In its broadest sense, this dimension of meaning encompasses humanity in all its temporal complexity. Meaning here becomes that which we call the cultural character of human life and its development. (Here we must also include nature, which makes determining this meaning extremely difficult.[270])

This complex structure of meaning is also embedded in historical culture. It represents the logical premise for any kind of historical thinking and forms the base upon which the activities of historical consciousness take place. It is a dynamic process in the interplay between experience and interpretation, between enduring and dealing with time.

All these dimensions of meaning are communicative and therefore interactive. Science can be understood as an intersection of this reciprocal interpenetration of dimensions through time and space. In academic study, meaning is conceptualized through research, explicated on an argumentative level, criticized and modified. Simply put, meaning is enhanced or advanced with regard to its cognitive assertiveness, its conceivability and perceptibility.

The Precarious Character of Historical Meaning　　One of the main themes of this work on metahistory is that the operations of the human mind involved in producing the meaning of history cannot be sufficiently understood if we look at them only as 'inherent' processes of historical consciousness. Rather, they occur in a complex interplay between 'inwardly projected' subjectivity and 'outwardly projected' objectivity of experience. The formation of meaning in the human mind is always tied to preset elements of meaning, so it is not a purely autonomous cultural processing of empirical facts.[271] Indeed, these presets, this claim for meaning, always require an active 'response'.

This has to do with the fact that the meaningfulness of human culture, in all its contradictory and unsettling circumstances, is always difficult to identify and is often perceived as problematic. *Meaning is always tied to meaninglessness.* This precarious form of meaning in the preset cultural elements of historical consciousness extends to the activities of this consciousness as a question and as a challenge in a broad and multifarious manner.

The many precarious preset elements of meaning that stimulate historical meaning are listed typologically as follows.

(a) We encounter meaning as the *powerful influence of tradition*. Historical thinking must deal with this influence reflexively and respond to tradition by alternating between respect and critique.[272]

(b) We encounter meaning in the form of *temporal alterity*. Current living conditions are not identical to those that existed at the time when the preset elements of meaning were established. Meaning lies within the divide of historical differences. In principle, all preset elements of meaning from the past must be interpreted in the present at the point where the living conditions of the present deviate from those in the past. The temporal movement of the human way of life that creates the phenomenon of 'history' extends into the activities of the human mind that are dedicated to this phenomenon and is shaped by it. Texts cannot be understood once and for all, but must be made understandable again and again. This is most certainly the case as regards the contexts.

(c) We encounter meaning historically in the form of *deficits in meaning*. Cultural achievements can appear limited and prompt a transgression of their limits. An example is the history of human and civil rights and the corresponding political culture of democratic legitimation of power. Initially they only applied to a limited group of citizens, but (even today) more and more people demand these rights. If we take the humanity criterion of the integral historical development seriously,[273] then we can judge almost all humanizing achievements as lacking. This criterion for meaning forces historical thinking to open up perspectives for the future that are characterized by chances for greater humanization.

(d) In view of the ever-condensing intercultural communication, there is a new potential for challenge: the *divergence in meaning* between different traditions in historical thinking. We could see this as a relativistic consequence and assume an enrichment of historical thinking through a plethora of differing perspectives. But is this form of pluralism really an advantage if it means there are no more transcultural perspectives in the formation of historical meaning that could be deciphered in an intercultural discourse? Then we are left with divergence, and chances to expand or intensify meaning, which lie in a communicative relationship between different concepts of meaning, remain unused.

(e) The *forgetting of meaning* is an experience of loss in historical culture that can be identified as such and then overcome through the appropriation of forgotten or repressed potentials for meaning. A well-known example is Max Weber's interpretation of modern capitalism as a determining force that turns human beings into the functionaries in a systematic process. For those subjected to this process, essential elements of a meaningful life are either withheld or even destroyed.[274] The historical memory of a time when this was not the case acts to fill the void of meaninglessness (for Weber, this is where capitalism acquires its religious bent). Cultural criticism of modernism is based on this kind of interpretive strategy: the historical process in which modern ways of life have developed is interpreted as destructive to meaning. The pre-modern period takes on a compensatory role as a source for meaning.

(f) Historical thinking can also *destroy meaning*. When this happens, the formation of meaning of the past is no longer taken seriously on a hermeneutic level, but instead is dismissed on the basis of ideological criticism, ruining or wasting the chances for orientation. A prominent example of this is Marx's interpretation of human and civil rights. He considered them to be merely a legal side effect of the capitalistic exploitation of humans by other humans. With this interpretation we lose the potential for meaning still found in the developmental process involved in a broad form of humanization. A similar example involves the more recent attempts of Chinese intellectuals to blame all the evils attached to the modern world, such as environmental destruction and loss of morality, on the Western Enlightenment.[275] Post-modern and post-colonial criticisms offer other examples. Regardless of its critical function, post-modernism destroys the meaning embedded in the processes of the universalization of human qualities. These critics disregard meaningful criteria for cultural orientation (including historical cognition) and toss them into the refuse of the past. Post-colonial critics project a destructive character onto the forces of modernization in Western culture,[276] and ignore the opposing tendencies without which the critique of modernism would no longer be plausible.

(g) *Traumatic annihilation of meaning* is the most radical challenge to historical culture. Here we must consider how the constitutive meaning of historical thinking is experienced as destroyed (that is, traumatized), not only for those immediately affected by the trauma but also for people born later who somehow relate to this meaning. It is necessary to process this experience through historical interpretation and to bring out its radical absurdity. In no way should historical thinking deal with such an annihilation of meaning with evasive strategies. If ignored, the trauma will only have an uncontrollable effect on the human unconscious.[277]

Meaning as a Problem   Today, there is nothing self-evident or obvious about 'the meaning of history'. The concept of a singular 'meaning of history' is seen as problematic and completely absurd. And yet we must assume there is such a meaning if we want to think historically in a meaningful way. The nagging doubt that comes with this assumption points to two things: a desire for meaning that fundamentally and continuously arises from human life, and an inability to fulfil such a desire. From this divide the capacity for inner-temporal differences to come about in the cultural forming of meaning can develop.

It is here, for example, that the future is imagined as the place for the fulfilment of meaning that the present demands but cannot produce. In order to make this future plausible, we can look to the past to find traces of this possible fulfilment and see this loss of fulfilment as characteristic of the present. All critical and emancipatory assessments of history follow this concept of time.

Or conversely, fears about the future lead us to imagine the past as a world filled with meaning. The present is seen as lacking in meaning, which can only be endured by remembering that things used to be different. We act in the hope that the world could be different. An example of this way of thinking is the way in which meaning is determined in the works of Max Weber and Jacob Burckhardt.[278]

Meaninglessness   The most pressing question in historical theory is how we must deal with meaninglessness and the absurd. Both are a constitutive part of the experience of time that drives human historical consciousness. As already pointed out, they can extend into historical thinking itself. The inner absurdity of human culture all too often, or always really, drives historical thinking to the idea of the end of time, an eschaton, where there is no more history. The desire for meaning can then only be fulfilled beyond or outside of history. Historical thinking sets its own limits in the dynamics of human life, which are driven by contradictions ('unsocial sociability'). We must look beyond these limits in order that historical thinking, though rooted within meaninglessness, might yet move forwards.

Trauma   As explained earlier, traumatic experiences play a particular role in the formation of historical meaning. These experiences have a destructive character and therefore they represent a radical challenge to historical think-ing. How can we think about these experiences – as they can only acquire meaning through thinking – without neglecting their particular quality?[279]

A convincing response to this question has to retain the meaninglessness of the thoughts. This means *demanding a degree of ambivalence about the category of meaning*, for which there are not many convincing concepts in historiog-raphy.[280] They are more readily available in art and religion. For historical thinking this means keeping a keen eye on human suffering in the cultural practices in which suffering is endured and overcome, as part of historical thinking itself. In so doing, we give these practices a specifically historical resonance. What would this look like?

Mourning An example of these cultural practices would be *mourning*. Its cognitive potential and temporal breadth in historical culture have not been sufficiently perceived or realized.[281] Mourning is a mental reaction to loss that affects our own identity. The paradigm of this is the loss of a loved one. With this loss, a part of our self that developed from our identification with this person dies, too. In the reifying language of psychoanalysis, we speak of the introjection of an 'object' in one's own self. Mourning is coping with this loss of self in the loss of another. Mourning means accepting this loss. Through grief, the person lost to us is removed from our inner self, while we gain a new but separate self. The absence of the loved one is not simply verified; rather, he or she is made present as absent. The lost person does not simply disappear from the mental chambers of those left behind, but gains his or her own place in the living world of memory.

In older cultures, the act of mourning addresses and makes present the other dimension of human existence in which humans live their life after death. In archaic societies, for example, the dead are transformed into ancestors through the rituals of mourning. Often this other dimension is regarded as more real and more significant than the dimension of the living. This is less often the case in modern societies, although the past remains alive through memory and can enormously influence the human unconscious.

The mental capacity for dealing with loss through mourning is not limited to grieving a personal relationship. Mourning can extend to loss that extends back past our own lifespan. This is the experience of historical loss, which also concerns our own (personal and social) identity. Crimes against humanity, for example, can represent such experiences of loss because they put our own humanity at risk. Being human is always a part of historical identity, though in varying ways, such as ethnically specific, universally exclusive, or universally inclusive, and varying constellations. Historical mourning realizes this loss of self in the temporal perspective of the formation of the historical self. Through the painful awareness of our loss of humanity, we direct this pain towards a virtual place within the space of historical consciousness. Mourning transcends the loss of our humanity towards a willingness to act for the following reason: such loss must and can never occur again. The future must grant more space for humanity. In this historical act of mourning, human dignity becomes a crucial motivational power in historical culture that transforms the past into the future through interpretation. The past is not losing the horror of how meaning can be made into something insane. The opposite is true: from the horrors of insanity we gain a perspective of how to stop and overcome the madness.

Overpowering of Meaning   In light of the growing significance of the experience of meaninglessness and absurdity – we need only consider the inflationary use of the concept of trauma – we should not overlook the opposing phenomenon: the experience of meaning as something overpowering, an experience that also belongs within the realm of culture. Traditionally this is understood as a numinous experience,[282] or as '*kairos*' (time fulfilled). Such experiences take place in the modern period, too; for example, as described by Marcel Proust:

> No sooner … than a shudder ran through me and I stopped, intent upon the extraordinary thing that was happening to me. An exquisite pleasure had invaded my senses, something isolated, detached, with no suggestion of its origin. And at once the vicissitudes of life had become indifferent to me, its disasters innocuous, its brevity illusory – this new sensation having had on me the effect which love has of filling me with a precious essence; or rather this essence was not in me, it was me. I had ceased to feel mediocre, contingent, mortal.[283]

In contrast to trauma, which dispels all concepts of meaning in life into a disturbing meaninglessness, this is a positive 'trauma', an overpowering rise above meaning. It also dispels the preset elements of meaning in daily life that for the most part seem insufficient. Here they do not negate but rather surpass themselves. The 'true meaning' appears beyond the efforts of the human mind to come to terms with the suffering and contradictions of life and stimulate action with concepts of happiness.

And where do we locate conceptually historical thinking in light of these experiences? It lies somewhere in between: both experiences, the destroying and the overwhelming, stimulate historical thinking, but historical thinking does not develop directly from either one. Historical thinking cannot give direct meaning to trauma, nor can it operate as overpowering meaning. It incorporates meaninglessness as an element in the interpretive potential of historical consciousness and feeds off the hope for a fulfilment of meaning as highest endeavour in the lives of human beings.

Meaning between Past, Present and Future   This 'in between' appears in the temporal relationship between human beings of the past, who have had these extreme experiences, and human beings of the present, who (can) relate to these historical extreme experiences. On one side we have the level of experience of those affected and on the other side the interpretive level of the observer. The latter also concerns an experience: the experience of the experience, so to speak. In this act of re-experiencing, the meaning that was suffered and lived in the past is shared across time as something relevant to the present. This meaning, whether negative or positive, demands some kind of response. It invites us to overcome meaninglessness or to adopt the fulfilment of meaning.

The absurdity of the Holocaust, for example, extends from the victims of that time to human beings who were born after the events. This is not just an intergenerational issue. It affects all historically thinking people because it concerns a crime against humanity. Accordingly, it affects the humanity of human beings born in a later period. It is in the nature of the absurdity of this historical experience that it demands to be considered as an essential part of historical identity in the conceptualizing of the meaning of our own humanity.

The same is true for the experiences of fulfilment of meaning in the past if they also concern the notion of our own humanity. An example of this is the 'Declaration of the Rights of Man and of the Citizen' from the French Revolution. For those who lived through this period, the moment was experienced as *kairos*, as hope fulfilled. It also has come to represent a benchmark for future generations.[284] Those born at a later period experience this *kairos* historically as a call for human beings to recognize the idea of 'the rights of man' as binding, as a tradition to continue and an idea to realize. In their historical interpretation, they place themselves within a broad developmental process that includes both past and future. In this process, the validity of human rights is universalized on an intercultural level, or at least it should be. At the same time, these ideas concerning legal control over political power structures become embedded in the social and cultural realms.

2. Once Again: The Limitations of Science

We must be clear: historical scholarship does not produce the meaning that historians have uncovered or unlocked from the past. Rather, it is based much more on the preset elements of meaning in an unprethinkable (*unvordenkliche*: a concept from Schelling on the most fundamental precondition for everything) time when culture began to mark the human world. History transforms the preset concepts of meaning into cognitive output.[285] They develop a specific formation of meaning that is critical for their field of study through methodical thinking. Within the context of meaning as something occurring in culture, which is an integral part of academic study, we can characterize this output as *reason in use*. To put it emphatically, historical scholarship stands for the rationality of historical thinking. Of course human reason is not limited to this kind of thinking. Moreover, not everything that occurs within this domain can be called reasonable. But in scientific form, human reason gains cognitive precision and conciseness. This precision in thought, derived from academic study, extends into the practical context of historical culture. As we have seen earlier, metahistory can and must provide didactics with the driving impulses to determine our goals for learning history.

The use of reason in academic study also has a thoroughly practical side, as we have seen earlier. But we also realize that this practical side has definite limitations. Clearly we understand that not all scholarly historical knowledge depends on its practical and cultural application. In view of the many activities, institutions and processes that operate or occur in historical culture, the opposite is the case. In the endeavour of scholarship, cognitive processes whose results are self-serving and whose sole purpose is knowledge production without any recognizable practical function are often dominant. Ironically, the plethora of academic footnotes in scientific publications represents a lack of practical relevance. Generally though, we need to keep in mind the disciplinary matrix of historical studies in which this lack of practical relevance becomes a condition (among others) for progress in the field.[286]

Conversely, there are many and pronounced needs for orientation that cannot be met through the cognitive achievements of historical knowledge (the needs that lead us to art and religion). And the unconscious depths of human subjectivity remain difficult if not impossible to reach with academic and institutional achievements of historical thinking.

And yet we must enquire into these domains that lie beyond methodically regulated cognition. Only then might we discern what science can and cannot do, and how the possibilities can be broadened or expanded. At any rate, we must avoid a reflexive self-isolation of historical cognition. How else are we able to properly perceive the contribution that academic study can make to the possible improvements of human life?[287]

The limits of historical scholarship lie where historical thinking is rooted in the present course of history as the unprethinkable (or pre-conscious) occurring of meaning.[288] Only in rare instances can one have inspiring experiences of this meaningfulness (or its opposite).[289]

Great historians like Jacob Burckhardt have found ways to express this inspiration (when dealing with the fundamental questions of what they do). He is one of few historians who have been able to express 'despair and lamentation' as elements of the historical experience. Despite this, or maybe because of this, he was able to discern a focus or direction in historical thinking beyond our individuality (meaning, beyond the competence of historical cognition). Burckhardt conferred on history a 'spirit of humanity' ('*Geist der Menschheit*') as it built its new dwelling, soaring above, yet closely bound up with all these manifestations (meaning the crisis-shaken character of the present, J.R.).[290] History here is 'a marvelous spectacle, though not for contemporary earthly beings', meaning, history for Burckhardt is not something we can access on a clear cognitive level. Despite or maybe because of this evading nature, this idea of history is the only one that makes sense to Burckhardt.

The relevant perspectives of historical orientation arise from an irrefutable necessity of the human mind to come to terms with the conflicting factors in our 'unsocial sociability' (Kant's '*ungesellige Geselligkeit*'). The greatest desire of the human mind is to appease the inner contradictions, the inconsistencies in our daily lives. This is expressed in ideas of a quality of life that goes beyond all the concrete forms of contingency in life. These ideas could be identified in a comprehensive concept for happiness in the form of a general principle of justice or a fundamental liberation from suffering.

Here lies yet another limit of historical thinking. Such emphatic intentions transcend the realm of historical experience and the forming of meaning, though not by losing sight of them. Science participates in these intentions, as its claims of reason imply the idea that reason determines the lives of human beings, acting as a stimulus in daily life. This idea is high-minded. It goes beyond all experience. With the power of hope and desire, it can inspire us in our dealings with experience and knowledge.

Historical reason takes its orientational power from both of these areas of meaning that lie beyond its discursive dealings with the experience of time and that are overlooked in the day-to-day business of research. In the modus of a methodically systematic approach to information, it considers the area of historical experience from two perspectives: from the absoluteness or unconditionality of the meaning of human culture, and from the possibility to actively form the living circumstances according to fundamental concepts of humanity. Both can stimulate academic study in the pursuit of knowledge.

By marking both limits, the unprethinkability and the emphasis or effusiveness of the defining criteria for meaning in historical thinking, we prevent the narrowing of this thinking. Rather, we locate it in the lives of human beings. Recognizing limitations opens up possibilities to work with them and even to transcend them. In manoeuvring between them, historical thinking can contribute to the humanization of human beings. Let us concede that historical thinking is moved by the absurdity in life and is sustained by the fundamental trust in the preset elements of meaning in interpreting and dealing with time. Historical thinking might then lead to interpretive work that lends weight to our own humanity.

Notes

268. See this volume, 105sq.
269. See this volume, 16sqq.
270. See this volume, 75sqq.

271. Emil Angehrn emphasized this elementary fact as '*Sinnbildung gründet im Sinngeschehen*' ('the forming of meaning is founded in the happening of meaning'). E. Angehrn. 2011. 'Sinngeschehen und Sinnbildung', *Erwägen Wissen Ethik* 22(4), 490–493, quote, 492.

272. See A. Assmann. 1999. *Zeit und Tradition*, Cologne: Böhlau; J. Rüsen. 2012. 'Tradition: A Principle of Historical Sense Generation and its Logic and Effect in Historical Culture', *History and Theory*, theme issue 'Tradition' 51(4), 45–59.

273. See this volume, 89.

274. Above all in his examination of the Protestant ethic and the spirit of capitalism.

275. Strikingly presented in Wei-Ming Tu, 'Confucian Humanism as a Spiritual Resource for Global Ethics', 1–8.

276. An example of this is in the work of Vinay Lal. 2005. 'Much Ado about Something: The New Malaise of World History', *Radical History Review* 91, 124–130; idem. 2005. 'The Concentration Camp and Development: The Pasts and Future of Genocide', *Patterns of Prejudice* 39(2), 220–243; idem, 'The Politics of Culture and Knowledge after Postcolonialism', 191–205. See also S. Seth. 2011. 'Where is Humanism Going?', *The Unesco Courier* (October–December), 6–9.

277. See Rüsen, 'Krise, Trauma, Identität', 145–179, especially 171–179.

278. M. Weber. 1992. *The Protestant Ethic and the Spirit of Capitalism*, London: Routledge, 122 sqq. For Burckhardt see Rüsen: *Konfigurationen des Historismus*, 276–328 ('Der ästhetische Glanz der historischen Erinnerung – Jacob Burckhardt').

279. See this volume, 28sqq.

280. A counter example worth noting is in S. Friedländer. 1998–2006. *Das Dritte Reich und die Juden*. Vol. 1: *Die Jahre der Verfolgung 1933–1939*. Munich: C.H. Beck; vol. 2: *Die Jahre der Vernichtung: Das Dritte Reich und die Juden, 1939–1945*. Munich: C.H. Beck. (*Nazi Germany and the Jews*, 2 vols, New York: Harper Collins, 1997, 2007.); also see idem. 2007. *Den Holocaust beschreiben*, Göttingen: Wallstein.

281. See B. Liebsch and J. Rüsen (eds). 2001. *Trauer und Geschichte*, Cologne: Böhlau; and B. Liebsch. 2006. *Revisionen der Trauer*, Weilerswist: Velbrück Wissenschaft; J. Rüsen. 2008. 'Leidensverdrängung und Trostbedarf im historischen Denken', in T.R. Peters and C. Urban (eds), *Über den Trost*, Ostfildern: Matthias Grünewald Verlag, 76–84; J. Rüsen. 2008. 'Emotional Forces in Historical Thinking', *Historein. A Review of the Past and Other Stories* 8, 41–53; B. Bevernage. 2012. *History, Memory, and State-sponsored Violence*, New York: Routledge, 147–167 ('History and the Work of Mourning').

282. Otto, *The Idea of the Holy: An Inquiry into the Non-rational Factor in the Idea of the Divine and its Relation to the Rational*.

283. M. Proust. 1992. *Remembrance of Things Past*, book 1, *Swann's Way*. New York: Modern Library, 48.

284. Kant, in considering the enthusiasm with which his contemporaries greeted the French Revolution, interpreted it as a '*Geschichtszeichen*' (sign of history) that represented a '*Tendenz des menschlichen Geschlechts im ganzen*' ('tendency found within the human species in general') (I. Kant. 1968. 'Der Streit der Fakultäten', in W. Weischedel (ed.), *Werke in zehn Bänden*, vol. 9, Darmstadt: Wissenschaftliche Buchgesellschaft, A 142–144).

285. See this volume, 45.

286. See this volume, 43.

287. This can be considered a challenging concept of whether and how yesterday can become better. See E. Schulin. 1998. '"Ich hoffe immer noch, dass gestern besser wird" – Bemerkungen zu einem von Jörn Rüsen gewählten Motto', in H.W. Blanke, F. Jaeger and T. Sandkühler (eds), *Dimensionen der Historik*, Cologne: Böhlau, 3–12; J. Rüsen. 2003. *Kann gestern besser werden?*, Berlin: Kulturverlag Kadmos; G. Essen. 2007. '"Can Yesterday Get Better?" The Trouble with Memory and the Gift of the Eucharist', in H. Schildermann (ed.), *Discourse in Ritual Studies*, Leiden: Brill, 277–297.

288. See this volume, 63.

289. These experiences can be had with historical events (e.g., declarations of human rights) and people (e.g., Buddha, St Francis, Gandhi, Mandela), although they lie in a meta- or pre-historic realm, that is, they break beyond the borders of time and space, becoming direct or immediate experiences. Nonetheless, they are effective in thought processes that pertain to setting and events as they occurred.

290. Burckhardt, *Weltgeschichtliche Betrachtungen*, 325 (*Force and Freedom*, New York: Pantheon Books, 1943, 370); Burckhardt, *Über das Studium der Geschichte: Der Text der 'Weltgeschichtlichen Betrachtungen'*, 294 f.

Bibliography

Adorno, T.W. 1966. *Negative Dialektik*. Frankfurt am Main: Suhrkamp. [*Negative Dialectics*. New York: Continuum International, 2007.]

Angehrn, E. 1991. *Geschichtsphilosophie*. Stuttgart: Kohlhammer.

Angehrn, E. 2010. *Sinn und NichtSinn: Das Verstehen des Menschen*. Tübingen: Mohr/Siebeck.

Angehrn, E. 2011. 'Sinngeschehen und Sinnbildung: Hermeneutische Überlegungen', *Erwägen Wissen Ethik* 22(4), 490–493.

Ankersmit, F. 2012. *Meaning, Truth, and Reference in Historical Representation*. Ithaca, NY: Cornell University Press.

Antweiler, C. 2007. *Menschliche Universalien: Kultur, Kulturen und die Einheit der Menschheit*. Darmstadt: Wiss. Buchgesellschaft.

Antweiler, C. 2011. *Mensch und Weltkultur: Für einen realistischen Kosmopolitismus im Zeitalter der Globalisierung*. Bielefeld: Transcript. [*Inclusive Humanism: Anthropological Basics for a Realistic Cosmopolitanism*. Göttingen: Vandenhoeck & Ruprecht unipress; Taipei: National Taiwan University Press, 2012.]

Aristoteles. 1982. *Poetik: Griechisch/Deutsch*. Stuttgart: Reclam [English translation: http://www.perseus.tufts.edu/hopper/text?doc=Perseus%3Atext%3A1999.01.0056%3Asection%3D1447a]

Arnason, J.P., S.N. Eisenstadt and B. Wittrock (eds). 2005. *Axial Civilisations and World History*. Leiden: Brill.

Assmann, A. 1999. *Erinnerungsräume: Formen und Wandlungen des kulturellen Gedächtnisses*. Munich: C.H. Beck.

Assmann, A. 1999. *Zeit und Tradition: Kulturelle Strategien der Dauer* (= *Beiträge zur Geschichtskultur*, vol. 15). Cologne: Böhlau.

Assmann, A. and U. Frevert. 1999. *Geschichtsvergessenheit, Geschichtsversessenheit: Vom Umgang mit deutschen Vergangenheiten nach 1945*. Stuttgart: Deutsche Verlagsanstalt.

Assmann, A. and H. Friese (eds). 1998. *Identitäten*. Frankfurt am Main: Suhrkamp.

Assmann, J. 1992. *Das kulturelle Gedächtnis: Schrift, Erinnerung und politische Identität in frühen Hochkulturen*. Munich: C.H. Beck. [*Cultural Memory and Early Civilization: Writing, Remembrance, and Political Imagination*. Cambridge: Cambridge University Press, 2011.]

Assmann, J. 1995. *Politische Theologie zwischen Ägypten und Israel*, 2nd ed. Munich: Hanser.

Badt, K. 1971. *Eine Wissenschaftslehre der Kunstgeschichte*. Cologne: Dumont.

Barricelli, M. 2007. *Schüler erzählen Geschichte: Narrative Kompetenz im Geschichtsunterricht*. Schwalbach/Taunus: Wochenschau.

Bauer, W. 1927. *Einführung in das Studium der Geschichte*, 2nd ed. Tübingen: Mohr.

Baumgartner, H.M. 1972. *Kontinuität und Geschichte: Zur Kritik und Metakritik der historischen Vernunft.* Frankfurt am Main: Suhrkamp.

Beard, C.A. 1935. 'That Noble Dream', *The American Historical Review* 41(1), 74–87.

Becker, C.L. 1935. 'Every Man His Own Historian', in idem, *Every Man His Own Historian: Essays on History and Politics.* New York: F.S. Croft & Co, 233–255.

Bédarida, F. (ed.). 1995. *The Social Responsibility of the Historian.* Oxford: Berghahn Books.

Benjamin, W. 1977. 'Der Erzähler: Betrachtungen zum Werk Nikolai Lesskows', in idem, *Gesammelte Schriften,* vol. II.2, edited by R. Tiedemann and H. Schweppenhäuser. Frankfurt am Main: Suhrkamp, 438–465. ['The Storyteller: Reflections on the Works of Nikolai Leskov', in idem, *Illuminations,* edited by H. Arendt. New York: Schocken Books, 1969, 83–109, quoted from D.J. Hale (ed.), *An Anthology of Criticism and Theory 1900–2000.* Malden, MA: Blackwell Publishing, 2006] [Available online at: http://www.massey.ac.nz/ massey/fms/Colleges/College%20of%20Humanities%20and%20Social%20Sciences/EMS/ Readings/139.105/Additional/The%20Storyteller%20-%20Walter%20Benjamin.pdf.]

Benjamin, W. 1991. 'Über den Begriff der Geschichte', in idem, *Gesammelte Schriften,* edited by R. Tiedemann and H. Schweppenhäuser, vol. I.2. Frankfurt am Main: Suhrkamp, 691– 704. ['Theses on the Philosophy of History', in idem, *Illuminations,* edited by H. Arendt. New York: Schocken, 1969, 253–264.] [Available online at: http://www.composingdig italmedia.org/f15_mca/mca_reads/benjamin-theses-on-the-philosophy-of-history.pdf.] ['On the Concept of History', available online at: http://members.efn.org/~dredmond/ ThesesonHistory.html; https://www.marxists.org/reference/archive/benjamin/1940/his tory.htm.]

Bernheim, E. 1908. *Lehrbuch der Historischen Methode und der Geschichtsphilosophie: Mit Nachweis der wichtigsten Quellen und Hülfsmittel zum Studium der Geschichte,* 5th ed. Leipzig: Duncker & Humblot.

Bevernage, B. 2012. *History, Memory, and the State Sponsored Violence: Time and Justice.* New York: Routledge.

Bodin, J. 1966. *Method for the Easy Comprehension of History.* New York: Octagon Books.

Borries, B. von, H.-J. Pandel and J. Rüsen (eds). 1991. *Geschichtsbewußtsein empirisch.* Pfaffenweiler: Centaurus.

Borries, B. von and J. Rüsen (eds). 1994. *Geschichtsbewußtsein im interkulturellen Vergleich: Zwei empirische Pilotstudien.* Pfaffenweiler: Centaurus.

Brieler, U. 1998. *Die Unerbittlichkeit der Historizität: Foucault als Historiker.* Cologne: Böhlau.

Burckhardt, J. 1949. *Weltgeschichtliche Betrachtungen: Historisch-kritische Gesamtausgabe,* compiled and edited by R. Stadelmann. Pfullingen: Neske. Alternative edition: *Gesamtausgabe,* vol. 7: *Weltgeschichtliche Betrachtungen: Historische Fragmente aus dem Nachlaß,* edited by A. Oeri and E. Dürr. Stuttgart: Deutsche Verlagsanstalt, 1929. [*Force and Freedom: Reflections on History.* New York: Pantheon Books, 1943.]

Burckhardt, J. 1982. *Über das Studium der Geschichte: Der Text der 'Weltgeschichtlichen Betrachtungen': Aufgrund der Vorarbeiten von Ernst Ziegler nach den Handschriften,* edited by P. Ganz. Munich: C.H. Beck.

Carr, D. 2011. 'Which Way is East? Rüsen's *Historik*', *Erwägen Wissen Ethik* 22(4), 508–509.

Cavalli-Sforza, L.L. 2000. *Genes, Peoples, and Languages.* New York: North Point Press.

'Chinese and Western Historical Thinking'. 2007. Forum in *History & Theory* 46(2), 180–232.

Chladenius, J.M. 1985. *Allgemeine Geschichtswissenschaft, worinnen der Grund zu einer neuen Einsicht in allen Arten der Gelahrtheit geleget wird.* Vienna: Böhlaus Nachf. (Excerpts in H.W. Blanke and D. Fleischer (eds). 1990. *Theoretiker der deutschen Aufklärungshistorie,* 2 vols. Stuttgart, Bad Cannstatt: Frommann Holzboog, 226–274.)

Christian, D. 2004. *Maps of Time: An Introduction to Big History.* Berkeley: University of California Press.

Cicero, M.T. 1976. *De oratore: Über den Redner.* Stuttgart: Reclam.

Cloete, D. and A. Mason. 1981. *Vusi Goes Back: A Comic Book about the History of South Africa*. Johannesburg: Prezanian Comix in association with the Environmental and Development Agency (EDA) Trust.

Danto, A.C. 1974. *Analytische Philosophie der Geschichte*. Frankfurt am Main: Suhrkamp. [*Analytical Philosophy of History*, 2nd ed. Cambridge: Cambridge University Press, 1968.]

De Baets, A. 2009. *Responsible History*. Oxford: Berghahn Books.

D'Haenens, A. 1983. *Oralité, Scribalité, Electronalité: La scribalité occidental depuis le moyen Âge*. Louvain-la-Neuve.

Dilthey, W. 1989. *Introduction to the Human Sciences* (= *Selected Works*, vol. 1). Princeton, NJ: Princeton University Press.

Droysen, J.G. 1977. *Historik: Historisch-kritische Ausgabe*, vol. 1., edited by P. Leyh. Stuttgart, Bad Cannstatt: Frommann Holzboog.

Dux, G. 1997. 'Wie der Sinn in die Welt kam, und was aus ihm wurde', in K.E. Müller and J. Rüsen (eds), *Historische Sinnbildung: Problemstellungen, Zeitkonzepte, Wahrnehmungshorizonte, Darstellungsstrategien*. Reinbek bei Hamburg: Rowohlt Taschenbuch Verlag, 194–217.

Dux, G. 2000. *Historischgenetische Theorie der Kultur. Instabile Welten: Zur prozessualen Logik im kulturellen Wandel*. Weilerswist: Velbrück Wissenschaft. [*Historico-genetic Theory of Culture: On the Processual Logic of Cultural Change*. Bielefeld: Transcript, 2011.]

Eggert, M.K.H. 2006. *Archäologie: Grundzüge einer Historischen Kulturwissenschaft*. Tübingen: Francke.

Eisenstadt, S.N. (ed.). 1987–1992. *Kulturen der Achsenzeit: Ihre Ursprünge und ihre Vielfalt*. Parts I, II and III. Frankfurt am Main: Suhrkamp. [*The Origins and Diversity of Axial Age Civilization*. Albany, NY: SUNY Press, 1986.]

Emrich, W. 1957. *Die Symbolik von Faust II: Sinn und Vorformen*. Bonn: Athenäum.

Erdheim, M. 1984. *Die gesellschaftliche Produktion von Unbewußtheit: Eine Einführung in den ethnopsychoanalytischen Prozeß*. Frankfurt am Main: Suhrkamp.

Essen, G. 1996. 'Geschichte als Sinnproblem: Zum Verhältnis von Theologie und Historik', *Theologie und Philosophie* 71, 321–333.

Essen, G. 2007. '"Can Yesterday Get Better?" The Trouble with Memory and the Gift of the Eucharist: Systematic Theological Reflections on the Presence of the Past', in H. Schildermann (ed.), *Discourse in Ritual Studies*. Leiden: Brill, 277–297.

Feder, A. 1921. *Lehrbuch der historischen Methodik*, 2nd ed. Regensburg: Kösel & Pustet.

Flaig, E. 1996. 'Verstehen und Vergleichen: Ein Plädoyer', in O.-G. Oexle and J. Rüsen (eds), *Historismus in den Kulturwissenschaften: Geschichtskonzepte, historische Einschätzungen, Grundlagenprobleme*. Cologne: Böhlau, 262–287.

Flaig, E. 1999. 'Soziale Bedingungen des kulturellen Vergessens', in *Vorträge aus dem Warburg-Haus*, vol. 3. Berlin: Akademie Verlag, 31–100.

Flaig, E. 2007. 'Ohne Wahrheit keine Wissenschaft: Überlegungen zur Wendung nach den Wenden', in C. Kühberger et al. (eds), *Wahre Geschichte – Geschichte als Ware: Die Verantwortung der historischen Forschung für Wissenschaft und Gesellschaft*. Contribution for an international meeting, 12–14 January 2006, Alfried Krupp Wissenschaftskolleg Greifswald. Rahden/Westf.: VML, Leidorf, 49–80.

Flaig, E. 2009. *Weltgeschichte der Sklaverei*. Munich: C.H. Beck.

Fludernik, M. 1996. *Towards a 'Natural' Narratology*. London: Routledge.

Fludernik, M. 2001. 'New Wine in Old Bottles? Voice, Focalization and New Writing', *New Literary History* 32, 619–638.

Foner, E. 2002. *Who Owns History? Rethinking the Past in a Changing World*. New York: Hill and Wang.

Fowler, J.W. 1991. *Stufen des Glaubens: Die Psychologie der menschlichen Entwicklung und die Suche nach Sinn*. Gütersloh: Gütersloher Verlagshaus Gerd Mohn. [*Stages of Faith: The Psychology of Human Development and the Quest for Meaning*. New York: HarperOne, 1981.]

Freud, S. 1964. *Totem und Tabu: Einige Übereinstimmungen im Seelenleben der Wilden und der Neurotiker.* Frankfurt am Main: Fischer Bücherei. [*Totem and Taboo.* London: W.W. Norton, 1989.]

Freud, S. 1975. *Der Mann Moses und die monotheistische Religion: Schriften über die Religion.* Frankfurt am Main: Fischer Taschenbuch. [*Moses and Monotheism.* London: Hogarth Press, 1939.]

Freud, S. 2000. 'Das Ich und das Es', in idem, *Studienausgabe*, vol. 3: *Psychologie des Unbewußten.* Frankfurt am Main: Fischer Taschenbuchverlag, 273–330. [*The Ego and the Id.* Seattle: Pacific Publishing Studio, 2010.]

Friedländer, S. 1986. *Kitsch und Tod: Der Wiederschein des Nazismus.* Munich: Deutscher Taschenbuchverlag. [*Reflections of Nazism: An Essay on Kitsch and Death.* New York: Harper & Row, 1984.]

Friedländer, S. 1998–2006. *Das Dritte Reich und die Juden.* Vol. 1: *Die Jahre der Verfolgung 1933–1939*; vol. 2: *Die Jahre der Vernichtung: Das Dritte Reich und die Juden, 1939–1945.* Munich: C.H. Beck. [*Nazi Germany and the Jews.* 2 vols. New York: Harper Collins, 1997, 2007.]

Friedländer, S. 2007. *Den Holocaust beschreiben: Auf dem Weg zu einer integrierten Geschichte.* Göttingen: Wallstein.

Fröhlich, K. and J. Rüsen. 1991. 'Menschenrechte im Systemkonflikt', in idem. (eds), *Menschenrechte im Prozeß der Geschichte: Historische Interpretationen, didaktische Konzepte, Unterrichtsmaterialien.* Pfaffenweiler: Centaurus.

Fulda, D. 1996. *Wissenschaft aus Kunst: Die Entstehung der modernen deutschen Geschichtsschreibung 1760 bis 1860.* Berlin: de Gruyter.

Fulda, D. 2002. 'Strukturanalytische Hermeneutik: eine Methode zur Korrelation von Geschichte und Textverfahren', in D. Fulda and S.S. Tschopp (eds), *Literatur und Geschichte: Ein Kompendium zu ihrem Verhältnis von der Aufklärung bis zur Gegenwart.* Berlin: de Gruyter, 39–60.

Fulda, D. and S.S. Tschopp (eds). 2002. *Literatur und Geschichte: Ein Kompendium zu ihrem Verhältnis von der Aufklärung bis zur Gegenwart.* Berlin: de Gruyter.

Füßmann, K. 1994. 'Dimensionen der Geschichtsdarstellung', in K. Füßmann, H.T. Grütter and J. Rüsen (eds), *Historische Faszination: Geschichtskultur heute.* Cologne: Böhlau, 27–44.

Gadamer, H.-G. 1990. *Wahrheit und Methode: Grundzüge einer philosophischen Hermeneutik*, 2nd ed. Tübingen: Mohr/Siebeck. [*Truth and Method*, 2nd ed. New York: Crossroad, 1991.]

Gieselmann, M. and J. Straub (eds). 2012. *Humanismus in der Diskussion: Rekonstruktionen, Revisionen und Reinventionen eines Programms.* Bielefeld: Transcript.

Giesen, B. 1991. *Die Entdinglichung des Sozialen: Eine evolutionstheoretische Perspektive auf die Postmoderne.* Frankfurt am Main: Suhrkamp.

Giesen, B. (ed.). 1991. *Nationale und kulturelle Identität: Studien zur Entwicklung des kollektiven Bewußtseins in der Neuzeit.* Frankfurt am Main: Suhrkamp.

Goertz, H.-J. 2001. *Unsichere Geschichte: Zur Theorie historischer Referentialität.* Stuttgart: Reclam.

Goertz, H.-J. 2007. 'Geschichte: Erfahrung und Wissenschaft', in idem, *Geschichte: Ein Grundkurs*, 3rd ed. Reinbek: Rowohlt, 19–47.

Goertz, H.-J. 2009. 'Was können wir von der Vergangenheit wissen? Paul Valéry und die Konstruktivität der Geschichte heute', *Geschichte in Wissenschaft und Unterricht* 60(12), 692–706.

Goethe, J.W. v. 1999. *Faust: Texte*, ed. A. Schöne. Frankfurt am Main: Deutscher Klassiker Verlag.

Goldhagen, D. 1996. *Hitlers willige Vollstrecker: Ganz gewöhnliche Deutsche und der Holocaust.* Berlin: Siedler. [*Hitler's Willing Executioners: Ordinary Germans and the Holocaust.* New York: Alfred A. Knopf, 1996.]

Grafton, A. 1998. *Die tragischen Ursprünge der deutschen Fußnote.* Munich: Deutscher Taschenbuchverlag.

Grass, G. 2002. *Im Krebsgang: Eine Novelle*, 3rd ed. Göttingen: Steidl. [*Crabwalk*. Orlando; Austin; New York; San Diego; Toronto; London: Harcourt, 2002.]

Große, J. 2008. 'Geschichtsphilosophie heute', *Philosophische Rundschau* 55, part I: 123–155; part II: 209–236.

Haffmans, P. and G. (eds). 2011. *Das Neue Testament viersprachig*. Berlin, Zürich: Haffmans & Tolkemit.

Halbwachs, M. 1985. *Das Gedächtnis und seine sozialen Bedingungen*. Frankfurt am Main: Suhrkamp.

Halbwachs, M. 1985. *Das kollektive Gedächtnis*. Frankfurt am Main: Suhrkamp. [*On Collective Memory*. Chicago: University of Chicago Press, 1992.]

Handro, S. and B. Schönemann (eds). 2002. *Methoden geschichtsdidaktischer Forschung*. Münster: LIT.

Hardtwig, W. 1991. 'Geschichtsreligion – Wissenschaft als Arbeit – Objektivität: Der Historismus in neuerer Sicht', *Historische Zeitschrift* 252, 1–32.

Hasberg, W. 2001. *Empirische Forschung in der Geschichtsdidaktik: Nutzen und Nachteil für den Unterricht*. 2 vols. Neuried: ars una.

Heer, N.W. 1971. *Politics and History in the Soviet Union*. Cambridge, MA: Cambridge University Press.

Herder, J.G. 1883. 'Briefe zur Beförderung der Humanität', no. 122, in idem, *Briefe zur Beförderung der Humanität* (= *Herders sämtliche Werke*, vol. 18), edited by B. Suphan. Berlin: Weidmann, 286–295. [*Philosophical Writings*, edited by M.N. Forster. Cambridge: Cambridge University Press, 2002, 415–420.]

Herder, J.G. 1991. 'Briefe zur Beförderung der Humanität', no. 27, in *Werke*, vol. 10, edited by H.D. Irmscher. Frankfurt am Main: Deutscher Klassiker Verlag. [*Letters for the Advancement of Humanity*. Cambridge: Cambridge University Press, 2002.]

Herder, J.G. 2002. *Ideen zur Philosophie der Geschichte der Menschheit*, part I, book 2, edited by W. Pross. Darmstadt: Wissenschaftliche Buchgesellschaft. [*Reflections on the Philosophy of the History of Mankind*. Chicago, London: University of Chicago Press, 1968.]

Hölkeskamp, K.-J., J. Rüsen, E. Stein-Hölkeskamp and H.T. Grütter (eds). 2003. *Sinn (in) der Antike: Orientierungssysteme, Leitbilder und Wertkonzepte im Altertum*. Mainz: Philipp von Zabern.

Howell, M. and W. Prevenier. 2004. *Werkstatt des Historikers: Eine Einführung in die historischen Methoden*. Cologne: Böhlau.

Huang, C.-C. 2000. 'The Defining Character of Chinese Historical Thinking', *History and Theory* 46, 180–188.

Humboldt, W. von. 1960. 'Über die Aufgabe des Geschichtsschreibers', in *Werke*, edited by A. Flitner and K. Giel, vol. 1: *Schriften zur Anthropologie und Geschichte*. Darmstadt: Wissenschaftliche Buchgesellschaft, 585–606. (*Gesammelte Schriften* [Akademie Ausgabe] IV, 35–56.) ['On the Historian's Task', in L. von Ranke, *The Theory and Practice of History*. Indianapolis: Bobbs Merrill, 1973, 5–23; also in *History and Theory* 6, 57–71.]

Internationales Archiv für Sozialgeschichte der deutschen Literatur (IASL). 2011. 36(1).

Jaeger, F. and J. Rüsen. 1992. *Geschichte des Historismus: Eine Einführung*. Munich: C.H. Beck.

Jaeger, S. 2002. 'Erzähltheorie und Geschichtswissenschaft', in V. Nünning and A. Nünning (eds), *Erzähltheorie transgenerisch, intermedial, interdisziplinär*. Trier: WVT (Wissenschaftlicher Verlag Trier), 237–263.

Jaspers, K. 1963. *Vom Ursprung und Ziel der Geschichte*. Munich: Piper. [*The Origin and Goal of History*. New Haven: Yale University Press, 1953.]

Jeismann, K.-E. 1985. *Geschichte als Horizont der Gegenwart: Über den Zusammenhang von Vergangenheitsdeutung, Gegenwartsverständnis und Zukunftsperspektive*. Paderborn: Schöningh.

Jung, C.G. 1990. *Die Beziehungen zwischen dem Ich und dem Unbewußten*. Munich: Deutscher Taschenbuchverlag.

Kant, I. 1968. 'Idee zu einer allgemeinen Geschichte in weltbürgerlicher Absicht', in W. Weischedel (ed.), *Werke in zehn Bänden*, vol. 9. Darmstadt: Wissenschaftliche Buchgesellschaft, 33–50, A 385–411. ['Idea for a Universal History with Cosmopolitan Purpose', available online at: http://www.everything2.com/index.pl?node_id=929350.]

Kant, I. 1968. 'Kritik der reinen Vernunft', in W. Weischedel (ed.), *Werke in zehn Bänden*, vol. 3. Darmstadt: Wissenschaftliche Buchgesellschaft. ['The Critique of Pure Reason', available online at: http://www.gutenberg.org/files/4280/4280-h/4280-h.htm.]

Kant, I. 1968. 'Metaphysik der Sitten', in W. Weischedel (ed.), *Werke in zehn Bänden*, vol. 7. Darmstadt: Wissenschaftliche Buchgesellschaft, 309–634, A III–190. ['The Metaphysiscs of Ethics', available online at: http://oll.libertyfund.org/titles/1443.]

Kant, I. 1968. 'Der Streit der Fakultäten', in W. Weischedel (ed.), *Werke in zehn Bänden*, vol. 9. Darmstadt: Wissenschaftliche Buchgesellschaft, 263–393, A 142–144. ['The Conflict of the Faculties', available online at: http://m.friendfeed-media.com/91c8689f09ed3844c1 dc69109084f41edf83c836.]

Karlsson, K.-G. 2003. 'The Holocaust as a Problem of Historical Culture: Theoretical and Analytical Challenges', in K.-G. Karlsson and U. Zander (eds), *Echoes of the Holocaust: Historical Cultures in Contemporary Europe*. Lund: Nordic Academic Press, 9–58.

Kermani, N. 2011. *Gott ist schön: Das ästhetische Erleben des Koran*, 4th ed. Munich: C.H. Beck.

Kierkegaard, S. 1962. *Die Krankheit zum Tode*. Reinbek: Rowohlt. [*The Sickness unto Death*. Princeton, NJ: Princeton University Press, 1983.]

Kleist, H. von. 1961. 'Über das Marionettentheater', in idem, *Sämtliche Werke und Briefe*, edited by H. Sembdner, vol. 2. Munich: Hanser, 338–345. ['On the Marionette Theatre', available online at: http://www.southerncrossreview.org/9/kleist.htm.]

Klotz, V. 1982. 'Erzählen als Enttöten: Vorläufige Notizen zu zyklischem, instrumentalem und praktischem Erzählen', in E. Lämmert, *Erzählforschung: Ein Symposion*. Stuttgart: Metzler, 319–334.

Kocka, J. 1975. 'Theorien in der Sozial und Gesellschaftsgeschichte: Vorschläge zur historischen Schichtenanalyse', *Geschichte und Gesellschaft* 1, 9–42.

Kocka, J. 1980. 'Theory and Social History: Recent Developments in West Germany', *Social Research* 47(3), 426–457.

Kocka, J. 1984. 'Zurück zur Erzählung? Plädoyer für historische Argumentation', *Geschichte und Gesellschaft* 10, 395–408.

Kocka, J. 1986. 'Theory Orientation and the New Quest for Narrative: Some Trends and Debates in West Germany', in *Storia della Storiographia* 10, 170–181.

Kocka, J. 1989. *Geschichte und Aufklärung: Aufsätze*. Göttingen: Vandenhoeck & Ruprecht.

Kölbl, C. 2004. *Geschichtsbewußtsein im Jugendalter: Grundzüge einer Entwicklungspsychologie historischer Sinnbildung*. Bielefeld: Transcript.

Koselleck, R. 1979. *Vergangene Zukunft: Zur Semantik geschichtlicher Zeiten*. Frankfurt am Main: Suhrkamp. [*Futures Past*. Cambridge, MA: MIT Press, 1985.]

Koselleck, R. 1987. 'Historik und Hermeneutik', in R. Koselleck and H.-G. Gadamer, *Hermeneutik und Historik* (report from meeting of the Heidelberger Akademie der Wissenschaften, Phil.-hist. Klasse, Bericht 1). Heidelberg, 9–28.

Koselleck, R. 2000. 'Historik und Hermeneutik', in idem, *Zeitschichten: Studien zur Historik*. Frankfurt am Main: Suhrkamp, 97–118.

Koselleck, R. 2000. *Zeitschichten: Studien zur Historik*. Frankfurt am Main: Suhrkamp.

Kueffer, C. 2013. *Ökologische Neuartigkeit: die Ökologie des Anthropozäns*, in ZiF-Mitteilungen, 21–30.

Küenzlen, G. 1997. *Der neue Mensch: Eine Untersuchung zur säkularen Religionsgeschichte der Moderne*. Frankfurt am Main: Suhrkamp.

Kühberger, C. and C. Sedmak. 2008. *Ethik der Geschichtswissenschaft: Zur Einführung*. Vienna: Turia + Kant.

Kuhn, T. 1967. *Die Struktur wissenschaftlicher Revolutionen*. Frankfurt am Main: Suhrkamp. [*The Structure of Scientific Revolutions*. Chicago: The University of Chicago, 1962.]

Kulke, H. 1998. 'Geschichtsschreibung als Heilung eines Traditionsbruchs? Überlegungen zu spätmittelalterlichen Chroniken Südasiens', in J. Rüsen, M. Gottlob and A. Mittag, *Die Vielfalt der Kulturen*. Frankfurt am Main: Suhrkamp, 422–440.

Lal, V. 2005. 'The Concentration Camp and Development: The Pasts and Future of Genocide', *Patterns of Prejudice* 39(2), 220–243.

Lal, V. 2005. 'Much Ado about Something: The New Malaise of World History', *Radical History Review* 91, 124–130.

Lal, V. 2011. 'World History and its Politics', *Economic and Political Weekly* 46(46), 40–47.

Lal, V. 2012. 'The Politics of Culture and Knowledge after Postcolonialism', *Continuum: Journal of Media and Cultural Studies* 26(2), 191–205.

Lämmert, E. 1955. *Bauformen des Erzählens*. Stuttgart: Metzler.

Lamprecht, K. 1910. *Paralipomena der Deutschen Geschichte*. Vienna: Verl. des 'Wissen für Alle'.

Laslett, P. 1965. *The World We Have Lost*. London: Methuen.

Lenz, I. 2010. 'Differenzen der Humanität: die Perspektive der Geschlechterforschung', in J. Rüsen (ed.), *Perspektiven der Humanität: Menschsein im Diskurs der Disziplinen*. Bielefeld: Transcript, 373–405.

Liebsch, B. 2006. *Revisionen der Trauer: In philosophischen, geschichtlichen, psychoanalytischen und ästhetischen Perspektiven*. Weilerswist: Velbrück Wissenschaft.

Liebsch, B. and J. Rüsen (eds). 2001. *Trauer und Geschichte* (= *Beiträge zur Geschichtskultur*, vol. 22). Cologne: Böhlau.

Lorenz, C. 1997. *Konstruktion der Vergangenheit: Eine Einführung in die Geschichtstheorie* (= *Beiträge zur Geschichtskultur*, vol. 13). Cologne: Böhlau.

Lübbe, H. 2012. *Geschichtsbegriff und Geschichtsinteresse: Analytik und Pragmatik der Historie*, 2nd ed. Basel and Stuttgart: Schwabe.

Lyotard, J.-F. 1986. *Das postmoderne Wissen: Ein Bericht*. Vienna: Passagen Verlag. [*The Postmodern Condition: A Report on Knowledge*. Minneapolis, MN: University of Minnesota Press, 1984.]

Marx, K. and F. Engels. 1966. 'Feuerbach (Kritische Ausgabe)', in *Deutsche Zeitschrift für Philosophie* 14, 1199–1254 [*The German Ideology*, part I: Feuerbach, available online at: https://www.marxists.org/archive/marx/works/download/Marx_The_German_Ideology.pdf.]

Medick, H. 1984. '"Missionare im Ruderboot"? Ethnologische Erkenntnisweisen als Herausforderung an die Sozialgeschichte', *Geschichte und Gesellschaft* 10, 295–319.

Meier, C. 1973. 'Die Entstehung der Historie', in R. Koselleck and W.-D. Stempel (eds), *Geschichte: Ereignis und Erzählung* (= *Poetik und Hermeneutik*, vol. 5). Munich: Fink, 251–306.

Müller, J. 1997. *Entwicklungspolitik als globale Herausforderung: Methodische und ethische Herausforderung*. Stuttgart: Kohlhammer.

Müller, J. 2002. 'Ethische Grundsatzprobleme in der Entwicklungspolitik: Der Imperativ menschlicher Solidarität und die Entwicklungsethnologie', in F. Bliss, M. Schönhuth and P. Zucker (eds), *Welche Ethik braucht Entwicklungszusammenarbeit?* Bonn: Politischer Arbeitskreis (PAS).

Müller, K.E. 1984. *Die bessere und die schlechtere Hälfte: Ethnologie des Geschlechterkonflikts*. Frankfurt am Main: Campus.

Müller, K.E. 1987. *Das magische Universum der Identität: Elementarformen sozialen Verhaltens: Ein ethnologischer Grundriß*. Frankfurt am Main: Campus.

Müller, K.E. 1999. *Die fünfte Dimension: Soziales Raum-, Zeit und Geschichtsverständnis in primordialen Kulturen*. Göttingen: Wallstein.

Müller, K.E. 2003. 'Sein ohne Zeit', in J. Rüsen (ed.), *Zeit deuten: Perspektiven, Epochen, Paradigmen*. Bielefeld: Transcript, 82–110.

Müller, K.E. 2009. *Die Siedlungsgemeinschaft.* Göttingen: Vandenhoeck & Ruprecht unipress.

Mutschler, F.-H. 1997. 'Vergleichende Beobachtungen zur griechisch-römischen und altchinesischen Geschichtsschreibung', *Saeculum* 48, 213–253.

Mutschler, F.-H. 2007. 'Sima Qian and His Western Colleagues: On Possible Categories of Description', *History and Theory* 46, 194–200.

Nagl-Docekal, H. (ed.). 1996. *Der Sinn des Historischen: Geschichtsphilosophische Debatten.* Frankfurt am Main: Fischer Taschenbuch Verlag.

Neumann, E. 1986. *Ursprungsgeschichte des Bewußtseins.* Frankfurt am Main: Fischer Taschenbuchverlag. [*The Origins and History of Consciousness.* Princeton, NJ: Princeton University Press, 1973.]

Niethammer, L. 2000. *Kollektive Identität: Heimliche Quellen einer unheimlichen Konjunktur.* Reinbek: Rowohlt.

Nietzsche, F. 1988. 'Vom Nutzen und Nachteil der Historie für das Leben' (= *Unzeitgemäße Betrachtungen,* part II [1874]), in idem, *Sämtliche Werke: Kritische Studienausgabe in 15 Einzelbänden,* vol. 1. Munich: Deutscher Taschenbuchverlag, 243–334. ['On the Uses and Disadvantages of History for Life', in idem, *Untimely Meditations,* translated by R.J. Hollingdale. Cambridge: Cambridge University Press, 1983, 83–100.]

Nippel, W. (ed.). 2000. *Virtuosen der Macht: Herrschaft und Charisma von Perikles bis Mao.* Munich: C.H. Beck.

Nippel, W. 2012. 'Das forschende Verstehen, die Objektivität des Historikers und die Funktion der Archive: Zum Kontext von Droysens Geschichtstheorie', in S. Rebenich and H.-U. Wiemer (eds), *Johann Gustav Droysen: Philosophie und Politik, Historie und Philologie.* Frankfurt am Main: Campus, 337–377.

Noak, C. 1994. 'Stufen der Ich-Entwicklung und Geschichtsbewußtsein', in B. von Borries and H.-J. Pandel (eds), *Zur Genese historischer Denkformen: Qualitative und quantitative empirische Zugänge.* Pfaffenweiler: Centaurus, 9–46.

Nora, P. 1990. *Zwischen Geschichte und Gedächtnis.* Berlin: Wagenbach. ['Between Memory and History: Les Lieux de Mémoire', *Representations* 26, special issue 'Memory and Counter-Memory', 1989, 7–24.]

Novick, P. 1988. *That Noble Dream: The 'Objectivity Question' and the American Historical Profession.* New York and Cambridge: Cambridge University Press.

Nünning, A. 1995. *Von historischer Fiktion zu historiographischer Metafiktion.* Vol. 1: *Theorie, Typologie und Poetik des historischen Romans*; Vol. 2: *Erscheinungsformen und Entwicklungstendenzen des historischen Romans in England seit 1850.* Trier: WVT (Wissenschaftlicher Verlag Trier).

Oesterdiekhoff, G.W. 1992. *Traditionales Denken und Modernisierung: Jean Piaget und die Theorie der sozialen Evolution.* Opladen: Westdeutscher Verlag.

Oesterdiekhoff, G.W. 2010. 'Die Humanisierung des Menschen: Anthropologische Grundlagen der Kulturgeschichte der Menschheit', in J. Rüsen (ed.), *Perspektiven der Humanität: Menschsein im Diskurs der Disziplinen* (= *Der Mensch im Netz der Kulturen-Humanismus in der Epoche der Globalisierung,* vol. 8). Bielefeld: Transcript, 221–256. ['Man on the Way: Towards Intellectual Growth and Humanity – Anthropological Foundations of History and Social Change', in J. Rüsen (ed.), *Approaching Humankind: Towards an Intercultural Humanism.* Göttingen: Vandenhoeck & Ruprecht unipress; Taipei: National Taiwan University Press, 2013, 69–91.]

Otto, R. 2004. *Das Heilige: Über das Irrationale in der Idee des Göttlichen und sein Verhältnis zum Rationalen,* 2nd ed. Munich: C.H. Beck. [*The Idea of the Holy: An Enquiry into the Non-rational Factor in the Idea of the Divine and its Relation to the Rational.* London and New York: Oxford University Press, 1970.]

Paravicini, W. 2008. *Die Wahrheit der Historiker.* Munich: Oldenbourg.

Pinker, S. 2011. *The Better Angels of Our Nature: Why Violence Has Declined.* New York: Viking Adult. [*Gewalt: Eine neue Geschichte der Menschheit.* Frankfurt am Main: S. Fischer, 2011.]

Proust, M. 1992. *Remembrance of Things Past*, book 1, *Swann's Way*. New York: Modern Library. [*In Swanns Welt: Auf der Suche nach der verlorenen Zeit*. Part 1. Frankfurt am Main: Suhrkamp, 1981.]

Ranke, L. von. 1874. *Geschichten der romanischen und germanischen Völker von 1494–1514*, *Sämtliche Werke*, vol. 33. Leipzig: Duncker & Humblot.

Ranke, L. von. 1874. *Zur Kritik neuerer Geschichtsschreiber*, 2nd ed. *Sämtliche Werke*, vol. 34. Leipzig: Duncker & Humblot.

Ranke, L. von. 1877. *Über die Verwandtschaft und den Unterschied der Historie und der Politik*, *Sämtliche Werke*, vol. 24: *Abhandlungen und Versuche*. Leipzig: Duncker & Humblot, 280–293.

Ranke, L. von. 1958. *Die großen Mächte: Politisches Gespräch*, edited by T. Schieder. Göttingen: Vandenhoeck & Ruprecht. ['The Great Powers: Dialogue on Politics', in L. von Ranke, *The Theory and Practice of History*. Indianapolis: Bobbs Merrill, 1973, 65–130.]

Ranke, L. von. 1971. *Über die Epochen der neueren Geschichte* (= *Aus Werk und Nachlaß*, vol. 2), edited by T. Schieder and H. Berding. Munich: Oldenbourg.

Ranke, L. von. 1973. *The Theory and Practice of History*. Indianapolis: Bobbs Merrill.

Ranke, L. von. 1975. *Vorlesungseinleitungen* (= *Aus Werk und Nachlaß*, vol. 4), edited by V. Dotterweich and W.P. Fuchs. Munich: Oldenbourg.

Reill, P.H. 2005. *Vitalising Nature in the Enlightenment*. Berkeley: University of California Press.

Rickert, H. 1896. *Die Grenzen der naturwissenschaftlichen Begriffsbildung: Eine logische Einleitung in die historischen Wissenschaften*. Heidelberg: Mohr/Siebeck.

Rickert, H. 1924. *Die Probleme der Geschichtsphilosophie: Eine Einführung*, 3rd ed. Heidelberg: Winter.

Ricoeur, P. 1984–1988. *Time and Narrative*. 3 vols. Chicago: University of Chicago Press.

Ricoeur, P. 1988. *Zeit und Erzählung*. vol. 1: *Zeit und historische Erzählung*. Munich: Fink.

Ries, K. (ed.). 2010. *Johann Gustav Droysen: Facetten eines Historikers*. Stuttgart: Franz Steiner.

Rieß, P., S. Fisch and P. Strohschneider. 1995. *Prolegomena zu einer Theorie der Fußnote*: Münster: Lit.

Rohbeck, J. 2000. *Technik, Kultur, Geschichte: Eine Rehabilitierung der Geschichtsphilosophie*. Frankfurt am Main: Suhrkamp.

Rohbeck, J. and H. Nagel-Docekal (eds). 2003. *Geschichtsphilosophie und Kulturkritik: Historische und systematische Studien*. Darmstadt: Wissenschaftliche Buchgesellschaft.

Runia, E. 2007. 'Burying the Dead, Creating the Past', *History and Theory* 46, 313–325.

Rüsen, I. 2008. '"Das Gute bleibt – wie schön!" Historische Deutungsmuster im Anfangsunterricht', in J. Rüsen, *Historisches Lernen: Grundlagen und Paradigmen*, 2nd ed. Schwalbach/Taunus: Wochenschau, 144–159.

Rüsen, J. 1969. *Begriffene Geschichte: Genesis und Begründung der Geschichtstheorie J.G. Droysens*. Paderborn: Schöningh.

Rüsen, J. 1976. *Für eine erneuerte Historik: Studien zur Theorie der Geschichtswissenschaft*. Stuttgart: Frommann Holzboog.

Rüsen, J. 1983. *Historische Vernunft: Grundzüge einer Historik I: Die Grundlagen der Geschichtswissenschaft*. Göttingen: Vandenhoeck & Ruprecht. [English translation available online at: https://www.academia.edu/14081879/Reason_and_History.]

Rüsen, J. 1986. *Rekonstruktion der Vergangenheit: Grundzüge einer Historik II: Die Prinzipien der historischen Forschung*. Göttingen: Vandenhoeck & Ruprecht.

Rüsen, J. 1989. *Lebendige Geschichte: Grundzüge einer Historik III: Formen und Funktionen des historischen Wissens*. Göttingen: Vandenhoeck & Ruprecht.

Rüsen, J. 1990. 'Grundlagenreflexion und Paradigmenwechsel in der westdeutschen Geschichtswissenschaft', in idem, *Zeit und Sinn: Strategien historischen Denkens*. Frankfurt am Main: Fischer Taschenbuch, 50–76.

Rüsen, J. 1993. *Konfigurationen des Historismus: Studien zur deutschen Wissenschaftskultur*. Frankfurt am Main: Suhrkamp.

Rüsen, J. (ed.). 1999. *Westliches Geschichtsdenken: eine interkulturelle Debatte*. Göttingen: Vandenhoeck & Ruprecht. [*Western Historical Thinking: An Intercultural Debate*. New York and Oxford: Berghahn Books, 2002.]

Rüsen, J. 2000. 'Vom Nutzen und Nachteil der Ethnologie für die Historie: Überlegungen im Anschluß an Klaus E. Müller', in S. Schomburg-Scherff et al. (eds), *Die offenen Grenzen der Ethnologie: Schlaglichter auf ein sich wandelndes Fach*. Festschrift Klaus E. Müller. Frankfurt am Main: Lembeck, 291–309.

Rüsen, J. (ed.). 2001. *Geschichtsbewußtsein: Psychologische Grundlagen, Entwicklungskonzepte, empirische Befunde*. Cologne: Böhlau.

Rüsen, J. 2001. 'Historisches Erzählen', in idem, *Zerbrechende Zeit: Über den Sinn der Geschichte*. Cologne: Böhlau, 43–105.

Rüsen, J. 2001. 'Krise, Trauma, Identität', in idem, *Zerbrechende Zeit: Über den Sinn der Geschichte*. Cologne: Böhlau, 139–179.

Rüsen, J. 2001. *Zerbrechende Zeit: Über den Sinn der Geschichte*. Cologne: Böhlau.

Rüsen, J. 2002. *Geschichte im Kulturprozess*. Cologne: Böhlau.

Rüsen, J. 2002. 'Historische Methode und religiöser Sinn: Dialektische Bewegungen in der Neuzeit', in idem, *Geschichte im Kulturprozeß*. Cologne: Böhlau, 9–41.

Rüsen, J. 2003. 'Die Kultur der Zeit: Versuch einer Typologie temporaler Sinnbildungen', in J. Rüsen (ed.), *Zeit deuten: Perspektiven, Epochen, Paradigmen*. Bielefeld: Transcript 2003, 23–53.

Rüsen, J. 2003. 'Geschichte verantworten', in idem, *Kann gestern besser werden? Essays zum Bedenken der Geschichte*. Berlin: Kulturverlag Kadmos, 47–87. ['Responsibility and Irresponsibility in Historical Studies: A Critical Consideration of the Ethical Dimension in the Historians' Work', in D. Carr, T.R. Flynn and R.A. Makkreel (eds), *The Ethics of History*. Evanston, IL: Northwestern University Press, 2004, 195–213.]

Rüsen, J. 2003. *Kann gestern besser werden? Essays zum Bedenken der Geschichte*. Berlin: Kulturverlag Kadmos.

Rüsen, J. 2003. 'Was ist Geschichte? Versuch einer Synthese', in idem, *Kann Gestern besser werden? Essays zum Bedenken der Geschichte*. Berlin: Kadmos, 134ff. [Shortened version: 'History: Overview', in N.J. Smelser and P.B. Baltes (eds), *International Encyclopedia of the Social & Behavioral Sciences*. Amsterdam: Elsevier, 2001, 6857–6864.]

Rüsen, J. 2004. 'Der Ethnozentrismus und seine Überwindung: Ansätze zu einer Kultur der Anerkennung im 21. Jahrhundert', in M. Kastner, E.M. Neumann-Held, C. Reick (eds), *Kultursynergien oder Kulturkonflikte? – eine interdisziplinäre Fragestellung*. Lengerich: Pabst Science Publishers 2007, 103–117 ['How to Overcome Ethnocentrism: Approaches to a Culture of Recognition by History in the 21st Century', in *Taiwan Journal of East Asian Studies* 1(1), 59–74; also in *History and Theory* 43, theme issue 'Historians and Ethics', 118–129].

Rüsen, J. 2004. 'Interpreting the Holocaust: Some Theoretical Issues', in K.-G. Karlsson and U. Zander (eds), *Holocaust Heritage: Inquiries into European Historical Culture*. Malmö: Sekel, 35–62.

Rüsen, J. 2004. 'Tradition and Identity: Theoretical Reflections and the European Example', *Taiwan Journal of East Asian Studies* 1(2), 135–158.

Rüsen, J. 2005. *History: Narration, Interpretation, Orientation*. New York: Berghahn Books.

Rüsen, J. 2006. 'Faktizität und Fiktionalität: Sinnbewegungen des historischen Denkens in der Nachbarschaft zur Theologie', in idem, *Kultur macht Sinn: Orientierung zwischen Gestern und Morgen*. Cologne: Böhlau, 119–133.

Rüsen, J. 2006. 'Zivilgesellschaft und Religion: Idee eines Verhältnisses', in idem, *Kultur macht Sinn: Orientierungsprobleme zwischen Gestern und Morgen*. Cologne: Böhlau, 227–239.

Rüsen, J. 2008. 'Der Teil des Ganzen: über historische Kategorien', in idem, *Historische Orientierung: Über die Arbeit des Geschichtsbewusstseins, sich in der Zeit zurechtzufinden*, 2nd ed. Schwalbach/Taunus: Wochenschau, 168–187.

Rüsen, J. 2008. 'Die Individualisierung des Allgemeinen: Theorieprobleme einer verglei-chenden Universalgeschichte der Menschenrechte', in idem, *Historische Orientierung: Über die Arbeit des Geschichtsbewußtseins, sich in der Zeit zurechtzufinden*, 2nd ed. Schwalbach/ Taunus: Wochenschau, 188–231.

Rüsen, J. 2008. 'Emotional Forces in Historical Thinking: Some Metahistorical Reflections and the Case of Mourning', *Historein: A Review of the Past and Other Stories* 8, 41–53.

Rüsen, J. 2008. *Historisches Lernen: Grundlagen und Paradigmen*, 2nd ed. Schwalbach/Taunus: Wochenschau.

Rüsen, J. 2008. *Historische Orientierung: Über die Arbeit des Geschichtsbewusstseins, sich in der Zeit zurechtzufinden*, 2nd ed. Schwalbach/Taunus: Wochenschau.

Rüsen, J. 2008. 'Leidensverdrängung und Trostbedarf im historischen Denken', in T.R. Peters and C. Urban (eds), *Über den Trost: Für Johann Baptist Metz*. Ostfildern: Matthias Grünewald Verlag, 76–84.

Rüsen, J. 2008. 'Vom Geist der Geisteswissenschaften', in C. Goschler, J. Fohrmann, H. Welzer and M. Zwick (eds), *Arts and Figures: GeisteswissenschaftlerInnen im Beruf*. Göttingen: Wallstein, 25–31.

Rüsen, J. 2008. 'Was ist Geschichtskultur? Überlegungen zu einer neuen Art, über Geschichte nachzudenken', in idem, *Historische Orientierung: Über die Arbeit des Geschichtsbewusstseins, sich in der Zeit zurechtzufinden*, 2nd ed. Schwalbach/Taunus: Wochenschau, 211–234.

Rüsen, J. (ed.). 2010. *Perspektiven der Humanität: Menschsein im Diskurs der Disziplinen*. Bielefeld: Transcript. [Shortened English version: *Approaching Humankind: Towards an Intercultural Humanism*. Göttingen: Vandenhoeck & Ruprecht unipress; Taipei: National Taiwan University Press, 2013.]

Rüsen, J. 2010. 'Klassischer Humanismus: eine historische Ortsbestimmung', in J. Rüsen (ed.), *Perspektiven der Humanität: Menschsein im Diskurs der Disziplinen*. Bielefeld: Transcript, 273–316 ['Classical Humanism: A Historical Survey', in J. Rüsen (ed.), *Approaching Humankind: Towards an Intercultural Humanism*. Göttingen: Vandenhoeck & Ruprecht unipress, 2013, 161–184.]

Rüsen, J. 2011. 'Diskursive Bewegungen in der Historik: Versuch einer Antwort an meine Kritiker', *Erwägen Wissen Ethik: Streitforum für Erwägungskultur* 22(4), 604–619.

Rüsen, J. 2011. 'Historik: Umriss einer Theorie der Geschichtswissenschaft', *Erwägen Wissen Ethik: Streitforum für Erwägungskultur* 22(4), 477–490.

Rüsen, J. 2012. 'Die vier Typen des historischen Erzählens', in idem, *Zeit und Sinn: Strategien historischen Denkens*, 2nd ed. Frankfurt am Main: Humanities Online, 148–217.

Rüsen, J. 2012. 'Humanism: Anthropology, Axial Times, Modernities', in O. Kozlarek, J. Rüsen and E. Wolff (eds), *Shaping a Humane World: Civilizations, Axial Times, Modernities, Humanisms*. Bielefeld: Transcript, 55–79.

Rüsen, J. 2012. 'Tradition: A Principle of Historical Sense Generation and Its Logic and Effect in Historical Culture', *History and Theory*, theme issue 'Tradition' 51(4), 45–59.

Rüsen, J. 2012. *Zeit und Sinn: Strategien historischen Denkens*, 2nd ed. Frankfurt am Main: Humanities Online.

Rüsen, J. 2013. 'Die Macht der Gefühle im Sinn der Geschichte: Theoretische Grundlagen und das Beispiel des Trauerns', in J. Brauer and M. Lücke (eds), *Emotionen, Geschichte und historisches Lernen: Geschichtsdidaktische und geschichtskulturelle Perspektiven*. Göttingen: Vandenhoeck & Ruprecht, 27–44.

Rüsen, J., M. Fehr and T.W. Rieger (eds). 2005. *Thinking Utopia: Steps into Other Worlds*. New York: Berghahn Books.

Rüsen, J. and K.-J. Hölkeskamp. 2003. 'Einleitung: Warum es sich lohnt, mit der Sinnfrage die Antike zu interpretieren', in K.-J. Hölkeskamp, J. Rüsen, E. Stein-Hölkeskamp and H.T. Grütter (eds): *Sinn (in) der Antike: Orientierungssysteme, Leitbilder und Wertkonzepte im Altertum*. Mainz: Philipp von Zabern, 1–16.

Rüsen, J. and H. Laass (eds). 2009. *Humanism in Intercultural Perspective: Experiences and Expectations*. Bielefeld: Transcript.

Rüsen, J. and H. Laass (eds). 2009. *Interkultureller Humanismus: Menschlichkeit in der Vielfalt der Kulturen*. Schwalbach/Taunus: Wochenschau.

Rüsen, J. and J. Straub (eds). 1998. *Die dunkle Spur der Vergangenheit: Psychoanalytische Zugänge zum Geschichtsbewußtsein* (= *Erinnerung, Geschichte, Identität*, vol. 2). Frankfurt am Main: Suhrkamp.

Rüsen, J. and J. Straub (eds). 2010. *Dark Traces of the Past: Psychoanalysis and Historical Thinking*. New York: Berghahn Books.

Schlözer, A.L. 1990. *Vorstellung seiner Universalhistorie. Mit Beilagen* (= *Beiträge zur Geschichtskultur*, vol. 4), edited by H.W. Blanke. Hagen: Margit Rottmann Medienverlag.

Schneider, C., C. Stillke and B. Leineweber. 1996. *Das Erbe der Napola: Versuch einer Generationengeschichte des Nationalsozialismus*. Hamburg: Hamburger Edition.

Schneider, N. 1986. 'Kunst und Gesellschaft: Der sozialgeschichtliche Ansatz', in H. Belting et al. (eds), *Kunstgeschichte: Eine Einführung*. Berlin: Reimer, 244–263.

Schreiber, W., A. Körber, B. v. Borries, R. Krammer, S. Leutner-Ramme, S. Mebus, A. Schöner and B. Ziegler (eds). 2006. *Historisches Denken: Ein Kompetenz-Strukturmodell*. Neuried: ars una.

Schulin, E. 1998. '"Ich hoffe immer noch, dass gestern besser wird" – Bemerkungen zu einem von Jörn Rüsen gewählten Motto', in H.W. Blanke, F. Jaeger and T. Sandkühler (eds), *Dimensionen der Historik: Geschichtstheorie, Wissenschaftsgeschichte und Geschichtskultur heute. Jörn Rüsen zum 60. Geburtstag*. Cologne: Böhlau, 3–12.

Seixas, P. (ed.). 2004. *Theorising Historical Consciousness*. Toronto: University of Toronto Press.

Seth, S. 2004. 'Reason or Reasoning? Clio or Siva?', *Social Text* 22(1), 85–101.

Seth, S. 2011. 'Where is Humanism Going?', *The Unesco Courier* (October–December), 6–9.

Simmel, G. 1923. *Die Probleme der Geschichtsphilosophie: Eine erkenntnistheoretische Studie*, 5th ed. Munich: Duncker & Humblot.

Stanzel, F.K. 1979. *Theorie des Erzählens*. Göttingen: Vandenhoeck & Ruprecht.

Straub, J. 1998. 'Personale und kollektive Identität: Zur Analyse eines theoretischen Begriffs', in A. Assmann and H. Friese (eds), *Identitäten: Erinnerung, Geschichte*, Frankfurt am Main: Suhrkamp, 73–104.

Straub, J. 2004. 'Identität', in F. Jaeger and B. Liebsch (eds), *Handbuch der Kulturwissenschaften: Grundlagen und Schlüsselbegriffe*, vol. 1. Stuttgart: Carl Ernst Poeschel, 277–303.

Tillmanns, J. 2012. *Was heißt historische Verantwortung? Historisches Unrecht und seine Folgen für die Gegenwart*. Bielefeld: Transcript.

Tu, W.-M. 2009. 'Confucian Humanism as a Spiritual Resource for Global Ethics', *Peace and Conflict* 16(1), 1–8.

Weber, M. 1968. 'Die drei Typen der legitimen Herrschaft', in idem, *Gesammelte Aufsätze zur Wissenschaftslehre*, 3rd ed., edited by J. Winckelmann. Tübingen: Mohr, 475–488. ['The Three Types of Legitimate Rule', *Berkeley Publications in Society and Institutions* 4(1), 1958, 1–11.]

Weber, M. 1922. *Gesammelte Aufsätze zur Religionssoziologie*, vol. 1. Tübingen: Mohr.

Weber, M. 1922. 'Die Wirtschaftsethik der Weltreligionen: Einleitung', in idem, *Gesammelte Aufsätze zur Religionssoziologie*, vol. 1. Tübingen: Mohr/Siebeck, 237–275.

Weber, M. 1964. *Wirtschaft und Gesellschaft: Grundriß der verstehenden Soziologie*. Studienausgabe, edited by J. Winckelmann. Cologne: Kiepenheuer & Witsch.

Weber, M. 1968. *Gesammelte Aufsätze zur Wissenschaftslehre*, 3rd ed., edited by J. Winckelmann. Tübingen: Mohr/Siebeck. [*The Methodology of the Social Sciences*. New York: The Free Press, 1949.]

Weber, M. 1968. 'Die "Objektivität" sozialwissenschaftlicher und sozialpolitischer Erkenntnis', in idem, *Gesammelte Aufsätze zur Wissenschaftslehre*, 3rd ed., edited by J. Winckelmann.

Tübingen: Mohr/Siebeck, 146–214. ["'Objectivity" in Social Science and Social Policy', in idem, *The Methodology of the Social Sciences*. New York: The Free Press, 1949, 50–112.]

Weber, M. 1992. *The Protestant Ethic and the Spirit of Capitalism*. London: Routledge. [Available online at: http://www.d.umn.edu/cla/faculty/jhamlin/1095/The%20Protestant%20Eth ic%20and%20the%20Spirit%20of%20Capitalism.pdf.]

Wehler, H.-U. 1987. *Deutsche Gesellschaftsgeschichte*. vol. 1: *Vom Feudalismus des Alten Reiches bis zur Defensiven Modernisierung der Reformära 1700–1815*. Munich: C.H. Beck.

Welsch, W. 2011. *Immer nur der Mensch? Entwürfe zu einer anderen Anthropologie*. Berlin: Akademie.

Welzer, H. 2002. *Das kommunikative Gedächtnis: Eine Theorie der Erinnerung*. Munich: C.H. Beck.

White, H. 1973. *Metahistory: The Historical Imagination in Nineteenth Century Europe*. Baltimore: The Johns Hopkins University Press. [*Metahistory: Die historische Einbildungskraft im 19. Jahrhundert in Europa*. Frankfurt am Main: Fischer, 1992.]

Wiesel, E. 1966. *The Gates of the Forest*. New York: Avon Books.

Index

MAKING SENSE OF HISTORY

Studies in Historical Cultures
General Editor: Stefan Berger
Founding Editor: Jörn Rüsen

Bridging the gap between historical theory and the study of historical memory, this series crosses the boundaries between both academic disciplines and cultural, social, political and historical contexts. In an age of rapid globalization, which tends to manifest itself on an economic and political level, locating the cultural practices involved in generating its underlying historical sense is an increasingly urgent task.